"We Love Mr King"

The **ISEAS – Yusof Ishak Institute** (formerly Institute of Southeast Asian Studies) is an autonomous organization established in 1968. It is a regional centre dedicated to the study of socio-political, security, and economic trends and developments in Southeast Asia and its wider geostrategic and economic environment. The Institute's research programmes are grouped under Regional Economic Studies (RES), Regional Strategic and Political Studies (RSPS), and Regional Social and Cultural Studies (RSCS). The Institute is also home to the ASEAN Studies Centre (ASC), the Nalanda-Sriwijaya Centre (NSC) and the Singapore APEC Study Centre.

ISEAS Publishing, an established academic press, has issued more than 2,000 books and journals. It is the largest scholarly publisher of research about Southeast Asia from within the region. ISEAS Publishing works with many other academic and trade publishers and distributors to disseminate important research and analyses from and about Southeast Asia to the rest of the world.

"We Love Mr King"

Malay Muslims of Southern Thailand in the Wake of the Unrest

Anusorn Unno

YUSOF ISHAK INSTITUTE

First published in Singapore in 2019 by
ISEAS Publishing
30 Heng Mui Keng Terrace
Singapore 119614
E-mail: publish@iseas.edu.sg
Website: <http://bookshop.iseas.edu.sg>

All rights reserved. No part of this publication may be reproduced, stored in a retrieval system, or transmitted in any form or by any means, electronic, mechanical, photocopying, recording or otherwise, without the prior permission of the ISEAS – Yusof Ishak Institute.

© 2019 ISEAS – Yusof Ishak Institute, Singapore

The responsibility for facts and opinions in this publication rests exclusively with the author and his interpretations do not necessarily reflect the views or the policy of the publishers or their supporters.

ISEAS Library Cataloguing-in-Publication Data

Anusorn Unno.
"We Love Mr King" : Malay Muslims of Southern Thailand in the Wake of the Unrest.
1. Malays (Asian people) —Thailand, Southern.
2. Sovereignty—Thailand, Southern.
3. Islam and politics—Thailand, Southern.
I. Title.
II. Title: Malay Muslims of Southern Thailand in the Wake of the Unrest.
DS570 M3A63   2019

ISBN 978-981-4818-11-7 (soft cover)
ISBN 978-981-4818-12-4 (ebook, PDF)

Cover photos: Ceremonial footed tray.
Photos courtesy of Anusorn Unno.

Typeset by Superskill Graphics Pte Ltd
Printed in Singapore by Mainland Press Pte Ltd

*For all those who have lost their lives
in the southern unrest*

Contents

List of Tables and Figures	ix
Acknowledgements	xi
Main "Dramatis Personae"	xiii
Introduction	1
Chapter 1: Guba	**12**
1.1. Guba of Raman District	13
1.2. Guba and the Raman Sultanate	20
1.3. "Wild Guba"	25
Chapter 2: Winds of Change	**33**
2.1. The Unrest	34
2.2. Security Forces Operations	46
2.3. Okhrae Dalae	51
2.4. A Moment of Fear and Distrust	55
Chapter 3: Subjectivities on the Rise	**67**
Part 1: Formal Subjectivities	68
3.1. Muslims	68
3.1.1. The Return of Babo and the Advent of Islamic Strands	69
3.1.2. A Formal Islamic Way of Life	76
3.1.3. Diverse Muslims	77
3.2. Thai Citizens	82
3.2.1. Disciplining the Children	82
3.2.2. Training the Men	87
3.2.3. Taking Care of the Population	93
3.3. Royal Subjects	106
3.3.1. Royal Initiatives	107
3.3.2. Royal Recognition	111
3.3.3. Royal Involvement with the Recent Unrest	113

Part 2: Local Subjectivities	120
3.4. The Subordinates	120
3.4.1. Khru Razak and His Legacy	120
3.4.2. Official Leaders	131
3.4.3. Grey Figures	141
3.5. Faara: A Girl of Multiple Subjectivities	148

Chapter 4: The Clashes — 162
4.1. Different Strands of Islam — 163
4.2. Islam and Malay Beliefs and Rituals — 173
4.3. Malay-Muslim Identity and Thai Citizenship — 182

Chapter 5: Living Lives with Multiple Subjectivities — 190
5.1. Negotiating with Allah and Interpreting Islam — 191
5.2. Modifying the Malay World — 194
5.3. Outsmarting the State — 196
5.4. Observing the Insurgents' and Strongmen's Rules — 201
5.5. "Puloh Yaakob": Encountering de facto Sovereignty — 203

Chapter 6: Engaging with the Sovereigns — 212
6.1. Women of Allah — 214
6.2. "We Love Mr King": Crafting Subjectivity and Enacting Agency through the Exceptional Sovereign — 221

Conclusion: Sovereignty in Crisis — 236

Bibliography — 241

Index — 249

About the Author — 258

List of Tables and Figures

Table 2.1:   The Unrest in Guba and Adjacent Areas, 2004–16   37

Table 3.1:   Thailand's 2010 Fiscal-Year Budget for the Programme
             for Solving Problems in and Developing the
             Southern Border Provinces   94

Table 4.1:   *Bomohs* in Guba and Their Services and
             Specializations   181

Figure 1.1: Guba   14
Figure 1.2: Raman in Nationalist Historiographies   23

Figure 3.1: Khru Razak   124
Figure 3.2: Faara   153

Figure 6.1: The Thai Flag   223
Figure 6.2: Ceremonial Footed Tray: เรารัก (*rao rak*) = We Love   225
Figure 6.3: Ceremonial Footed Tray: นายหลวง (*nay luang*) =
             Mr King   225

Acknowledgements

This book has emerged out of my long-time research in Thailand's Deep South. It began in 2007 with a Summer Pilot Research Grant I received from the University of Washington's Department of Anthropology, enabling me to travel across the region to assess the feasibility of doing fieldwork amid the unrest and to select a field site for a PhD dissertation. I was able to identify at least three villages that were suitable for the research I sought to conduct. However, the village that struck me as most appropriate was Guba. This is not only because it lends itself to the examination of research questions but more importantly because it possesses necessary conditions for fieldwork — the interlocutors' hospitality and open-mindedness — that make it possible for a Thai Buddhist like me (and the only Thai Buddhist in the village during my sojourn) to carry out a thirteen month period of fieldwork there. After I graduated and then taught at Thammasat University's Faculty of Sociology and Anthropology, I continued to conduct research in Guba from which material in this book was also drawn. I am therefore deeply indebted and thankful to the people of Guba and especially the family with whom I stayed, although I cannot name their real names given the sensitivity of the issues discussed.

I am grateful to my PhD supervisory committee. Celia Lowe, committee chair and also my adviser, not only encouraged me to work on the southern unrest since the beginning of my PhD study but also provided me with relevant theories and ethnography as well as organized dissertation writing workshops in Indonesia. Charles F. Keyes offered his insightful knowledge about Thai society and also introduced me to important works on Thailand's Deep South and Malaysia; he also guided me if he felt that I was pushing an argument too far. Arzoo Osanloo was a real help on subjects related to Islam, and Carlo Bonura was a friendly and thoughtful discussant on southern Thai politics. I also received encouraging comments from Sara R. Curran, an external committee member who has conducted extensive research in northeastern Thailand. Without their help, I could not have finished my dissertation. I am also thankful to the National Science Foundation for the Doctoral Dissertation Improvement Grant that financially supported my fieldwork in Guba in 2008–09.

For the research projects, I am thankful to the Ministry of Culture's Department of Cultural Promotion for providing me with a grant to study Malay beliefs and rituals in light of Islamic reform in Guba in 2012–13. I am thankful to the Thailand Research Fund, which provided me with a grant to study multiple forms of sovereignty in Guba in 2014–15. In this project, I received insightful comments and suggestions from Chaiwat Sa-tha-anand, who served as the project's mentor and to whom I am thankful.

I received help and support from many people in writing this book. Christopher Joll not only strongly encouraged me to write the book but also provided me with a comprehensive list of scholarly literature on Islam in general and Thailand's Deep South in particular. His book on Muslim merit-making in the southernmost region is extensively used in the book, and I greatly appreciate it. I am thankful to Aryud Yahprung for promptly sending me his dissertation on Islamic reform and revival in southern Thailand. I am grateful to Michael Montesano for his support and encouragement in writing this book. Reviewers' comments and suggestions played a crucial role in transforming my flawed and awkward manuscript into something more presentable. They are really appreciated. I am also thankful to my wife, Chalita Bundhuwong, who spent late nights with me offering support while doing her own work while I was writing this book.

All praise goes to the people of Guba and the aforementioned persons. Any errors contained within are entirely mine.

Anusorn Unno
Bangkok, 6 December 2017

Main "Dramatis Personae" (Alphabetically)

Abidin	New Group practitioner
Aiman	The family's second son, a ritual and cultural specialist
Aryani	Mother of three whose husband was killed in the unrest
Azlan	Chairman of village 1 Red-Whiskered Bulbul club
Daessa	The family's rubber tapper, a member of various state-supported groups
Dahari	Southern Guba mosque committee member
Effendi	Rubber trader, a man of vast connections
Faara	Female schoolchild
Ishak	The family's paternal grandfather, former village 1 headman
Jaafar	A leading ritual specialist or *bomoh*
Jamal	The family's maternal younger brother
Jasim	Burong Kueteetae subdistrict headman, the most influential figure or strongman in Raman and nearby districts
Maeh	The family's mother
Mana	Former village 1 headman, village 1 headman's father-in-law
Meng	Village 1 headman
Mohammed	Arzeulee Subdistrict Administrative Organization village 1 member, a northern Guba mosque committee member
Najmudin	The family's extended member and employee
Nazri	Son of the Imam of northern Guba mosque
Osman	Khru Razak's right-hand man
Qasim	A leading ritual specialist or *bomoh* specializing in exorcism

Saifuldin	The family's oldest son, Arzeulee Subdistrict Administrative Organization deputy chief executive
Shaari	Male schoolchild
Shakib	Arzeulee Subdistrict Administrative Organization chief executive
Talib	Roadside teashop owner, village 2 assistant headman
Tok Zaki	Dakwah leader
Wae	The family's father
Yaakob	Hajj service provider, New Group practitioner
Zaidi	Dakwah practitioner

Introduction

During a hot, breezy afternoon in Guba — a Malay Muslim village in southern Thailand — a schoolchild halted and reoriented a routine conversation at a roadside pavilion by bringing in a decorated, footed tray.¹ The tray had been made for the opening ceremony and parade for Tadika Samphan, an intramural sports game among members of Taman Didikan Kanak Kanak (Tadika)² in Raman district of Yala Province. The tray contained tricoloured sticky rice that inscribed a sentence, "เรารักนายหลวง" (*rao rak nay luang*), purposely meant to mean "We love the king". It would not have drawn much attention from those at the pavilion if the word for "king" had been spelled as it should have been. Instead of "ในหลวง" (*nai luang*), "the king" — the most commonly used phrase for designating the Thai monarch³ — what was inscribed instead was "นายหลวง" (*nay luang*), a term that literally means "Mister Luang" and that, for Thai-speaking people, has nothing to do with the Thai monarch.

After my remarks on the title *nay luang*, the others at the pavilion had various reactions. Some were surprised and said they had never before realized that the *nay* spelling was incorrect, despite the virtual omnipresence of the phrase *rao rak nai luang* nationwide, especially after state-supported campaigns in 2006. Others — especially those who had been involved in making the decorated tray — seemed embarrassed, as they had been particularly attentive in making it, and it had already been displayed in the parade and at the official opening ceremony, where senior government officials had been present. "It should not have happened", one of them said in disappointment. Still, although some wondered if the incorrectly spelled phrase *nay luang* could be considered blasphemous to the highly revered Thai monarch, most of them did not take the issue seriously, considering it a small mistake they could joke about among themselves.

The misspelled *rao rak nay luang* would have simply passed as an illiteracy issue, a failure of formal education, or an unintended consequence of the state's propaganda had it not been written by a group of Malay Muslims from southern Thailand, in a period when Malay Muslims were attempting to negotiate their subjectivity in questions relating to the state, their ethnicity, and religion. Tadika Samphan, long held by the Tadikas in Raman district in cooperation with the mosques of each subdistrict (*tambon*), had been organized in Raman since 2007 by the Raman district office at the district (*amphoe*) level. Despite the district office's claims that the move had been made to ease the Tadikas' financial burden, Tadika personnel believed that the office's real purpose in taking over Tadika Samphan was to monitor traditional Islamic schools in the same way it did with *pondok* schools, which security agencies deemed to be a breeding ground for militant Islam or Islamic radicalism (Yegar 2002, p. 133), in part blamed for the recent unrest in the region (Liow 2006, pp. 90, 92, 107; Wattana 2006, pp. 125, 141).[4] Their discontent and unwillingness notwithstanding, Tadika personnel had no choice but to participate in the now district-controlled Tadika Samphan as "invited guests", unless they wanted to be suspected or accused of resisting the state or, worse, of being involved in the unrest.

While the state demanded allegiance, Tadika personnel remain committed to being Malay and Muslim. While cooperating with the administration of their district as Thai citizens, Tadika personnel and students have articulated their Malay heritage via their dress and parade decorations such as artificial silver and gold flowers, and their Muslim faith via the chanting of Koranic verses in Arabic. Importantly, despite increasing attempts on the part of Islamic reform movements to purify Islam at the expense of Malay culture (Anusorn 2016, pp. 22–44), the two spheres were jointly articulated on the decorated, footed tray. According to the person who designed the tray, the three colours of sticky rice symbolize the three pillars of life: red, the country; white, the religion; and yellow, the ethnicity, led by the raja or king. As the religion and the race refer to Islam and Malay, respectively, the message of the tray's symbolism is that one's life is jointly supported by Islam and Malay culture. Only the traditional meaning of the tray's conical shape, signifying Mount Meru, was discarded, given its association with Hinduism.

However, to articulate Islamic and Malay identities via a decorated, footed tray in the state-controlled Tadika Samphan competition raises a serious question that needs to be answered. The three colours of the sticky rice match the three colors of the Thai national flag, which signifies state ideology: the nation, the religion, and the monarch. But while the red stripes in the flag specifically refer to the Thai nation, the red sticky rice might refer to the Malay nation demanded by Malay separatist movements of previous decades. The yellow sticky rice, which symbolizes Malay ethnicity, is a difficult fit in the Thai nation, which is associated with ethnic Thais. And while the white stripes in the flag are closely associated with Buddhism, the white sticky rice is definitely intended to represent Islam. One must ask, then, how the people who made the tray were in compliance with the state's demands, while simultaneously retaining their ethno-religious subjectivity. In other words, how could they reconcile questions of subjectivity in relation to sovereignty that have plagued the region now making up Thailand's Deep South for centuries?

The region's sovereignty has come into question throughout the course of its history. From the fourteenth to the eighteenth century, sovereignty over the region was ambiguous. The region contained various Malay sultanates whose territorial reach was not clearly defined. At the same time, the Siamese kingdom regarded these sultanates as vassal states and demanded that its territorial sovereignty be imposed on the region as well. The Siamese attempted to impose a suzerain–vassal relationship,[5] but to no avail — Siam was forever dissatisfied with the Malay sultanates' contributions, whereas the sultanates felt that Siam's demands were onerous and sometimes intolerable, resulting in frequent warfare over the centuries (Nik Mahmud 1994, p. 3; Che Man 1990, p. 34; Nantawan 1976, pp. 198–99; Uhlig 1995, p. 214; Teeuw and Wyatt 1970, pp. 8–9, 16–17; Yegar 2002, p. 74). It was not until the early nineteenth century that the question of ambiguous sovereignty was put to rest, when Siam changed the status of the Malay sultanates from tributary states to integral principalities. Because they had been offered a certain degree of autonomy — the ability to enact laws, control over taxation, and supervision over local government bureaucracy — the principalities staged no uprisings for a period of time (Nik Mahmud 1994, p. 4; Che Man 1990, p. 35; Idris 1995, p. 198; Nantawan 1976, pp. 20, 198; Scupin 1980, p. 60, 1986, p. 119; Teeuw and Wyatt 1970, p. 22; Uthai 1988, p. 213; Yegar 2002, p. 76).

The peaceful period in the region did not last long. Faced with a threat to its territorial sovereignty by Western colonial powers, Siam in early twentieth century launched a new policy with respect to the Malay principalities — central administration and the establishment of a provincial system — to ensure that its sovereignty was fully imposed across the territory, and as a result the principalities' semi-independence was put to an end (Nik Mahmud 1994, pp. 28–29; Che Man 1990, pp. 35, 62; Farouk 1984, p. 236; Idris 1995, p. 199; Nantawan 1976, pp. 201–3; Uthai 1988, pp. 213–17). This policy was modelled on the colonial *Beamtenstaaten* of the Dutch East Indies (Anderson 1996, pp. 99–100) and resembled the methods used by the British in the western Malay states (Uthai 1988, p. 213). This pernicious form of internal colonialism represented "a permanent gain to the colonizers; no other calculations and assessments are necessary" (Che Man 1990, p. 241). Consequently, the Malay ruling elites occasionally revolted against Siam (Che Man 1990, p. 35; Idris 1995, p. 199; Nantawan 1976, pp. 202–203; Uthai 1988, pp. 214–16; Yegar 2002, p. 77).

Following the centralization policy, Siam launched a nation-building project that addressed sovereignty at the ideological level as well as the territorial one. Although King Chulalongkorn's (r. 1868–1910) *chat Thai* or "Thai nation" was inclusive of different nationalities (Keyes 1971, pp. 551–68, 1995, pp. 136–60), his successor King Vajiravudh's (r. 1910–1925) version of nationalism was limited exclusively to ethnic Thais (Anderson 1996, pp. 100–101), a policy that was followed by subsequent leaders. The People Party's government of Field Marshal Plaek Phibunsongkhram in 1939 promoted a pan-Thai movement or Maha Anachak Thai (Great Thai Empire) (Keyes 1995, pp. 136–60), whose ideology was to assimilate ethnic minorities into Thai culture (Scupin 1986, p. 126). The ethno-nationalistic ideology and assimilation policy were forcefully carried out under Phibun's government. In 1939, Phibun promulgated a royal decree, Thai Ratthaniyom (Thai Customs Decree), which attempted to create a unitary nation based on one ethnic identity and one religion. Any ethnic or religious attributes that were not in line with Thai ethnicity and Buddhism were susceptible to persecution. Malay Muslims of southern Thailand suffered more than other minorities as they were forced to pay homage to Buddhism as the state religion and were forbidden to wear Malay dress, to learn or speak the Malay language, or to have a Malay name (Nik Mahmud 1994, pp. 24, 30–31, 290; Che Man 1990, p. 65; Farouk 1984, p. 236; Nantawan 1977, p. 92; Scupin 1986, p. 126; Uthai 1988, pp. 252–53, 259–60; Yegar 2002, pp. 90–91).

Alienated from the Thai state, Malay Muslims of southern Thailand were attracted to the pan-Malay nationalism that was proliferating in Southeast Asia during and after World War II, leading to the foundation of many separatist movements in southern Thailand. Initially, these movements aimed to unify with their Malay brethren on the peninsula under the British-controlled Federation of Malaya. But after the possibility of such unification passed, forming their own independent Malay nation became their new goal. In the wake of Islamic resurgence in many parts of the world, the Malay separatists in Thailand integrated Islam more deeply into their ethnic-based nation (Che Man 1990, pp. 68–70, 1995, pp. 242–46; Farouk 1984, p. 239; Uthai 1984, p. 231; Yegar 2002, pp. 145–46). The separatist movements reached their peak in the 1960s and 1970s (Forbes 1982, p. 1061) before waning in the 1990s due partly to changes in Thai government policies and internal rifts in the movements (Croissant 2005, p. 23).

The unrest, however, has resurrected since 2004, after separatists robbed a cache of weapons from Krom Luang Narathiwat Ratchanakarin Military Camp in Narathiwat Province. In addition to the anonymity of the perpetrators and the lack of concrete demands (Croissant 2005, pp. 21–22), what distinguishes the recent unrest from earlier insurgent activity are the increasing appropriation of Islam (Liow 2006, pp. 90, 92, 107; Wattana 2006, pp. 125, 141) and the fact that most casualties are now Malay Muslim civilians (Deep South Incident Database 2017). The unrest has claimed more than 6,500 lives and injured thousands more, and the violence continues unabated (Srisompob and Supaporn 2016). Although several factors — ranging from the political conflict (McCargo 2006, pp. 39–71), radical Islam (Liow 2006, pp. 90, 92, 107; Wattana 2006, pp. 125, 141), and shifting government policies (Croissant 2005, p. 30) to the influence of vested interest groups and crime rings (Askew 2007, pp. 5–37) — have contributed to the recent unrest, prompting questions about what it is and who is behind it, the unrest is still largely a political conflict rooted in ethnic and religious differences. In other words, it remains a question of the sovereignty of the Thai state over an Islamic Malay population that has never been resolved.

Political science and other academic fields have long focused on issues of sovereignty. However, since around the 1990s sovereignty has come under reconsideration and is now a cross-disciplinary topic in the social sciences and humanities. The work of Giorgio Agamben has largely been responsible for this change. Agamben argues that the problem of sovereignty is often reduced to the question of who within the political order is invested with what power, whereas the threshold of the political order, which he calls the "state of exception", is never called into question (Agamben 1998, p. 12). Agamben credits Carl Schmitt with highlighting the link between sovereignty and the state of exception by defining the sovereign as "he who decides on the state of exception" (Agamben 1998, p. 11; see also Agamben 2000, p. 40, 2005, p. 1). In addition, he maintains that sovereign power is manifest as the person who has exclusive power to decide who can be killed with impunity without himself committing homicide (Agamben 1998, p. 142). As such, rather than examining the political order, to understand sovereignty one should look at the threshold of the political order or at the state of exception, as it is a hidden point where sovereignty is founded on the production of bare life (Agamben 1998, p. 83) — life that "may be killed and yet not sacrificed" (Agamben 1998, p. 8).

While the impact of Agamben's notion of sovereignty is wide ranging, it has a specific location in anthropology. Thomas Blom Hansen and Finn Stepputat (2006, pp. 296–300, 304; see also Hansen and Stepputat 2005, p. 36) maintain that the emergence of sovereignty as a central concern in anthropology has been informed by the work of Agamben, which they think is capable of tackling the two long-standing impasses in their field of study. On the one hand, the traditional emphasis on kingship, sacrifice, and ritual in primitive societies has proven incapable of addressing the complex relationship between royal sovereignty and modern forms of governance. On the other hand, Michel Foucault's notion of "cutting off the king's head in the social sciences" is unable to determine, for instance, how to account for the proliferation of legal discourse premised on the idea of the state as a centre of society, if power is really dispersed. Agamben's notion of sovereignty, Hansen and Stepputat argue, is promising in overcoming such impasses, in that it shifts the focus from sovereignty as an ontological basis of power and order to sovereignty as a tentative and emergent form of authority grounded in violence and designed to generate loyalty, fear, and legitimacy. They then proposed multiple forms of "de facto sovereignty" — "the ability to kill, punish, and discipline with impunity" — that are in constant competition with one another in such places as colonial territories, postcolonial societies, and war zones. The state is not the natural and self-evident centre and origin of sovereignty but one among several sovereign bodies including criminal gangs, political organizations, vigilante groups, insurgents, quasi-autonomous police, and self-appointed strongmen and leaders.

Taking cues from such an anthropologically grounded, reconsidered notion of sovereignty, I maintain that the unrest in Thailand's Deep South is a result of the convergence of different forms of "de facto sovereignty" all attempting to impose their will over the Malay Muslim residents of the region. While the Thai state and the monarchy demand allegiance and loyalty from the region's residents as its citizens and its subjects, respectively, the residents at the same time are committed to Islam and their Malay identity, whose demands are often not in accordance with those of the Thai state and monarchy. Additionally, local insurgents demand the support of the residents using religion and ethnicity as their justification, and strongmen and criminal gangs for their part reinforce their rules via violence. All these factors only serve to compound the unrest.

This book is an ethnography of the Malay Muslims of Guba in the wake of the unrest that newly emerged in the 2000s. It examines how the unrest plays out on the ground, focusing on how it is experienced and explained by the residents. It also examines how different forms of de facto sovereignty — the Thai state, the monarchy, Islamic religious movements, the insurgents, influential figures like local strongmen and *kratom* cocktail producers/sellers[6] — impose their rules and subjectivities on and demand allegiance from the residents, and how the residents deal with and appropriate these impositions. The phrase *rao rak nay luang* inscribed on the decorated, footed tray is one example of such impositions, specifically regarding the Thai state's sovereignty articulated through the sovereign monarch.

The material in this book is drawn primarily from my three ethnographic research projects conducted in Guba in 2008–15. One project, involving research for a PhD dissertation conducted in 2008–09, examines how residents negotiate different forms of sovereignty (Anusorn 2011). The ensuing projects elaborate on specific themes — Malay rituals against the backdrop of Islamic reform, which I researched in 2012 (Anusorn 2013), and different forms of de facto sovereignty, especially as imposed by local strongmen, which I researched in 2013–14 (Anusorn 2015). As a native Thai speaker also capable in Malay, I used both languages in conducting my fieldwork, depending on the informants' fluency in Thai and their language preference. Given the sensitivity of the issues covered, the names of my informants and of some places mentioned in the book have been changed to ensure confidentiality. Part of section 6.2 — "We Love Mr King": Crafting Subjectivity and Enacting Agency through the Exceptional Sovereign. — has been published in *Thammasat Review* 19, no. 2 (2016), under the title "'Rao Rak Nay Luang': Crafting Malay Muslims' Subjectivity through the Sovereign Thai Monarch". The book's chapters are arranged as follows.

Chapter 1 examines the history of Guba village with reference to the Raman Sultanate. According to local lore, the village was founded as a place to raise elephants and horses that the Raman Sultanate deployed in its wars with the Patani Sultanate. Although the Patani Sultanate is predominant in the historiography of the Deep South, Guba's residents identify themselves with the Raman Sultanate and understand Patani to have been their enemy. The recent past has also dissociated the village from the broader history of the region. An influential figure in the village was involved in anti-government activities in the 1970s, but these had nothing to do with separatism, as separatist movements did not operate in the village during their peak in the 1980s. Guba's unique history and its recent past have significantly shaped how the recent unrest played out in the village and how the residents responded to and made sense of it.

Chapter 2 examines how Guba's residents have experienced the recent unrest. The chapter explores the unrest through the everyday lives of the residents, focusing on how they have perceived and explained it. The chapter also examines how security forces operate in the area, how the residents respond to and make sense of these forces, and how the insurgents operate in the area. These phenomena have combined to create fear and distrust among the residents, forcing them to reconsider their subjectivity in relation to ethnicity, religion, and the state.

Chapter 3 specifically addresses questions of subjectivity in relation to sovereignty that the residents find themselves pressured to answer. On the one hand, the dissemination of certain strands of Islamic thinking encourages residents to live the life of "good Muslims", following new discourses of morality. This process was intensified by the insurgents using certain Islamic teachings to justify or facilitate their operations. On the other hand, the Thai state has launched various "help and care" programmes to ensure the loyalty of residents in the wake of the recent unrest. This effort has been reinforced by royal initiatives intended to attract the allegiance of the residents, seen as royal subjects, to the monarchy. The residents simultaneously have been forced to observe the rules set by local strongmen and other influential figures such as *kratom* cocktail producers and sellers, whose power over life and death became more pressing as the unrest spread. The chapter ends with an exploration of how multiple subjectivities, tied to different forms of sovereignty, were imposed on the body of a schoolgirl in a state ceremony that for many residents was itself a cause of tension and conflict.

Chapter 4 examines tensions and conflicts among different sources of subjectivity, in other words different forms of sovereignty. It examines how tensions between Guba's mosque group and a religious movement locally called Dakwah occasionally surface and how certain Islamic teachings invoked by the insurgents often generate confusion and debate among the village residents. The chapter also examines how certain Malay beliefs and rituals deemed incompatible with strict versions of Islam have been abandoned or adjusted. The chapter explores how Malay ethnicity and Islam have at times been in conflict with state ideology, which is implicitly associated with Thai ethnicity and Buddhism. The residents are therefore forced to address these tensions and conflicts directly.

Chapter 5 explores how Guba's residents manage the different forms of sovereignty they are confronted with. In the case of Islam, it explores how those engaged with illegal businesses and activities deemed sinful selectively draw on and interpret Islamic teachings to justify their actions and arguments. It also examines how ordinary village residents — especially women — interpret Islamic precepts to render their everyday practices religiously permissible. In terms of Malay beliefs and rituals, the chapter examines how they have been modified to be in line with strict versions of Islam. The chapter then explores how the residents encounter the state, focusing on how they outsmart it. In the case of the insurgents, the chapter explores how residents in charge of local security and ordinary villagers observe the insurgents' rules while leaving some room of negotiation. The chapter then explores how village residents obey local strongmen and other influential figures almost without exception. The chapter ends with an exploration of a wedding ceremony, focusing on how the rules of different forms of sovereignty are simultaneously imposed and negotiated.

Chapter 6 examines how residents craft subjectivity and enact agency through the sovereigns. It explores how, through strict observance of religious duties, one female resident became a pious Muslim ascribed with agency to act in religious and related matters. Then it examines how the inscription of the sentence *rao rak nay luang* on a ceremonial footed tray enabled a group of residents to engage state authorities as royal subjects with authority. It is the king's two states of exception — the embodiment of the Thai state in a state of exception and a human being stripped of the god-king features — that made such engagement possible. While highlighting the potential of such submissive subjectivity and mediated agency, however, the chapter also points to the conditions and limits involved, especially with respect to the sovereign monarch.

The conclusion recapitulates previous chapters with a focus on the question of sovereignty in crisis. Thailand's Deep South has had to juggle conflicting sovereignties for centuries. Emerging from the ambiguous sovereignty of the sultanates, the region is now plagued with the undifferentiated sovereignty of the unitary state. Although the Kingdom of Thailand was created to enable the Thai state to exercise its sovereignty in a state of exception and had the king as the embodiment, several problems remain unresolved. For Malay Muslims to flourish in Thailand, the Thai state's sovereignty needs to be exercised in a fragmented or flexible manner.

Notes

1. Such a tray, or *phanphum* (พานพุ่ม), is a cone-shape offering made of auspicious materials such as flowers, cooked sticky rice, candles, joss sticks, and other items.

It is usually used in ceremonies, especially official ones, as a symbol of respect, reverence, and loyalty to revered persons including the king, the queen, the Buddha, historical persons, teachers, and so on. For state ceremonies involving parades, these trays are carried out in the parades and then set down in front of pictures or symbols of the persons being honoured in the ceremony.

2. In the abbreviation "Tadika", *ta* stands for *taman*, which means a park; *di* stands for *didikan*, which means education or upbringing; and *ka* stands for *kanak-kanak*, which means children. Tadika therefore literally means "children's education park". However, in practice Tadika is a traditional Islamic educational institution that is located in the mosque compound and has undergone significant changes since the 1990s. Originally, Tadikas were run independently by the mosque under the supervision of the imam and supported by the community. Later, in 1997, according to the central Thai government's Department of Religion's Order on Mosque Centers for Islam and Ethics Instruction, Tadikas were required to register in exchange for government support, such as teachers' wages of 2,000 baht per instructor per year. However, seven years later, only around 40 per cent of Tadikas in Thailand's Deep South had registered, due to the negligible amount of the wage offered and the complicated registration process. (The Deep South comprises Yala, Pattani, and Narathiwat Provinces, as well as certain districts in Songkhla Province.) In 2004, the central government increased the wage and also allocated budget for mosque administration to attract more Tadikas to register. It also created a curriculum of Islamic studies for Tadikas, which are now officially called the Mosque Center for Islamic Studies (Tadika) (ศูนย์การศึกษาอิสลามประจำมัสยิด [ตาดีกา]). The curriculum, which is in line with the National Education Act of 1979, covers eight areas — six areas are about Islam and the two others are the Malay and Arabic languages (Abdulaziz 2013, pp. 31–46). Tadikas therefore now fall under the supervision of the Ministry of Education, although they are still run and administered by the mosque. They are also designed to be equivalent to primary schools or "worldly education", and as such they operate on weekends so that children can attend.

3. Although King Bhumibol Adulyadej passed away on 13 October 2016, given his seventy years on the throne and King Vajiralongkorn's "quiet" succession, Thais still consider *nai luang* to refer to King Bhumibol. Unless stated otherwise, *nai luang* in this book will likewise be intended to refer to King Bhumibol.

4. *Pondok* schools have long been a target of suspicion and distrust on the part of the central Thai government. Being aware of the central role of *pondok* schools in Malay Muslim communities and how these schools had obstructed the 1921 Compulsory Education Law and the cultural assimilation policies pushed forth in 1939, the Sarit Thanarat government, in connection with its overall strategy of national integration, proclaimed a policy in 1961 aimed to change the *pondoks'* traditional method of instruction and to weaken their impact. Under the new law, all *pondoks* were required to convert into private Islamic schools and to teach a standard government-designed curriculum, with the Thai language as the

medium of instruction, in order to "create and improve Thai consciousness, [and] cultivate loyalty to the principal institutions such as the nation, the religion, and the monarchy" (Che Man 1990, pp. 97–98; see also Che Man 1995, pp. 237–38; Idris 1995, p. 203; Nantawan 1977, pp. 94–95; Uthai 1988, p. 226; Yegar 2002, p. 133). Although most *pondoks* followed the law, some did not and remain a target of suspicion and distrust on the part of security agencies, especially in the recent unrest in which "radical Islam" has played a significant role.

5. Stanley Jeyaraja Tambiah defined the relationship between Sukhothai and its successor, Ayutthaya, and their vassal states as "galactic polity". In this polity model, Sukhothai was an "exemplary centre" where political symbolism was well demarcated but where an effective administrative structure was absent in outlying areas (Tambiah 1976, pp. 102–31). The Malay sultanates were not integral parts of Sukhothai but rather loosely circumscribed tributary polities. Sukhothai was able to enforce sovereignty over the Malay sultanates only spasmodically and with difficulty, depending on the current strength of the monarchy. In the Ayutthaya period, the sultanates likewise maintained a substantial degree of sovereignty, although during the latter part of the Ayutthaya dynasty, Siamese kings incorporated Nakhon Si Thammarat as a first-class province, which reflected a greater degree of Siamese sovereignty in the region (Nik Mahmud 1994, p. 3; Scupin 1980, pp. 58–59, 1986, p. 117).

6. *Kratom* (*Mitragyna speciosa*) is a species of tree whose fresh leaves are consumed to cure sickness, relieve pain, and, it is believed, boost one's energy. People in the Deep South have continued to consume these leaves even after the Kratom Act was passed in 1943 criminalizing such consumption. In the 1990s, the use of *kratom* leaves became more recreational than medicinal. Young males especially now consume *kratom* leaves in the form of cocktails — boiling the leaves in water and adding cough syrup, cola, and ice. *Kratom* cocktails are popular especially among young Muslim men because the effects are similar to those of alcohol, which is prohibited in Islam. The addictiveness of *kratom* leaves and the proliferation of their consumption have become matters of grave concern among residents of the Deep South. In a survey of Deep South residents conducted in July–August 2016, respondents identified the most urgent issue requiring action (81.3 per cent) to be drug addition (primarily *kratom* consumption), followed by the need for safety zones in communities (74.5 per cent) and the improvement of law enforcement and juridical procedures (68.5 per cent) (Center for Conflict Studies and Cultural Diversity 2016, p. 10). As shown later in this book, residents of Guba are frustrated by the *kratom* addiction problem because any solution necessarily involves state authorities and producers/sellers, all of whom are capable of using violence with impunity.

1

Guba

Late one afternoon, the back of the house of the family I stayed with was converted into a place to perform a ritual in response to a misfortune that had befallen the family's horse. Seven offering trays were placed in the middle of the space, and they were surrounded by family members, relatives, and acquaintances; Jaafar, Guba's leading ritual specialist, acted as leader. After Jaafar finished the first part of the ritual, Aiman, the horse's owner and also known to be a ritual specialist, continued the ritual by touching each tray while chanting to give the offerings to revered spirits. The spirits include family ancestors, art masters, the village founder, the Prophet and a Raman sultan, each of whom represents an authority figure in each domain of importance to the residents, namely kinship, art or tradition, community, religion and polity, respectively. While the authority figures representing the first four domains are non-controversial, that representing polity vividly points to conflict and that side of the conflict residents associate themselves with — Raman rulers vis-à-vis Patani rulers. Aiman told me later that, unlike people on the east coast of Thailand's Deep South who associate themselves with the Patani Sultanate, Guba residents are tightly connected to the Raman Sultanate in various ways. Guba was founded as a place for training the war horses and elephants that Raman rulers used in their wars with Patani, and Guba's founder had been appointed by a Raman ruler. In addition, Raman rulers also adopted several Guba children, and many Guba residents worked in the palace. The bonds between the people of Guba and Raman's rulers are deep and cordial and still strongly felt to the present day.

That Guba associated itself with Raman rather than rival Patani is crucial. Thailand's Deep South is often indiscriminately regarded as a region of the ancient kingdom of Patani, with Langkasuka[1] as its predecessor. Other interior polities, especially Raman, were considered by Thai and Malay nationalist historiographies as "a unilateral Siamese initiative" in Siam's attempt to dissolve Patani into more manageable petty states. Separatists of past decades as well as present-day insurgents have invoked this historical construct to justify their means and goals. However, according to some historical evidence, Raman already existed as a local sultanate with tin mining as its economic backbone when Siam dissolved Patani in 1810 and replaced it with a confederation of petty states (King 2006, pp. 83–86; 2009, pp. 485–87). Guba residents' deep and strong connection with the Raman palace ethnographically reinforces such existence and significance of Raman.

As such, rather than presenting a grand history of Patani vis-à-vis Siam, widely examined in most literature on Thailand's Deep South, this chapter, after a brief introduction to Guba as an administrative unit, examines the past as well as the present of Guba through the framework of Raman vis-à-vis Patani. This local history significantly shapes how the unrest that resurfaced in 2004 arose in Guba and how the residents responded to it.

1.1. Guba of Raman District

Guba is a locality comprising parts of two villages (administratively numbered 1 and 2, or *mu* 1 and *mu* 2) in Arzeulee subdistrict, Raman district, Yala Province.[2] Its northern and central parts are part of village 1, the other part of which is Pahong Gayu. Southern Guba is part of village 2, which has Yula, another locality, as its major component. In 2017, southern Guba had 78 households and 411 residents. Central Guba had 90 households and 504 residents, while northern Guba had 27 households and 162 residents. The remaining 73 households and 207 residents of village 1 are situated in Pahong Gayu, and 189 households and 787 residents of village 2 are situated in Yula. Out of 5,467 *rai*[3] of village 1's total area, central and northern Guba combine to make up an area of 3,876 *rai*. Southern Guba covers an area of 1,654 *rai* out of 6,873 *rai* of village 2's total area. See Figure 1.1.

Guba residents speak Malay and embrace Islam. Some are natives and others are from other places, mostly through marriage. Most residents' ancestors lived on Thai soil, but some have ancestors from Malaysia. They speak the Raman Malay dialect, which differs from standard Malay, and many of the older generation cannot read or write Malay, either in Latin script (Rumi) or Arabic script (Yawi).[4] However, the younger generation can read and write standard Malay, which they learn in the Tadika and religious

FIGURE 1.1
Guba

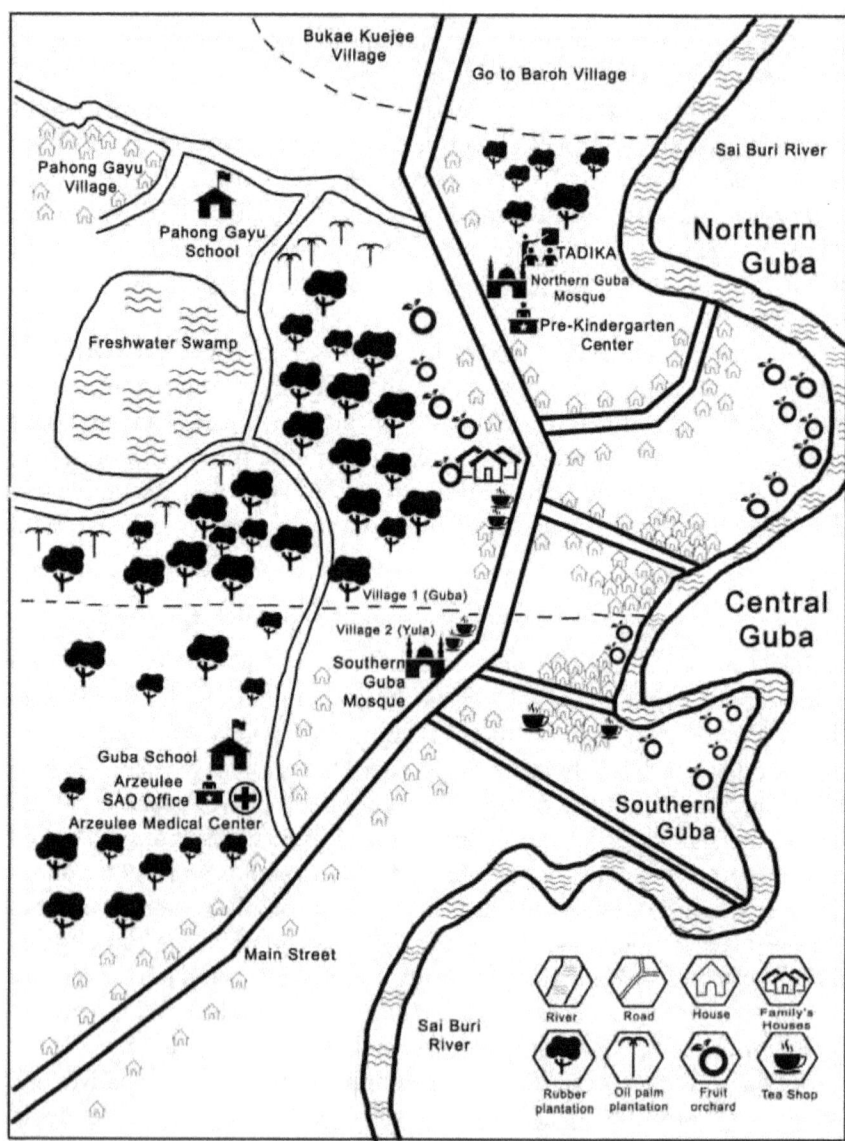

classes. Moreover, unlike their parents and the older generation in general, younger people are also fluent in Thai, which they study in school, which is the medium of the curriculum, and to which they are exposed via mass media. As such, although the Malay language is still a crucial part of the

Malay identity of the younger generation, this does not necessarily mean that it must compete with the Thai language as its opposition, as was the case for some of the older generation.

Likewise, although Guba residents are Sunni Muslims who since around the 1970s have experienced an "Islamic revival" like other Malay Muslims in southern Thailand, the way they have revived Islam is distinctive. The revival has occurred neither through a network of *ulama* or Kaum Muda (New Group) religious teachers, nor via the Salafi movement led by Ismail Lutfi; these two Islamic strands constitute Islamic revival and reform in much of the rest of the region (Aryud 2014, pp. 5–9, 83–189). Rather, it was a religious teacher studying Islam in Saudi Arabia — whose Islamic teaching could be regarded as Kaum Tua (Old Group) as opposed to Kaum Muda (New Group) — who initiated and significantly accounted for the "revival" of Islam in Guba. Additionally, the vibrancy of non-Islamic Malay beliefs and rituals in the region adds complexity to the manner in which Islam is actually revived there. I will specifically examine how different strands of Islam spread into Guba in Chapter 3; and in Chapter 4 I will discuss how these strands clashed with each other, and how Malay belief and rituals survived the revival of Islam in Guba.

As for the local economy, almost all households participate in the rubber economy as their main source of income. In 2017, 153 of 195 households owned rubber plantations with an average of 9.7 *rai* per household; only 16 households owned no farmland. In addition to tapping rubber, households with large plantations hire other residents, especially the landless, to tap their rubber, receiving half of the gain in return. Large rubber plantation owners also hire fellow residents, especially the young, to collect and transport rubber scrap. There are six rubber traders in Guba. In addition to buying and selling rubber products, they also have their own rubber plantations and hire other residents to tap rubber for half the profits.

In addition to rubber, Guba residents participate in other kinds of agriculture, including growing fruits and vegetables and keeping cows and goats, as supplementary sources of income. In the past, the residents grew rice for household consumption. However, due to the robust growth of the rubber economy and changes in geographic landscapes brought about by government development projects, the residents ceased growing rice and focused primarily on rubber in the mid-1980s. Some residents participate in the non-agricultural economy; for instance, there are five grocery shops in the area. However, such businesses are intended to be a supplementary source of income, as all shop owners also have rubber plantations on which they place greater emphasis. Likewise, although there are six teashops in the area, only one of them functions as the owner's main source of income. Although some residents seek jobs in neighbouring Malaysia, most of them hire themselves out tapping rubber in Malaysian-owned rubber plantations, with a few working in the restaurant business. A few others work as government officials or have motorcycle repair shops as their primary occupation. Except for one motorcycle repairman, these non-agricultural workers are of the younger generation, and most of them stay in bigger towns or other places and visit home on weekends, holidays, or other occasions. As such, as with many other villages in Thailand's Deep South, Guba's economy is based on rubber.

Guba's robust rubber-based economy plays a crucial role in shaping village life. Many residents were not born in Guba but moved here after getting married to local people and finding that there were more jobs in Guba than in their own villages. Job opportunities, however, distract children from school, partly accounting for school drop-outs. Saha, a ten-year-old boy, said that apart from boredom in school and what he felt was too much homework, "I quit school because I found hanging around in the village much more fun. I can play whatever and whenever I want. I also can work to support myself. I hire myself out in many jobs in the village, such as picking rubber scrap. I can earn 100 baht from working for just three to four hours." It is common to see many children and youngsters hanging around in the village when class is in session.

In addition, there is a robust "unauthorized" business in Guba, namely the *kratom* cocktail business, as discussed in the introduction. *Kratom* leaf is classified as an addictive Category 5 substance with a penalty for those possessing, distributing, selling, or consuming it. However, despite the illegality of the business, there are five *kratom* cocktail producers/sellers in Guba, and the reason why this business is robust is complex. In addition to the huge profits, the absence of law enforcement officers in the area due to the recent unrest has created an excellent opportunity for illegal business ventures. Additionally, soldiers stationed in the area are either regular *kratom* customers or act to "protect" the business. And more, village 1's headman has adopted a neutral stance on the issue, for fear of provoking those who control the business.

As a result, *kratom* cocktail customers come and go all day long in Guba and even into the night. Most customers are male teenagers and young men, and many of them are from faraway villages and subdistricts where headmen have cracked down on the trade. Many Guba residents said that at least 70 per cent of male teenagers in the village are *kratom* cocktail customers, whether regularly or periodically.

Kratom consumption has changed the way male teenagers live their lives. Some residents said that, in the past, these teenagers would not simply hang around in the village; they would venture to nearby towns or even farther afield. One resident said that he would spent most of his childhood outside Guba and returned home only during important religious events. Male youngsters also paid more attention to girls by, for example, teasing them when they passed by. But, these days, many male teens prefer staying in the village and gathering in places such as riverside forest areas drinking *kratom* cocktails; they have even lost interest in the opposite sex. Some Guba residents have claimed that *kratom* had taken over the lives of male teens, and, while worrisome, they have no idea how to deal with it, not daring to challenge those who control the *kratom* cocktail rings — men who are above the law and can punish or kill with impunity those who challenge them, an issue I will address in Chapter 5. The situation becomes more complicated when many army troops stationed in village schools are themselves regular customers and protectors of the trade. Some residents even see the *kratom* trade as a plot on the part of the Thai state to weaken and eventually eliminate the Malay population from the Deep South.

Guba's political situation is also complex. As mentioned earlier, Guba is divided into two parts in terms of administration — village 1 and village 2. Different parts of Guba are regarded and treated differently by government agencies, which at times leads to problems and conflicts. For example, tap water in village 1 is provided by two different sources — the village tap water project, overseen by the village 1 headman, and tap water provided by the village 2 mosque. Households in the eastern part of central and northern Guba use the village tap water, whereas those in the western part obtain water from the mosque, which is nearby to them. These households often face different kinds of problems depending on where they source their water, which are difficult to solve. In addition to higher service charges, residents in the eastern part of Guba have to pay for repair costs, whereas residents in the western part do not have these expenses; but people cannot switch their service, which depends on their home's location. Likewise, residents in the western part of Guba, which is in the area of village 1, who obtain their water from the mosque, have no say in initiating improvements in the service because the mosque is located in village 2. Tap water services in Guba are therefore chronically out of order, and there is no easy way to fix them due to the administrative divide.

Administrative anomalies also pose serious problems when it comes to religious practice. In the past, all residents went to the same mosque to perform religious services. However, as the mosque was located in southern

Guba, it was then registered as village 2's official mosque. Although the majority of mosque attendees, who were from central and northern Guba, saw no difficulty in attending village 2's mosque, Mana, a former village 1 headman who lives in northern Guba, found it a serious problem when it comes to administration. He then managed to build a new mosque in northern Guba and registered it as village 1's official mosque.

The new mosque's primary attendees are northern and central Guba residents who are also village 1 residents. However, many northern and central Guba residents still attend southern Guba's mosque as they have become accustomed to, although the mosque is village 2's official mosque. Likewise, some southern Guba residents who are village 2 residents attend northern Guba's mosque, which belongs to village 1. Although such factors as proximity, habit and familiarity also account for people's choice in which mosque to attend, the main factor has to do with religious and political factions, an issue I will return to later.

In addition to the question of which administrative units are coupled with which official mosques, different parts of Guba are also demarcated by the residents' different religious orientations. Southern Guba residents are said to be more pious Muslims than their neighbours in central and northern Guba. Many southern Guba children are sent to Islamic boarding schools in nearby districts and provinces and also abroad, and many of them become religious teachers and leaders after completing their study and returning home. By contrast, only a handful of central and northern Guba children attend Islamic boarding schools, and none of them hold important religious positions. As Dahari, a northern Guba resident, put it:

> At the time there were only me and Saifuldin [his close friend] from central and northern Guba who attended a *pondok* in southern Guba. Most students were from southern Guba. And they formed their own group called "southern Guba kids", and they called us "northern Guba kids". And we stayed and played separately.

Besides the mosque, the other public spaces in Guba are the teashops. There are seven teashops, five along the main road and two along side streets in central Guba. The two latter teashops are open from early morning to dusk. One teashop along the main road is open only in the morning, selling hot drinks and a variety of local breakfast items. Next to it is another teashop, which is open from afternoon to evening, concentrating on hot drinks and local sweets. It also sells food for dinner. These two teashops are located in southern Guba. Two more teashops on the main road, located in central Guba, are open from dusk to late at night. One of them concentrates on drinks and a variety of factory-made snacks, whereas the other one does not pay much attention to its business except in the month of Ramadan, when it is the only teashop that sells specialties such as papaya salad, mango salad and grilled meatballs. The fifth teashop along the main road, which is located in northern Guba, was recently opened. It belongs to Mana's only son and is open in the morning for hot drinks and breakfast.

Each teashop has a different set of regular customers. The one along the main road in southern Guba that is open in the morning is always crowded with female customers, who come to buy breakfast such as *nasi kerabu* (rice salad) for their families. And, given that the shopkeeper is a woman, female customers always occupy the main table inside the shop, drinking tea and eating breakfast. However, these women are relatively wealthy villagers; poorer female residents prefer buying food to eat at home with their families. The adjacent teashop, which is open from the afternoon on, is a gathering place for people interested in politics, whereas the shop in central Guba selling various factory-made snacks is always crowded with boys and male teenagers as well as middle-aged men. One of the teashops in central Guba belongs to the mother of Mana's son-in-law and is largely patronized by customers who belong to Mana's political faction. Most men in Guba go to a teashop once a day, but some go twice, once in the morning and then in the evening or at night.

Public pavilions (*salas*) are the other places where Guba residents get together. Usually, they are simply places for people to hang out and chat, but they are also used for other purposes such as government distribution of medicines, the transaction of "unauthorized" business, and resting for troops during their village patrols. Pavilions are usually made of wood and roofed with dried nipa leaves or tiles; they are located in front of houses along the main road or on walkways in the inner part of the village. Their sizes vary, ranging from a small pavilion that can accommodate about five people to a big one that can fit up to twenty people. Each pavilion has regular users, and they tend to be full from late afternoon until dusk. The one in front of the house where I stayed is located along the main road and can accommodate up to fifteen people. What is special about this pavilion is that, whereas other pavilions are used exclusively by certain groups of residents, this one is also used by passers-by especially when it's raining; it is also occasionally used by government officials for distributing medicines and by troops for resting during their village patrols. In addition, while other pavilions are usually occupied only in the late afternoon, this pavilion is in use all day long until late at night by different groups of people, especially male teenagers.

It is noteworthy that Guba's lively and vibrant teashops and pavilions draw many outsiders to the village. Mahathir, a resident of Yala Province's Bannang Sata district who married a Guba woman, said that he liked visiting Guba because there is a lot of fun and liveliness here. As he put it,

> I love to visit and stay in Guba because there is a lot of fun here. It's very quiet in my village in Bannang Sata due to the curfew. Most shops are closed when darkness falls, and the open ones are almost empty. But here in Guba many teashops are open even late at night and a lot of people still hang around there.

The liveliness and vibrancy of teashops and pavilions in Guba point to two important issues. First, the social life of Guba residents as Muslims revolves far beyond religious institutions such as the mosque, which is always considered the first building block of any Muslim community. Teashops and pavilions, as I will show later, are spaces for expanding and reinforcing social networks, carrying out political activities and transacting business, especially the illegal sort. Second, while most teashops in other localities are closed at night (and pavilions empty of people) for safety reasons, teashops in Guba stay open. This is partly because central Guba, where night teashops and roadside pavilions are located, does not suffer from the unrest, whereas people in southern Guba are more pious, leaving them susceptible to the ideas of radical and sometimes manipulative clerics who promote the aims of the insurgency. Besides piety, local history also shapes how the unrest unfolded in Guba.

1.2. Guba and the Raman Sultanate

Guba has mythical origins. These origin stories are widely told and are meaningful to local residents, but there is no historical evidence to support them. There are at least three versions of Guba's origin story. One asserts that the word "Guba" is a corruption of the word *lembing*, which means "spear". The myth has it that, in the past, a war party passed through the area. A spear positioned on the back of one of the party's elephants fell off the beast's back and was not retrieved. The locality was then called Lembing to commemorate the incident. However, residents of later generations pronounced the term incorrectly, eventually resulting in "Guba". Another myth has it that, in the past, Guba was a paddy field crowded with buffaloes. When people moved in and created a settlement, they called the place "Guba" in reference to the location's original inhabitants; "Guba" is a pronunciation of the standard Malay word *kerbau*, which means "buffalo".

These two myths are rejected by most residents. The first myth downplays the word "Guba" as a corrupt pronunciation, which is nothing to be proud of, and the second myth associates Guba with an animal, which is nothing to be proud of either. It is the third myth that most residents accept, as it refers to the village founder, who, in addition to having admirable personal attributes, had a close relationship with the Raman Sultanate.

This third myth has it that, in 1810, a Patani ruler appointed his relative Toh Nik as Raman's ruler.[5] But later Toh Nik declared Raman's independence from Patani. The Patani ruler then sent troops to defeat Raman, but without success, as Raman had a strong army to defend itself. Patani did not give up on its effort to retake Raman, leading to constant wars between the two powers for many years. As elephants and horses were important in the warfare of the time, Toh Nik assigned his relative, a woman named Guba, and her family to take charge of raising and training elephants and horses in an area adjacent to present-day Guba. Toh Nik also appointed Guba as the settlement's leader. Later, the residents moved to where Guba is today and named the location to commemorate its founder. It is said that Guba was a beautiful and smart woman who was versed in magic and skilful in the use of various weaponry. Given her admirable attributes, combined with her kin relation with Toh Nik, this story then satisfies most people in Guba as an appropriate explanation for how their settlement was founded and named.

In addition to the dominant myth of origin, there are family stories that link Guba to the Raman Sultanate. Aiman said that his great-great-grandfather was a mahout for the Raman palace and was in charge of catching and training wild elephants for warfare. He added that this mahout's daughter was adopted by the sultan of Raman. Although she did not live in the palace, she was allowed to come and go as she pleased, and she underwent important royal ceremonies such as ear piercing with special instruments. The sultan often visited her, and she was tasked with holding welcoming ceremonies for him. Aiman said that in addition to this woman, who was his great-grandmother, some other residents of Guba, all females, were adopted children of various Raman sultans.

Besides these links, Guba is also connected to the Raman palace via other channels. Jaafar, for example, said that his grandmother was a chef at the palace, because her culinary skills were superb. She had received many gifts from the sultan, although these gifts had all been lost or disposed of. In particular, it is said that a highly skilled goldsmith had been assigned by a Raman sultan to produce golden items such as necklaces and rings for him and other royal family members. The goldsmith's home is located in front of the southern Guba mosque, but today it stands abandoned. Almost all of his descendants moved to other places and sold all golden items he made.

Given Guba's commitment and loyalty to Raman, a sultan in return gave the residents a royal *longkong* tree as a gift. The tree was planted in the forest along the Saiburi River, in an area that's now a rubber plantation. After Guba died, her body is said to be buried in the village cemetery along the river. Although there is no ritual specifically or regularly held for Toh Nik, the first Raman sultan, or Guba, the settlement's founder, these two legendary figures are acknowledged in rituals the residents hold for their ancestor spirits as well as in other rituals. The ritual held in response to the misfortune with the horse, related at the beginning of this chapter, is an example of such rituals.

The myth of origin and the family stories told in Guba and how they relate to the Raman sultanate are crucial when taking into account the nationalist historiographies of Patani vis-à-vis Siam. On the one hand, Malay nationalist historiographies emphasize Patani's legitimate right to retain sovereignty over territory, language, tradition, and religion in opposition to Siam's invasion. On the other hand, Thai nationalist historiographies highlight Siam's legitimate right to establish sovereignty over the region in opposition to local rulers' rebellions. The former narrative employs a theme of tragedy, with Patani's loss and suffering, whereas the latter resorts to a theme of paternalism, with harmony and unity in the Siamese kingdom and, later, the Thai state as the ultimate goal. Differences in emphases, plots and themes notwithstanding, these nationalist historiographies are not at odds in terms of historical facts. Both sides tend to draw on the same facts but frame them differently to serve their respective political goals. This holds true in the case of Raman, which had never been mentioned in these nationalist historiographies until Patani was dissolved into a confederation of petty states by Siam in 1816.

As shown in Figure 1.2, Raman first appeared in an overall history of Patani vis-à-vis Siam in 1816 as one of seven provinces that were administered as third- or fourth-class provinces under the supervision of the Thai royal commissioner of Songkhla, in an attempt on the part of Siam to reduce Patani's strength and dilute its semi-independent status by applying a policy of divide and rule. Raman then disappeared in 1901 when the seven provinces were replaced by the Area of the Seven Provinces, under the control of the area commissioner; Siam now attempted to bring these Malay states under its direct control. Monthon Pattani (Pattani Circle) was

FIGURE 1.2
Raman in Nationalist Historiographies

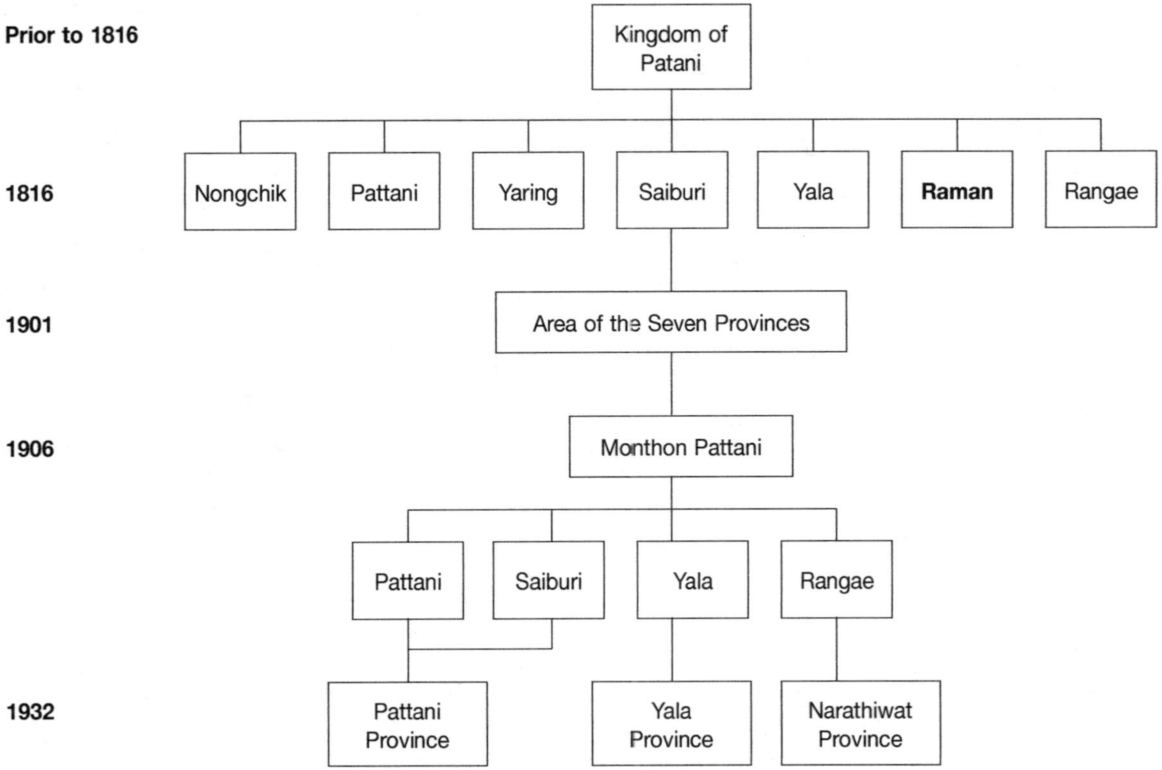

Prior to 1816: Kingdom of Patani

1816: Nongchik, Pattani, Yaring, Saiburi, Yala, **Raman**, Rangae

1901: Area of the Seven Provinces

1906: Monthon Pattani — Pattani, Saiburi, Yala, Rangae

1932: Pattani Province, Yala Province, Narathiwat Province

Sources: Nik Mahmud 1994, Idris 1995, Nantawan 1976, Uthai 1988.

established in 1906 as part of Siam's provincial administrative reform effort, and then the former seven provinces were reorganized into four provinces, with Raman becoming a component of Yala. After the 1932 revolution abolished Siam's absolute monarchy and created a constitutional monarchy, all the *monthons* were dissolved and a new provincial administration was introduced. Raman thus became a district of Yala Province, under the direct supervision of the Ministry of Interior (Che Man 1990, p. 35; Idris 1995, p. 199; Nik Mahmud 1994, pp. 28–29; Nantawan 1976, pp. 200–203; Uthai 1988, pp. 211–17; Yegar 2002, p. 77). This political status has remained in place to the present day.

While the overall history of Patani vis-à-vis Siam has been widely examined by scholars and others, people in Guba are not that familiar with it. Moreover, the Patani history that is circulated in Guba is not the one framed within wars between Patani and Siam whereby the former is the justifiable defender and the latter the illegitimate invader. Rather, it is framed within the wars between Patani and Raman, with the former the invader and the latter the defender. As mentioned earlier, the dominant myth of origin positions Guba as the place where elephants and horses were trained for Raman's wars against Patani. Family stories have reinforced the mythic bonds, as some Guba residents are said to be the descendants of adopted children of Raman sultans and many of them worked at the palace. In the general perception of Guba residents, Patani is therefore a competitor, if not an enemy, rather than a trustworthy friend of Raman, and they associate themselves with the latter. Nevertheless, one story does circulate about a Raman sultan captured by Siam and taken into custody in Bangkok; this story frames the conflict between Raman and Siam, not between Raman and Patani.

In addition, even among Guba residents with some knowledge of regional history, there are differences of opinion on it. On one side, some residents who subscribe to Malay nationalist/separatist historiographies glorify the history of Patani vis-à-vis Siam. Saifuldin, for example, claims that because Thailand's Deep South was once part of the Patani kingdom, the region should return to sovereign status. On the other side, some residents reject such restoration. Effendi, for example, said that prior to Patani was the kingdom of Langkasuka, where Hinduism and Buddhism were the major religions. Patani as well as Islam came later, and as such it would not be right to re-establish the southernmost region of Thailand with the Islamic Patani Sultanate as the basis. Given its position as a competing polity in the myth of origin and family stories, Patani occupies a difficult place in Guba residents' historical perceptions. As a result, it is not easy for present-day insurgents to invoke a sympathetic history of Patani vis-à-vis Siam in their operations in Guba.[6]

Besides the myth of origin and family stories, the recent past also shapes the way in which the current unrest in the region has played out in Guba.

1.3. "Wild Guba"

Elderly Guba residents said that in the past the settlement was like a "wild territory". Frequent gunfights took place among those vying for local power, with law enforcement officers being virtually absent from the area. Ishak, a former village 1 headman who at the age of eighty-three still carries a pistol, showed me the bullet scars on his shin, arm and forehead, and recounted to me the gunfights and ambushes that gave him the scars. He recounted such incidents:

> In the past, Guba was very scary because there were always gunfights and killings in the area. Some three to four figures with their subordinates competed with each other to take control over the area. I was also one who got involved in this kind of fight. During my thirty-some years of being a village headman, I was ambushed and had gunfights four or five times with those who wanted to replace me. Sometimes I had to eat dinner with the lamp turned off to prevent being ambushed. In one instance, I was ambushed and had a gunfight with Umar, who is now running a teashop in the inner part of the village. He conspired with one former village headman to get rid of me so that the former headman could replace me. But I fought back, and he ran away for awhile before being caught and put in jail for many years.... Another important case involved a man who lived at the curve [in the road], who together with his subordinates wanted to kill me because he thought I was a subordinate of Khru Razak, whom they regarded as a bandit. This man had a close relationship with government officials in the district. So they wanted to kill me, but without success. And later I had Khru Razak's subordinates kill them.... There were also gunfights and killings by other people here. But these gunfights and killings were not necessarily about the competition for power. They may have been about conflicts over interests, personal revenge, family feuds. Instead of using judicial procedures, which was almost inaccessible at the time, these people took the law into their hands. That's why Guba was very scary, and people didn't want or didn't dare to come or pass by here in the past.

Ishak's personal account of "wild Guba" resonates with other elderly residents' memories. Daud, in his seventies, said that in the past almost every household had guns for the purpose of protecting themselves, because no police were stationed in the area and there was a chance that one might come into a problem with an influential figure. Daud said: "There were some people who wanted to be big guys here. You would get in trouble if you had problems with them. So you had to protect yourself if there was really a problem. You couldn't ask for help from the police."

In addition to gunfights and killings, the former "wildness" of Guba is also characterized by a wide range of illegal businesses in the area. Around the 1950s, there were two bullfighting and three cockfighting rings open regularly. Despite the fact that such activities were illegal, the organizers were not arrested. On the contrary, some policemen were regular attendees. There was also a gambling den for playing dice, and an opium shop. Whereas the bullfighting and cockfighting rings were operated by local residents, the gambling den and opium shop were run by Chinese from outside the settlement. The gambling den was operated by two Chinese brothers, who rented a house and used it as a place to buy scrap rubber as well as to gamble with dice. Their regular customers included local Guba residents, but sometimes policemen came to play dice as well. The Chinese brothers conducted their businesses in Guba for five years before moving to Raman district, where the economic opportunities were better. (After they left, the village 1 headman ran a gambling den along with a teashop, which stayed open even during the month of Ramadan.) As for the opium shop, that business was run by a Chinese man at a house he rented. He also built a makeshift cottage in the forest by the river to provide a more private location for his customers to smoke opium. He had about fifteen regular customers, all of them local men. The Chinese man conducted his opium business in Guba for about ten years before being abducted and murdered for his money and valuables one day while he was making his way home. There have been no opium shops in Guba since then. No other Chinese came to do business or stay in Guba after the 1960s, either.

Most Guba residents over fifty, especially men, either witnessed or were involved with these illegal businesses. Ishak said that he occasionally bet on the bullfights and cockfights, because it was fun. "People from other villages also came to bet here. There were many motorcycles parked along the roads. It was so vibrant," he added. Jamal said that he sometimes followed adults to the makeshift riverside cottage to see how they smoked opium. He said:

> There were always people smoking opium in the cottage. They bought opium from the Chinese and went there for smoking because the place

was very comfortable. They lay down on the cottage floor smoking opium with a long pipe. The opium smoking pipes belonged to the Chinese. He provided everything for those who wanted to smoke opium. I didn't smoke opium because I was still a kid at the time. I just followed adults to see how they smoked opium.

Villagers said that opium addicts didn't work to earn their living, and many of them were broke and ended up selling or pawning their possessions so they could pay the Chinese opium seller. Yaakob, a hajj service provider, vehemently commented on how some Guba residents were addicted to opium and ended up selling their property, especially their rubber plantations, to the Chinese. He said: "They were severely addicted to opium. They didn't work. They were lazy. They either slept or smoked opium all day long. They sold everything they had to get money to buy opium. You know why hundreds of *rai* of rubber plantations behind Pahong Gayu now belong to the company? It's because the villagers sold them to the Chinese and then the Chinese sold them to the company."[7] Although opium and gambling are sinful according to Islam, no religious leaders told the Chinese to shut down their businesses or forbade Muslim locals from getting involved in these activities.

The activities of Khru Razak also added to the "wildness" of Guba. Khru Razak was a resident of Luboh Luwah village, which is about 7 kilometres from Guba. Initially he was a government schoolteacher, or *khru* (ครู). But after earning the respect of the villagers through his contributions to the village and through various assistance he provided to his neighbours, he came under suspicion of state authorities as an "influential person"[8] who might become involved with the anti-government movements that were active in the region during the 1970s. Pressured by state authorities, Khru Razak decided to leave his home and hide in the forest together with dozens of his subordinates. In addition to fighting state authorities, however, Khru Razak and especially his subordinates were said to have gotten involved in a wide range of illegal activities including ransom, kidnapping and extortion. Although Khru Razak and his subordinates often moved around in the area, their stronghold was in a forest in Bukae Kujee, which is adjacent to Pahong Gayu. Guba, then, was Khru Razak's turf.

This "turf" status was interpreted in various ways by different Guba residents, depending on their relationship with Khru Razak and his subordinates. In his recollection of gunfights and ambushes described above, Ishak implied that he had a good relationship with Khru Razak. He said:

> We knew each other well and we had a good relationship. I helped him when I was asked for, but I was not his subordinate. I let him borrow a government tractor when he cut the road. I had authority to do so because I was a village headman at the time. I helped him a lot. And he helped me, too. When I had a problem with those at the curve, I asked him to send his subordinates to get these people and he did so accordingly. But I never joined him in any fighting with the police or joined his subordinates in extorting people. We were just good friends.

In this regard, Ishak knew how to make use of Khru Razak's influence.

However, other people suffered from Khru Razak's influence. Although Khru Razak's main targets of kidnapping and extortion were wealthy Chinese and Thais, ordinary people were also among his victims. Mariam, a southern Guba woman aged fifty-eight, said that her family had to give rubber sheets to Khru Razak's subordinates on a monthly basis, obtaining nothing in return. She added that the family's cows kept in pens in the riverside forest were frequently stolen, and her family suspected that Khru Razak's subordinates were responsible for it. However, given Khru Razak's daunting influence, she said: "We had no choice but to accommodate their request and remain silent. Life was so difficult under Khru Razak's influence." "Wild Guba" under the influence of Khru Razak was not a liveable place for her family. I will specifically discuss Khru Razak and his "legacy" in Chapter 3.

It is noteworthy that the period in which Guba was "wild" — during the 1960s and 1970s — is a time when separatist movements were active in the region. As mentioned in the introduction, the Thai state's emphasis on nationalism and its policy of forced assimilation, coupled with pan-Malay nationalism in Southeast Asia during and after World War II, led to the founding of separatist movements in the region. Initially, these groups were independent of each other; there was no coordination between them, and some were organized spontaneously in response to specific incidents. However, after realizing that the lack of formal organization accounted for their respective failures, these groups came to the conclusion that they should be linked together within a formal organization. On 16 February 1948, Gabungan Melayu Pattani Raya (GAMPAR), or the Association of Malays of Greater Patani, was founded in Kota Bharu, Kelantan, Malaysia, and later was headed by Mahmmud Mayhiddin. Although GAMPAR was initiated and dominated by descendants of former regional sultans, its aim was no longer to fight for the restoration of power for these rulers. Rather, it was to combine Thailand's four southernmost provinces (Yala, Pattani, Narathiwat and Satun) into a single unit within the framework of the Malay Federation, a new goal inspired by the Malay national movement across peninsular and insular Southeast Asia prompted by the end of colonial rule (Che Man 1990, pp. 65-66; Farouk 1984, p. 237; Nantawan 1976, pp. 213-14; Nik Mahmud 1994, pp. 59-61; Uthai 1988, p. 26; Yegar 2002, pp. 108-10). Likewise, the aim of the Patani People's Movement (PPM), founded during the same period and led by Haji Sulong Abdul Kadir al-Fatani, was no longer merely the reinstitution of the authority of traditional rulers but the cessation of the southernmost provinces from Thailand and their unification with the sultanates of the Malay Peninsula (Che Man 1990, pp. 66-67; Yegar 2002, pp. 102-3). In addition to the new goal inspired by the Malay national movement, what distinguishes the two separatist movements from earlier struggles is that, rather than traditional rulers, they were led by religious elites, and rather than being organized around members of the ruling elite, they had a broad base of support among ordinary Malays (Che Man 1990, pp. 66, 132).

The two organizations, however, disintegrated after their respective leaders died in the early 1950s, and they were succeeded by a new generation of several separatist movements. Although diverse in their aims — some aspired to a greater degree of autonomy for Malays without separation from Thailand, many demanded immediate secession and independence, some wanted to install a sultan or raja as head of state, while others hoped to establish a republic — these movements shared their abandonment of the idea of incorporating Thailand's four southernmost provinces into the Malay Federation, and many of them were influenced by the worldwide Islamic resurgence. By 1970, there were about twenty such groups, and at the end of 1979 their estimated number rose to eighty-four. However, in the 1980s, only four of them — Barisan Nasional Pembebasan Patani (BNPP), Barisan Revolusi Nasional Melayu Patani (BRN), the Patani United Liberation Organization (PULO) and Gerakan Mujahidin Patani (GMP) — were still in operation, with PULO the largest and strongest. Although differing in ideology, strategy, and membership composition, these separatist movements shared common objectives. Apart from viewing the Thai government as a colonial power and stressing armed struggle to achieve a fully independent state, they wanted to establish a state based on Islamic values and lifestyle while preserving Malay identity and culture. To reinforce these common objectives, on 31 August 1989, they held a conference, which resulted in the founding of an umbrella organization,

Bersatu (Che Man 1990, pp. 70, 98, 105; 1995: 242–46; Farouk 1984, pp. 237–43; Nantawan 1977, p. 86; Uthai 1984, pp. 231; 1988, pp. 229–32; Yegar 2002, pp. 141–47).

Even during their peak in the 1960s and the 1970s, however, these separatist movements did not operate in Guba. The only thing local residents knew about these movements is that one of Bersatu's leaders, Poh Yeh, hid and operated on Budo Mountain, some 20 kilometres away from Guba, and even then he never came to Guba. In addition, although it is rumoured that Khru Razak once joined Poh Yeh's armed group on the mountain, he later left the group for contested reasons. Some said that the two did not share the same cause — Khru Razak fought the oppression and injustice of the state authorities, not for the separation or independence of Patani with Islam and Malay identity as the primary impetus. Others said that Khru Razak feared being apprehended by state authorities. Other rumours held that many with separatist notions who had joined Khru Razak later left him after finding that his struggle had nothing to do with separatism. To most Guba residents, the separatist movements of past decades are a faint, distant memory with which they had little association.

However, the recent unrest, whose origin most attribute to the theft of weapons from Krom Luang Narathiwat Ratchanakarin Military Camp in Narathiwat Province in 2004, has brought Guba residents to the front line of the long-standing battle. This is because, rather than state authorities, most of whom are Thai Buddhists, it is now Malay civilians who account for the majority of deaths (Deep South Incident Database 2017). Guba residents, who experienced earlier periods of unrest from a distance both historically and geographically, like their counterparts in the region now find themselves with the unrest on their doorsteps and their lives irrevocably changed — a topic I will examine in the next chapter.

Notes

1. Thailand's southernmost region first appears in recorded history as the ancient Malay kingdom of Langkasuka, which was founded in the first century AD (Che Man 1990, p. 32; Idris 1995, p. 195) or, in other accounts, in the second century (Teeuw and Wyatt 1970, p. 1). Langkasuka was considered an important commercial port for Asian mariners (Che Man 1990, p. 32) and attained importance in the sixth century when it began to send diplomatic and trading missions to China (Teeuw and Wyatt 1970, p. 2), whose records apparently sometimes confuse Langkasuka and Lang Chia Shu (Srisak 2004, pp. 150–205). Brahmanism is said to have entered Langkasuka in AD 200; the later spread of Buddhism, together with the spread of Srivijaya's power, made Langkasuka a stronghold of Buddhism as early as the seventh century (Idris 1995, p. 195). Like other small, ancient

states on the Malay Peninsula, Langkasuka's strength depended on the activities of the major powers in the region. When such powers as the Angkor Empire in Cambodia, the Mon Empire of Pagan, or Srivijaya intervened in the peninsula's affairs, the small states struggled to keep their independence; some maintained a precarious existence while others were submerged (Che Man 1990, p. 32). As a result, Langkasuka was strongest when the major powers to the north and the south were least active (Teeuw and Wyatt 1970, p. 2). Despite its importance, Langkasuka was never mentioned by name in the Thai records. It was mentioned as Patani or Tani and figured among a group of Buddhist states that centred around Nakhon Si Thammarat. In addition, the transition from Langkasuka to Patani is still a matter of speculation and dispute. In terms of date, some have estimated that the transition took place between the mid-fourteenth and mid-fifteenth centuries, at a time of expanding trade, increasing Thai interest on the peninsula, and the spread of Islam (Idris 1995, p. 196; Teeuw and Wyatt 1970, p. 3). In terms of the founder, the Kedah Annals attributes Patani's foundation to people from Kedah, whereas the Chronicles of Patani gives credit to a ruler from Kota Mahligai (Che Man 1990, p. 32).

2. Under the National Government Organization Act of 1991 (พระราชบัญญัติระเบียบบริหารราชการแผ่นดิน พ.ศ. 2534), Thailand was administratively divided into three levels: central, provincial and local. The central government consists of ministries, each of which is led by a minister who is appointed by the prime minister. The provincial government consists of provinces (จังหวัด, *changwat*), each of which is divided into districts (อำเภอ, *amphoe*), which fall under the Ministry of Interior's Department of Provincial Administration. Each province is led by a governor (ผู้ว่าราชการจังหวัด, *phu wa ratchakan changwat*), and each district is led by a district chief (นายอำเภอ, *nai amphoe*), both of whom are government officials appointed by the director general of the Department of Provincial Administration. For the local government, under the Local Government Act of 1914 (พระราชบัญญัติลักษณะปกครองท้องที่ พ.ศ. 2475) subdistricts (ตำบล, *tambon*) are established within each district, and each subdistrict is divided into villages (หมู่บ้าน, *mu ban*). Each subdistrict is led by a subdistrict headman (กำนัน, *kamnan*), and each village is led by a village headman (ผู้ใหญ่บ้าน, *phu yai ban*). Village headmen are elected by the village residents, and subdistrict headmen are elected by the village headmen of each subdistrict. Both subdistrict and village headmen are under the command of the district chief, and, in the absence of intervening circumstances, they can hold their office until they turn sixty. As of 2017, Thailand has 76 provinces, 878 districts, 7,255 subdistricts, and 75,032 villages.

3. A *rai* (ไร่) is a unit of area, equal to 1,600 square metres or 0.16 hectares.

4. The Malay language has been written using various scripts. Initially it was written in such scripts as Pallava and Kawi. When Islam came to the region in the fourteenth century via the Arabic language, these older scripts were gradually replaced by an Arabic script, which resulted in a Malay writing system called Yawi. However, with the influence of Western colonizers (the British and the Dutch)

in the seventeenth century, the Arabic script was gradually replaced by the Latin script, which resulted in a Malay writing system called Rumi. Although Rumi is in official use and seen in everyday life, Yawi largely remains the script for religious texts, as almost all Islamic texts were written using Arabic script. (For a history of the Malay language, see Collins 1998.)

5. According to Syukri (King 2009, p. 488), Toh Nik is an alias of Tuan Loh The, the first sultan of Raman. "Toh" is an abbreviation of "Datoh", which is a Malay honorific held by local rulers.
6. This also begs the question to scholars' use of "Patani" to identify local residents as "Patani Malays" (McCargo 2008, p. 183) and the insurgents as "Patani Warriors" (Askew and Helbardt 2012, pp. 779–80, 782, 789) — whether and to what extent it reflects how local residents regard themselves and the insurgents and how the insurgents regard themselves.
7. The "company" Yaakob mentioned is the largest car and motorcycle dealer and leasing company in Thailand's Deep South. The company was founded in 1939 by a descendant of a Chinese man who migrated to Pattani in about the 1910s. In addition to cars and motorcycles, which is its main business, the company also has other holdings such as rubber plantations, gas stations and department stores, although on a smaller scale.
8. In the Thai context, an "influential person" (*phu mi ittiphon*, ผู้มีอิทธิพล) is someone who holds informal power or influence over the others in his territory. Such a person can provide help and protection and also oppress or exploit, depending on the relationship. The influential person is usually involved in illegal business, which is the main source of his wealth, and he also always has a reciprocal relationship with state authorities, from whom he at least partly derives his informal power or influence. For studies of influential persons in terms of economy and politics, especially in Thailand's provinces, see McVey 2000.

2

Winds of Change

The separatist movements in Thailand's Deep South, which reached their peak in the late 1960s and 1970s, started to decline in the 1980s (Forbes 1982, p. 1061). On the one hand, the decline was brought about by changes in central government policy towards the region. The forced assimilation policy of the Phibun government was discontinued, Malays' cultural rights and religious freedoms were encouraged, many separatists were offered amnesty, and a "development as security" approach was implemented in the region. On the other hand, the decline also resulted from conflicts and ruptures within the separatist movements themselves and from the movements' failure to gain the broad support of the local Malay population (Croissant 2005, p. 23). This led observers to describe the separatist movements as "waning" (Rabasa 2003, p. 55) and "relatively quiet" (Tan 2003, p. 109). However, the unrest was resurrected around the turn of the millennium. A total of 1,975 violent incidents were recorded between 1993 and the end of November 2004. Of these, 21 per cent occurred before 2001, and 79 per cent took place from 2001 onward (Croissant 2005, p. 24). On 4 January 2004, about thirty armed men stormed Krom Luang Narathiwat Ratchanakarin Military Camp in Narathiwat Province, stealing 300 weapons and killing four soldiers. Incidents that occurred at Krue Se Mosque in Pattani and in Tak Bai, Narathiwat on 28 April and 25 October 2004, killing thirty-two and eighty-five Malay Muslims, respectively, aggravated the situation. These incidents combine to mark the year 2004 as the beginning of a new round, or "dramatic upsurge" (Askew and Helbardt 2012, p. 779), of unrest in the Deep South, which from 2004 to 2016 claimed 6,850 lives and 12,547 wounded and still goes on unabated (Deep South Incident Database 2016; Srisompob and Supaporn 2016).

Guba has not been immune to the resurrection of southern unrest. Drive-by shootings, roadside bombings, arson, and the distribution of threatening leaflets have not been uncommon to the settlement. However, Guba's specificity — its division into three different parts (northern, central, and southern), the "wildness" of its recent past, and its cordial memories and bonds with the Raman Sultanate demonstrated in the previous chapter — differentiates the ways in which the unrest has played out in the area. Mana, a former village 1 headman, said that he disagreed with the military in its classification of village 1 as a "red-zone village" (a zone in which insurgents operate), because southern Guba, where the insurgents vigorously operated, happens to be in village 2. Talib, a roadside teashop owner, said that his negative impression of Khru Razak makes it difficult for him to embrace the separatist ideology. In addition, Aiman said that Guba's cordial historical relationship with the Raman Sultanate poses obstacles to the insurgents' use of Patani history as a justification for their activities. "It's not easy for Guba people to appreciate the greatness of Patani, which is the enemy of their ancestors. Actually, they are freedom lovers", he added. However, some residents sympathize with the insurgents. Mohammed said that, although he had not supported the separatists in the past and remains unclear about Patani history, he is increasingly drawn to the insurgents' invocation of Islam as a creed that is constantly abused by the Thai state. The residents are therefore often put in difficult situations when it comes to the unrest.

This chapter examines the ways in which the recent unrest has played out in Guba against the backdrop of its distinct features. It also examines how Thai security forces have operated in the area, and how fear and distrust were created and spread among the residents in the wake of the recent unrest.

2.1. The Unrest

In the evening of 19 June 2005, Aryani, a mother of three, heard gunshots a short distance away. Wondering what had happened, she stepped out of her house, feeling sure that the incident was over. The road was now filled with motorcycles speeding back and forth, and neighbours huddled in front of their homes, all anxiously awaiting news about the gunshots. It did not take Aryani long to learn that the person who had been shot on the road at the far end of southern Guba was her husband, Badan. She recalls:

> I was shocked when I learned that it was my husband who was shot. I couldn't think about anything but crying. Then I went to see him. He lay

on the road with blood all over his body. But he was still alive. I hugged his body and cried. Then other villagers took him to the hospital and I followed them. It was very chaotic and confusing at the hospital while we were waiting. Then a doctor came to me and said my husband was dead. I cried and cried. I didn't know what to do at the time.

Aryani was uncertain about who the killers were and what was their motivation. After the incident, she consulted some fortune-tellers about the killers, but she kept what she learned to herself. However, her daughter, Suraina, believes that her father was killed by Okhrae Dalae.[1] She said,

> My dad has no enemies, but he was killed because he was a member of the village 2 security team [Chut Raksa Khwamplotphai Muban, Chor Ror Bor; ชุดรักษาความปลอดภัยหมู่บ้าน, ชรบ]. They killed him and took his pistol away but didn't touch his wallet or cell phone. They killed him because they thought he worked for the government.

Suraina said that the killers had come on two motorcycles, one carrying the shooting team and the other for those who scatter metal spikes on the road to block authorities. She added that some residents witnessed the incident, but they were too afraid to come out and tell the truth. The case is regarded by state authorities as insurgent-related activity. It was the first such shooting to take place in Guba since the new round of unrest broke out the year before. The shooters were never identified or apprehended, although various forms of assistance and compensation were given to the family.

Guba was still recovering from the killing of Badan when another shooting took place. Two weeks later, village 2 headman Majid was shot dead on the road in neighbouring village 5 while riding his motorcycle back from a monthly meeting at the Raman district office. He had had a close relationship with Badan, as he was by default the supervisor of the village 2 security team. The killing of Majid, who was a southern Guba resident, convinced residents that the unrest had now spread to Guba. Some locals said that, prior to the killings of Badan and Majid, some Okhrae Dalae had stayed and operated in southern Guba. Majid was aware of their operations and had asked them to go "play" somewhere else, but to no avail. On the contrary, Okhrae Dalae became angry with him and announced that his life would be in jeopardy if he persisted in interfering with them. Given these exchanges, many residents believed that Okhrae Dalae had killed Majid. As with Badan's case, the killing of Majid was regarded by state authorities as insurgency related, and there was no progress in apprehending the killers.

Majid's assistant, Ahmad, was then killed a few months later. Like Majid, Ahmad was a southern Guba resident. He had a close relationship with Majid, being one of his assistants responsible for maintaining order, and as a result he was on high alert after the killing of Badan and Majid. He stopped patronizing teashops in the evening and carried a carbine at all times. Despite his heightened sense of vigilance, however, Ahmad was shot dead in village 5 while returning home from errands. His death completed a series of killings of people in Majid's circle, whom, according to Guba residents, Okhrae Dalae considered their opponents. This series of killings marks the beginning of the recent unrest in Guba. See Table 2.1.

Shootings account for the greatest number of insurgent-related incidents. Between 2005 and 2016, there were nineteen such shootings in Guba, about half of them involving civilians in charge of security affairs. The remaining victims include state officials, state employees, and ordinary residents, all male. Except for the shooting of Uday in 2016, which involved a conflict in the *kratom* cocktail business, all the shootings are regarded by the authorities as related to the insurgency, and all the cases have been closed with no arrests of the perpetrators.[2] Except for the case of the village 1 headman, who fought back and survived the attack, and the case of the Yula military camp, in which soldiers hid themselves and fired back until the attackers retreated, all cases resulted in the death of the targets. In addition to the killings of Majid and his associates, two other shooting incidents are worthy of mention — those of police lieutenant Kriangkrai and of three members of the village 1 security team.

The killing of police lieutenant Kriangkrai is regarded by people in Guba as the most atrocious to have occurred during this period of new violence. Kriangkrai was neither a Guba resident nor a Muslim by birth. He was a Buddhist who had converted to Islam and come to live in southern Guba via his marriage to a southern Guba woman. His occupation as a police officer further dissociated him from other residents. Some said that he often flexed his power over them, for instance by disrupting the teenagers' *sepak takraw* games. In general, he was aloof and viewed his neighbours unfavourably. The estrangement only grew when the unrest began, and he became very cautious, aware that he might be a target. At some point, someone cut down some rubber trees in his family's rubber plantation as a warning. The incident made him even more alert — he managed to transfer his wife, who was a schoolteacher at Pa Ou school in village 5, to Guba school in village 2 to lessen the chance that she might be attacked, and he changed his routines to become less predictable. Despite his sense

TABLE 2.1
The Unrest in Guba and Adjacent Areas, 2004–16

Categories	Cases
Shooting	(1) Badan, member of village 2 security team (2005) (2) Majid, village 2 headman (2005) (3) Ahmad, village 2 assistant headman (2006) (4) Subhi (2006) (5) Murad, village 1 assistant headman (2006) (6) Former paramilitary ranger (2007) (7) Murshid (2008) (8) Police lieutenant Kriangkrai (2008) (9) Member of village 2 security team (2008) (10) Raman hospital janitor (2008) (11) Three members of village 1 security team (2008) (12) Wajdi (2009) (13) Teacher Nit (2011) (14) Zeh, former village 2 assistant headman (2011) (15) Yee, village 1 assistant headman (2012) (16) Reem (2012) (17) Yula military camp (2014) (18) Hum (2014) (19) Uday (2016)
Bombing	(1) Territorial defense volunteer car (2006) (2) Police car (2008) (3) Police car (2009) (4) Two soldiers (2010) (5) One soldier and one police officer (2010)
Theft of weapons	Theft of weapons in a northern Guba mosque (2005)
Scattering and posting of leaflets	Several times and places since 2005
Arson	(1) Telephone booth (2004) (2) Telephone booth (2004) (3) Office building of Arzeulee SAO (2006) (4) Guba school buildings (2007) (5) Police post (2008)
Tree felling	Several times and places since 2005
Metal spike scattering	Several times and places since 2005

of vigilance, however, he was eventually killed by a group of gunmen. His wife recalls the incident:

> It was in the late afternoon when the incident took place. Usually he did not make any stop when returning home — he just drove straight back

home from Raman police station. But on that day he stopped at my parents' house. I think he wanted them to close the house door. But when he got out his car, a group of men in a pick-up truck that had followed him shot him. They shot him to death and put his body in his car and set fire to it. My parents were in the house when this happened. They didn't dare to come out. And I think some villagers saw this, but they were too afraid to do anything. Even after the incident, no one said they saw the incident. There were construction workers around there, but they said they didn't see anything. I understand them. They don't want to put their life in trouble. They [the killers] are so cruel. They killed him and then burned him together with his car.

As in other cases, this killing is regarded by state authorities as related to the insurgency, and there was no progress in solving the case. However, Kriangkrai's death is distinctive in that, given his position as a police lieutenant, it is regarded as a "death in the line of duty", and as such he was posthumously promoted to a higher rank, and his wife received substantial government benefits and other forms of assistance and support. It is also noteworthy that Lieutenant Kriangkrai's funeral was poorly attended. Aiman said that only about eight people, mostly his immediate relatives, attended his funeral at the cemetery. This was partly because he had lived his life separate from his neighbours, and partly because people feared that Okhrae Dalae might misunderstand that they supported the lieutenant.

While the killing of Lieutenant Kriangkrai is distinctive in terms of its atrocity, the killing of three members of the village 1 security team is extraordinary in terms of scale. On the night of 17 December 2008, five members of the security team were headed back to Pahong Gayu in a pick-up truck after attending a meeting in Raman district. Three of them got out the pick-up at the house of one member, who was also a janitor at Pahong Gayu school. The other two drove the pick-up to their own homes nearby. While the school janitor went inside his home to prepare tea for his two friends, who sat chatting in front of the house, dozens of bullets were fired from the bushes on the opposite side of the road, killing the two security men who were sitting outside. The two security men who had driven off, after hearing the gunshots, returned to the house to help their friends. One of them was shot dead while opening the pick-up door in front of the house, while the other survived by hiding in the truck. The school janitor also survived, as he hid himself inside his house during the attack. The attack took place for about five minutes, and then the attackers fled the scene without leaving a trace, other than the three dead men. This was the most extensive gun attack that had occurred in village 1 to date.

In addition to the number of deaths, what is crucial about this killing is that it took place about a hundred metres away from a military camp, located in the front part of the Pahong Gayu school compound. No soldiers came out of the camp during the attack, nor did they come to the scene right away after the shooting ended, for fear of being trapped themselves. A Pahong Gayu resident said that the soldiers had asked a local boy who liked to hang out with them at the camp to go out and switch off the power to the camp so they could hide themselves in darkness. It was only after Mana, the village 1 headman, arrived at the scene with his assistants that the soldiers emerged from their camp to inspect the incident. As Mana put it:

> After the gunshots ended, I told my assistants that we should go to the scene to show the soldiers that we had nothing to do with the shooting. But when we arrived there, it was so quiet. There was no one there. I saw only the dead bodies, but there were no soldiers. I didn't know what to do and I was afraid too. So I told my assistants that we should stay in a house nearby and wait until the soldiers came out. We waited at the house about ten minutes, and then soldiers came out and we accompanied them.

There are at least three theories about the perpetrators and their motives. First, many residents claim that the killing was carried out by Okhrae Dalae as a lesson for the school janitor, whom they regard as a traitor. The story has it that the military wanted to build a military camp in village 1, specifically in the vicinity of Pahong Gayu school. Soldiers asked for Mana's cooperation, but they were denied on the grounds that there was no need for a military camp in village 1, because no insurgents operated there. However, later, the military camp was nevertheless built, in the front part of the school compound. It was believed that the school janitor, who was also a member of the village 1 security team, facilitated the process. Although he was not killed, the fact that the shooting took place at his home indicated that he was the real target. He left his home for three weeks after the incident for fear of being attacked again.

The second theory shifts the blame elsewhere. Some residents wondered why the soldiers let the shooting happen despite the fact that they are far better equipped than the insurgents. "Were they really scared, or did they in fact intentionally let them [the shooters] do it because they are the same group?" asked Ishak. He also wondered how a group of men can disappear without a trace despite the fact that there were many checkpoints in the area. He surmises that "they killed and then they fled into the camp. The paramilitary rangers did it with the cooperation of Pahong Gayu soldiers."

The third theory is more complicated. It had nothing to do with the school janitor or paramilitary rangers on a "dirty job"; rather, it was a matter of personal revenge. Zahrin, a Pahong Gayu resident, proposed this theory to me one day. He said:

> One member of the village security team had an enemy who is a paramilitary ranger. This man is not a Pahong Gayu native. He was from Than To district, and he had enemies there. I don't know what the conflict between him and the paramilitary ranger is about. But I heard that the paramilitary ranger was angry at him and came here with his gang to kill him.

Of the three theories, the first one aligns most closely with what government authorities believe actually happened. The killing is officially regarded as insurgency related, although the motive may not align exactly with that of the first theory. There was no progress in solving the case, although the relatives of the dead received compensation and various other forms of assistance.

Bombing is a secondary means of deadly attack employed by the insurgents. There have been five cases of bombings in Guba, and in each case the targets have been security authorities. The tactics are the same each time. Bombs are planted in the ground or under a road surface and are detonated when the target's car passes above it, or, on a footpath, when the target steps on it. Given that state officials have been the targets in each case, all cases are regarded as insurgency related. However, in one case, some Guba residents doubt the insurgents' involvement. This incident severely injured two Pahong Gayu soldiers, one losing a leg and the other losing an arm. While the official story has it that insurgents planted a bomb near a tree where soldiers frequently passed by and detonated it when two soldiers stepped on it, Saifuldin suspected that other soldiers were behind the bombing, which was motivated by revenge. He said: "They had conflict with each other, but I don't know what it is about. It is a personal matter. The insurgents have nothing to do with this."

While shootings and bombings intend to take life, other kinds of unrest have different aims. For example, the theft of weapons is primarily intended to take guns from civilians in charge of security affairs, not their lives. Amran, a former member of the village 1 security team, recalled an incident in which he and others were robbed of their guns while praying. He said:

> I was performing an evening prayer in the northern Guba mosque when a group of men entered the mosque and took my gun and others. They told us to sit still because they just wanted our guns. They didn't want to hurt us. And we followed their instructions as we didn't want to get killed, and the guns actually are not ours; the authorities gave them to us as members of the village security team and as assistant village headmen for the maintenance of order. So they took the guns and left the mosque without hurting anybody.

Amran believed that the robbers were Okhrae Dalae, as they spoke Malay — which is in line with the authorities' assumption. However, given that the robbery took place with no resistance, Amran and other members of the security team came under suspicion by the authorities of cooperating with the insurgents. Amran had to testify to the authorities that he had nothing to do with the insurgents; he just wanted to save his life. "Peaceful" weapons robberies like this are prevalent across the Deep South, and as a result many civilians in charge of security affairs are suspected of sympathizing with insurgents, or of being insurgents themselves.

Arson is another insurgent activity that is not aimed at taking life. It intends primarily to destroy state property and engender fear. However, it is noteworthy that while shootings, bombings and the theft of weapons have been on the rise during the recent unrest, arson has occasionally been committed long before. For example, Arzeulee subdistrict's primary health care building was burned down in the mid-1990s, and the residents believed that Okhrae Dalae was responsible, although in an earlier iteration. The first incident of arson in Guba since the new round of violence began in 2004 was the torching of a telephone booth in front of the southern Guba mosque, followed shortly thereafter by the torching of a telephone booth in the inner part of central Guba. No one saw the arsonists, but residents believed that they were Okhrae Dalae.

The biggest incident of arson has been the torching of a few Guba school buildings in 2007. A school janitor said that he heard something before the fire got underway. He did not see the arsonists but heard several gunshots, which kept him at bay. He also heard the arsonists say that no one was coming out to put out the fire unless they wanted to get killed. Indeed, no one came to put out the fire. In addition, no local officials rushed to the scene for fear of being trapped. It was not until sunrise, about seven hours after the fire was set, that authorities and villagers came to the scene, only to see the ruins of the school buildings. The school was closed for a week after the incident, and then opened with schoolchildren having class in tents and in one school building that was not burned. New structures were built and are now completed and in use. It is noteworthy that, while the media tends to portray the arson of school buildings as a big loss and cause of grief for local people, especially schoolchildren and teachers, in fact the newly built school buildings are always far better than the old ones, leading many residents to jokingly thank the arsonists, whoever they are, for making it possible for them to have new, vastly improved school buildings.

The felling of trees and scattering of metal spikes on roadways are not done independently but in conjunction with other acts of violence such as shootings, bombings, or arson. Their primary purpose is to block state authorities including soldiers, police officers, medical personnel and firefighters from performing their duties. For example, insurgents scattered many metal spikes on an access road after the shooting of a member of the village security team, to block soldiers and police from rapidly arriving at the scene. Likewise, some trees were cut down across the road after the Guba school buildings were set on fire to block fire trucks. Authorities attribute these kinds of activities to the insurgents, and local residents have no reason to doubt them.

The scattering or posting of leaflets, unlike other activities that are done anonymously, usually identifies the perpetrators.[3] Also, while other insurgent activities are vague as to motive, leaflets tend to state exactly what their purpose is. The contents of the leaflets are wide ranging, but they often include manifestos, warnings and clarifications.[4] Below is a leaflet distributed by the "Islamic Warriors of the Fatoni State", found at a roadside pavilion and written in Thai.

Manifesto of the Declaration Day

On 16 September 2006, Kafir Siam will hold a ceremony to show their will to promote a grand unification at Yala's central mosque. *They will invite our former allies, who now surrender to personal interest, as well as the Left (those taking side with Kafir Siam)* to join the declaration of their common standpoint. They will also invite Muslim ambassadors from all over the world to witness *this setup and image building. Earlier last month, Kafir Siam held a secret meeting with the Left at a resort near Bang Lang Dam.* They will also recruit more members of village security teams, village protection volunteers, and territorial defence volunteers, and they will set up three more regiments of paramilitary rangers. *This is to have us accuse and kill each other.* And when we are exhausted, these Kafir will step on us until we are down under the earth and we will be under their control forever.

> We, the Islamic warriors of the Fatoni State, pledge to declare our will that we will never stop killing Kafir Siam. Nor will we stop destroying their military, economic, political, educational, and social strategies until we regain our Fatoni land and establish the Fatoni Darussalam State. Let us Malay Muslims be a witness.
> Islamic Warriors of the Fatoni State (emphases in the original)

This leaflet addresses Malay Muslims in general. It tells fellow Malay Muslims that Kafir Siam, or non-Muslim Thais, are conspiring against them and how the "Islamic Warriors of the Fatoni State" are going to respond to this. Another leaflet mixes manifesto with warning; it was found along the road and was written in Thai.

Beware of Danger!

> Beware! Fatoni Muslims. From today on you need to *beware and be better prepared* as the enemy Kafir Siam will attack us by violent tactics with no mercy. *They will abduct, accuse, enclave, arrest, and employ other brutal means against us.* (This is the information we obtained from a highly confidential file of the army.)
>
> We cannot afford to be lighthearted and believe what General Sonthi[5] said about solving problems in the three southern border provinces by peaceful means. This is because the truth has already manifested itself through the merciless shootings of *tok imam*,[6] *ustaz*[7] and ordinary villagers just because they suspected these people and wanted to lay the blame on us. We cannot let them do this and do nothing ourselves. We need to do this to them before they do it to us. *If we kill, we kill for Allah. And if we are killed, let's make it a death for Allah Ta'ala.*
> Guardians of the People (emphases in the original)

This leaflet addresses local residents as "Fatoni Muslims", or Patani Muslims in general. On the one hand, it warns Muslims about prospective dangers and tells them to be prepared for such dangers. On the other hand, it declares what the "Guardians of the People" are going to do in response to such dangers.

The warning leaflets have different shades, ranging from mild reminders like the above examples to serious warnings and threats. Below is an example of a serious warning; the original was written in both Thai and Malay in Arabic (Yawi) script.

Warning

> *Beware!* Do not buy land properties (*konima*). This refers to properties of Kafir Siamese who lost the war and fled this land. Now Kafir Siamese

want to sell their farmlands, land and houses at low prices. This is like what Imam Nawawi[8] said.

Speaking of these properties, they are properties the Kafir Siamese gained from waging wars, [...]. These properties will be taken as stolen property, as they were wrongly gained according to Islamic principles. For example, if we buy the rubber plantations of the Kafir Siamese, the money Kafir Siamese get will become haram wealth and in the future will be seized and returned as property stolen from the Fatoni State. The Kafir Siamese came to this land empty-handed. So they have to leave this land empty-handed as well.

Do not buy these properties. Better to wait for them to be free of charge, because these properties actually belong to us. They don't belong to the Kafir Siamese.

From the Warriors of the Fatoni State (emphases in the original)

The leaflet directly tells Malay residents not to buy the properties that Thais are trying to sell, and to wait to get them for free instead. Although the tone is serious, it is also softened with friendliness. Significantly, the leaflet designates no punishment for those who disobey the advice. This is different from another leaflet, written in Thai, that clearly states the punishments that will be imposed on those who are disobedient:

The Punishment

1. Cooperate with the government (death)
2. The persons whom the religion hates (death)
3. Do not do what the religion forbids. If you insist on doing so, (death)

"Do not think you can run away from the hunting eye" (emphases in the original)

Although the addressee is not stated, it is clear that local Malay Muslims are the intended audience. The leaflet also makes it clear that those who cooperate with the Thai government or commit acts that Islam forbids will be targeted for death. It threatens that all are under surveillance; there is no place to hide. However, what the leaflet leaves unclear is its author. While the other leaflets quoted above include the names of the makers at the bottom, this leaflet does not provide any such information. The matter is therefore open to speculation; some claim that all these leaflets are produced by the same party. But the reason why they did not put their name on this last leaflet is that the content is quite strong, and they fear that it may generate hatred against them among Malay Muslims. Others say that the leaflet makers and distributors may be state authorities seeking to discredit or delegitimize the insurgents.

Given the issues of defamation and delegitimization, some leaflets seek to clarify earlier directives that may have been misunderstood or that may have been only rumoured. For example, in mid-May 2006 there were rumours in Guba and nearby villages that leaflets had been distributed forbidding any kind of work on Friday mornings on the ground that such behaviour was not in line with Islam. Further, the leaflets were said to instruct every Muslim male to go perform Friday noon prayers at the mosque. However, it was said that no movement or organization had signed its name at the bottom of the leaflet. Some people, in their curiosity, went around asking others if such a leaflet really existed and who had seen it. But these efforts were not successful; no one had actually seen the leaflet. However, about two weeks later, hundreds of leaflets were anonymously scattered in Guba and adjacent areas. These leaflets, which were signed by "Patani Mujahideen Warriors", said that their group had not produced or scattered any leaflets forbidding people from working on Friday mornings, especially tapping rubber at dawn, which is their primary occupation. They added that people could indeed work on Friday mornings. What they did request is that people get their work done before noon so that they, especially the men, could perform Friday noon prayers at the mosque.

Another kind of clarifying leaflet is issued after an incident in which Malay Muslims have been killed or injured. These seek to clarify that those behind the incident did not mean to hurt their fellow Malay Muslims. Other parties, usually Thai authorities, are to blame for such mishaps. Below is part of such a leaflet, written in Thai. It was found on the road by a passerby while on his way home from doing errands in Raman district.

> Bombs in commercial banks killed 1 customer and wounded 26 others. The estimated cost of damage is 2.6 million baht. *Our aim is to destroy Kafir Siam's economic system and their social-psychological condition.* We did not want to destroy life and body. *We deeply apologize to Muslims who were wounded by the bombs.* But we condemn the staff of some banks for not informing their customers after receiving our warning phone calls 15 minutes before the bombs were detonated.
>
> *Islamic Warriors of the Fatoni Darussalam State* (emphases in the original)

Most leaflets address Malay Muslims in general. However, some leaflets specifically address individuals. These leaflets are always serious warnings or deadly threats towards individuals whom the leaflet makers consider defectors or traitors. I have never seen this kind of leaflet but have spoken to people who have received them. Below is what Talib, a roadside teashop owner, said about a leaflet anonymously posted on the wall of his elder sister's teashop:

> A leaflet was posted on the wall of my elder sister's teashop at night. A plastic bag with a hard-boiled egg and rice grains in were also hung on the wall. The leaflet said that my elder brother, who is a policeman in Satun Province, is like a Thai dog because he works to serve the Thais. It also said that this betrays fellow Malay Muslims and ordered my elder brother to quit his job, otherwise he would be killed. A hard-boiled egg and rice grains are the symbol of death. People in the three southernmost provinces always bring these two things to the house of the dead to help the host perform the funeral ceremony. So this is a deadly threat against my elder brother.

The scattering and posting of leaflets was widespread in the initial stages of the recent unrest. It was always conducted secretly at night and often in public places such as roadside teashops, roadside pavilions and mosques. However, more recently, the distribution of leaflets has waned. Many residents said that the insurgents have shifted their strategy, focusing more on deadly attacks. Interestingly enough, the military increasingly employs leaflet scattering as a way to disseminate its own message, along with other kinds of operations.

2.2. Security Forces Operations

Along with the activities of the insurgents or Okhrae Dalae, Guba residents have experienced various security forces operations, mainly by army soldiers or Okhrae Hijau and paramilitary rangers or Okhrae Hitae.[9] Most residents encounter security forces in the form of troop patrols. Jamal said it was not long after the theft of weapons at the army base in Narathiwat Province in 2004 that he first saw a troop patrol in Guba. He recalled that, while sitting and chatting with his friends at the roadside pavilion in the afternoon as usual, he saw a convoy of military vehicles on the road. Part of the convoy stopped in front of the southern Guba mosque, while the remainder passed by the pavilion before stopping in front of the northern Guba mosque. Then soldiers got out of their vehicles, formed a line, and then patrolled along the road from the two ends. They stopped by some houses and greeted the residents; on occasion they walked down smaller lanes into the inner parts of central Guba before emerging and walking along the main road again. Then they patrolled past the pavilion. Jamal said that some of them smiled and greeted him and others in the pavilion in Thai, and he and his companions smiled back to reciprocate good social manners. The soldiers patrolled the area for about an hour and left without incident.

Troop patrols were not conducted regularly. Sometimes, soldiers came to patrol the area two or three days in a row, while other times they disappeared for a week before coming back again. "It is up to the situation", said one resident. "If their intelligence says that Okhrae Dalae are operating in the area, they will come to patrol frequently. But they will not come if they think there is nothing around here." Another resident has his own theory. He said: "It also depends on the situation in general. If the situation is deteriorating, they will patrol more frequently." Speculation notwithstanding, these residents said that troop patrol schedules are unpredictable. This held true even after military camps were set up in the area.

Another routine operation by security forces in the area is house searches. These differ from troop patrols in that they specifically target certain houses suspected of being hiding places, meeting points, safe havens, or operation sites of the insurgents. In addition, while troop patrols consist solely of soldiers, house searches are conducted by combined forces including soldiers (the main force), police officers (the secondary force), and public officials and civilians in charge of security affairs as assistants. This mixture of personnel is required because these operations need the cooperation of different government agencies, and the number of soldiers alone is not sufficient. It is also noteworthy that while troop patrols covered all three parts of Guba, house searches were often specifically focused on the southern part of the settlement, where the insurgents were thought to be most active.

A significant house search was done at the house of Babo[10] in southern Guba. In 2009, after the moon was seen and the declaration of the end of the month of Ramadan was made, Babo's house was crowded with people from Guba and nearby villages. They came to get blessings from Babo, their de facto religious leader, and also to celebrate the end of the month of Ramadan with their acquaintances. While joyfully chatting with each other, they were surprised and frightened by the sudden approach of a group of soldiers. The soldiers, without saying anything, walked into the house, past the living room where people were gathered, to the kitchen at the back of the house. They searched the kitchen for awhile and came back to the living room. Some people asked what was going on, as they personally knew some of the soldiers who were stationed at Pahong Gayu military camp. The soldiers replied that they were looking for Babo's son and his friends, who were suspected of involvement in the unrest and who had disappeared more than two years earlier (I discuss Babo's son, Ibrahim, later in this chapter). They thought that these suspects may come back home to celebrate the end of Ramadan with Babo and others. But the soldiers did not find anyone they wanted. They spoke a little bit before leaving, and the people at Babo's house were discontent. As Talib, who was present in the house, put it: "They [the residents] got pissed off. They said that the soldiers didn't respect Babo. They said that the soldiers should have said something to Babo or anyone sitting there, not just the sudden entering the house and walking straight to the back without saying anything. This is insulting."

Only a few house searches were successful (from the point of view of the security forces) — those being sought were found and arrested with no clash. One successful search took place in the late morning of 25 August 2008. A combined force searched a house belonging to Ghani in the inner part of central Guba. Ghani had just returned home from tapping rubber. He was arrested and taken to a military camp for interrogation and detention. The house search and the arrest generated resentment among residents, as they believed that Ghani was just an ordinary villager tapping rubber to earn his living and that he had nothing to do with the insurgency. They suspected that a hired spy, also a Guba resident, for some reason provided the authorities with false information. Ghani was detained for several weeks before being released without any charge.

Another "successful" house search took place in village 2. In the morning of 20 February 2009, people in village 2 saw about a hundred heavily armed soldiers and police scattering along the main road. Judging from previous experience, they knew that a major house search was going to take place but did not know for sure which part of the village and which house would be specifically targeted. It was not until after noon prayer that they learned more about it. Apparently, soldiers and police as well as public officials came to search a house, which, according to their intelligence, had been used as a meeting and hiding place for insurgents for three years. All the suspects were found and arrested with no clashes. However, what interested and concerned the residents was that two of the five suspects were male teenagers from southern Guba. Some people said that they knew these teenagers well and did not believe that they could be involved with the unrest, as they were accused of. Many added that these teenagers and other suspects should have run away or fought rather than surrendering to the authorities, because they would be beaten and tortured during interrogation, which people thought would be more painful than death.

It addition to conducting troop patrols and house searches, security forces in Guba also set up military camps and a police post. In 2005, a police post was set up along the main road and staffed with a police officer and some civilians in charge of security affairs. A checkpoint was set up in front. Usually, the post was stationed by the civilians. A police officer came once a day or so to check if everything was in order. The checkpoint usually was not in operation; it was only manned when security measures were tightened, especially after a violent incident had occurred in Guba or nearby. The post only operated for a short period of time before being closed down and moved away. A police officer who had been assigned to the post explained why it was closed:

> The [village 2] assistant headman who worked with me was shot dead. We had been friends since childhood. So I felt deeply saddened by his death. I was also disheartened about my work here. I told my superintendent that I could no longer work at the post. He agreed with my request. He did not find anyone else to replace me but cancelled the operation instead. The post then was deserted and the checkpoint was moved away from the road. There have been no police posts or checkpoints in the area since then.

The first military camp near Guba has a long, complex history largely centred around the tense relationship between soldiers of the Thai army and Mana, village 1 headman at the time, as mentioned earlier. In their efforts to "colour" or categorize villages in the Deep South, soldiers met with Mana and asked him about the situation in the village. They said that, according to their intelligence, insurgents were active in village 1, and as a result the village should be categorized as a "red-zone" village requiring full military operations. But Mana disagreed and argued that no insurgents operated in his village, challenging the soldiers to prove their case in court. The soldiers did not accept the challenge and left the meeting without saying anything.

A few days later, a military convoy passed by Guba, and then some soldiers from the convoy returned and stopped in the settlement. They got out of their military pick-up truck and said that someone had scattered metal spikes on the road. They suspected that someone in the village had done it and therefore wanted to inspect the motorcycles in the vicinity to check if any of them had been used in the operation, but the inspection was inconclusive. After learning about the incident, Mana rushed to the scene. He did not find any metal spikes in the road, but a soldier in an armoured personnel carrier (APC) pointed a machine gun at him as if he were a culprit. Trying to suppress his anger, Mana asked the soldiers where the metal spikes were. The soldiers said they had already cleared them up, although the police had not yet come to investigate the scene, according to normal procedures. Mana said that he did not believe the soldiers' story; in fact, he claimed: "They wanted to create a situation so that they could use it as a justification to set up a military camp in the village."

After the confrontation, soldiers came to meet with Mana again. This time, they wanted his cooperation in setting up a military camp in Guba. Mana disagreed again and said that it would bring violence to the village, which in his opinion was still calm and peaceful. Although the soldiers failed to get Mana's cooperation, a military camp was eventually established in the front part of the Pahong Gayu school compound in 2008. As mentioned earlier, this success was largely attributed to the efforts of a school janitor who was also a member of the village security team. About forty army soldiers were stationed at the camp, and they were tasked with various kinds of military operations. At first, they collected data about the nearby villages and residents and patrolled the villages on a regular basis. But later they patrolled the villages only once in awhile and became aloof. Sometimes they joined combined force in house searches, and sometimes they provided medical care and implemented development projects for the residents. Their primary daily military operations, as seen through the eyes of the residents, was to travel back and forth between their camps and other destinations in their APCs, pick-up trucks, and motorcycles.[11]

The military camp was in operation for four years but closed in 2012 due to changes in the security agencies' policy to protect schools. However, in late 2013 a new military camp was built in Yula settlement of village 2. Soldiers renovated an abandoned rubber smokehouse that had been built by the Office of the Rubber Replanting Aid Fund as common village property. However, only a few residents actually used the building, because most of them sell their product as rubber scrap, not rubber sheet. The smokehouse was eventually abandoned. Seeing this as an opportunity, soldiers informed the subdistrict headman and the chief executive of the Subdistrict Administrative Organization (SAO)[12] that they wanted to transform the smokehouse into a temporary military camp. However, the SAO chief disagreed on the grounds that the smokehouse was still in use by residents for penning cattle during flooding. He wanted the soldiers to hold a community forum allowing residents to express their opinion on the issue. But the soldiers did not follow this suggestion; rather, they approached the owner of the land on which the smokehouse was located and offered him a monthly rent of 3,000 baht. The landowner felt pressure to accept the offer despite his unwillingness.

Residents said that the soldiers of the Yula military camp mostly operated like those of the Pahong Gayu military camp but differed in that they patrolled more often, especially in rubber plantations and forests, and in that they were less friendly. These soldiers also used the Tadika in the northern Guba mosque as a temporary shelter, despite the residents' disagreement with this practice. It was not until one soldier committed suicide in the Tadika's bathroom that soldiers stopped using the facility as their temporary shelter. Initially, the Yula military camp was stationed mainly by army soldiers with some paramilitary rangers. However, later, due to changes in security policy, the soldiers were withdrawn and replaced exclusively by paramilitary rangers. Thus, a former smokehouse in Yula is now a fully operational paramilitary ranger regiment camp.

The unrest in Guba and nearby areas has decreased in more recent years but has not entirely ended. While bombings and the distribution of leaflets have waned, shootings have continued. And although troop patrols are not conducted as often as before and house searches occur only once in awhile as most suspected insurgents have fled to other areas, Guba is still closely monitored by security agencies, especially the paramilitary rangers or Okhrae Hitae stationed at the Yula military camp. Security agencies believe that insurgents or Okhrae Dalae still operate in Guba, especially its southern part.

2.3. Okhrae Dalae

Okhrae Dalae, or "insider", is the word Guba residents use to refer to the insurgents. It is a generic term that does not refer to any specific movements or organizations, such as BRN-Coordinate, which security agencies and related organizations consider the perpetrators of the recent unrest (McCargo 2008, pp. 171–74; for a study of BRN-Coordinate, see Helbardt 2015). Nor does it connote any virtue, like the term *juwae* (*pejuang* in standard Malay), which means "warrior" and which some sympathizers of the insurgents use to refer to them (Askew and Helbardt 2012, pp. 779–80). Okhrae Dalae simply refers to Malays in southern Thailand who are involved in the insurgency, without insinuating any opinion about them. While it remains unclear who exactly is behind each insurgency-related incident in the Guba area, the name "Ibrahim" comes up most often.

Ibrahim was the imam of the southern Guba mosque and Babo's eldest son. After spending about five years at a *pondok* in Balor subdistrict of Raman district, about 10 kilometres south of Guba, he studied Islam at Al-Azhar, a famous university in Cairo. Upon his return, he taught at the Thamavitya Mulniti School, a noted private Islamic school[13] in Yala Province, teaching Islam, Arabic language, and other related subjects. When the former imam of the southern Guba mosque, who was his older uncle, passed away, he was elected the mosque's new imam with the support of his father. On the surface, his life was simple. He taught at the school, staying in Yala Province during the week and returning home on Fridays to spend his weekends there. However, after one evening prayer in August 2006 at the southern Guba mosque, some people learned for the first time that his life is not simple as they had thought. Ibrahim was suspected of being involved in the insurgency, and he needed to leave home right away for a safer location. Below is Jamal's account of Ibrahim's address to his fellow mosque members after the evening prayer:

> When we finished the evening prayer, Imam asked us to stay there a minute longer as he had something to tell us. Some twenty people were there waiting for his talk. Imam had tears in his eyes when he began to speak. He said that after this dawn prayer he had to leave because he was suspected of being involved with the unrest. He knew this from his friends who are his colleagues at the school and who are also suspected of being involved with the unrest. There were three of them. His friends told him that the authorities would arrest him unless he escaped. So he decided to leave, but he wanted to tell the story and say goodbye to his friends here before. Then he cried and hugged everyone, including me. After the dawn prayer, he left his home. It has been two years [in 2009] since he left home, and he has never returned. Or at least no one here has seen him since then. No one but his close relatives and Babo know where and how he is now.

Ibrahim did not state clearly whether or not he was indeed involved with the insurgency as accused, leaving his friends and acquaintances in confusion and uncertainty. Some residents said that they did not believe the accusation. When asked why he felt compelled to flee if he was not involved, one person said: "Because he doesn't believe that he will get justice. You know, they [the state authorities] will beat you until you admit that you did it." Talib said that he was even more surprised when learning later from a government notice that Ibrahim was a core leader of the insurgency. As he put it, "I couldn't believe my eyes when one day I saw Ibrahim on a poster as a leader of the insurgents. You know, the poster that the authorities distributed showing that he would be a deputy prime minister and his friend would be an interior minister if Patani State was successfully founded. It's unbelievable!"

However, some residents were not surprised to learn that Ibrahim was involved with the unrest. Mohammed, for one, said that he used to be a southern Guba mosque committee member. But he quit the appointment after noticing that, over a three-year period, Ibrahim always talked about the founding of Patani State during the mosque committee meetings. Ibrahim had said their dream of founding Patani State was coming nearly true, as many countries especially in the Middle East had provided them with a variety of assistance including money, weapons and military training. He asked other committee members to cooperate with him to facilitate this goal. Mohammed disagreed with Ibrahim, as he had had a bitter experience with separatist movements in the past. However, he did not express his objection in the meetings because, he said, "I don't want to be in trouble." The only thing he could do was to quit his position on the grounds that he was a northern Guba resident, and now northern Guba had its own mosque.

Mohammed, who now is a northern Guba mosque committee member, added that it was not only Ibrahim but also many other residents who were involved with the unrest. He said that some southern Guba mosque committee members openly supported Ibrahim in the meetings, some of them being Okhrae Dalae. He said that he knew some of them to be active in the insurgency, but there were many others he was uncertain about. So he cannot talk about the unrest openly for fear of being targeted.

Another resident who is always mentioned in connection with Okhrae Dalae is Hing, from southern Guba. He went to Guba school for his primary education and was a "good boy" in the eyes of his teachers. As Roh, one of his teachers, put it: "I know Hing well. He is a good boy. He always helps carry out school activities, and he loves playing sports. He is quiet but sincere." After finishing grade 6 at the school, he went to study religion at a *pondok* in Balor subdistrict. He completed level 10 at the *pondok* and then became a *cikgu* (teacher) at a Tadika in Kero subdistrict, about 3 kilometres east of Guba. He also liked playing football and is therefore known as Ustaz Hing and Black Beckham.

Most people did not know that Hing was involved with the insurgency, as they mostly saw him teaching children and playing football. Later, they learned that he had disappeared because of his involvement, but they did not know where he was or in what condition. People gradually came to learn that he was a suspect in many insurgency-related incidents. According to state intelligence, he was a Platoon 1 Commander of the Runda Kumpulan Kecil (RKK)[14] in Raman and was behind many insurgent incidents, making him one of the most wanted insurgents with a high bounty on his head.

After years of operations, in December 2013 he and his company were surrounded by soldiers and police in Rueso district of Narathiwat Province. The stand-off played out for several hours before he and three of his company (one of whom was also a southern Guba resident) were killed. Seven were captured alive, two of whom were Yula residents. The bodies of Hing and his companion from southern Guba were buried at the southern Guba cemetery with hundreds of people attending. Although his death resulted in a declining number of insurgency-related incidents in Guba, there are still some Okhrae Dalae in the area.

According to Talib, the village 2 assistant headman, local Malays who are involved with the unrest can be divided into three groups. First are the ideological leaders, which primarily include Imam Ibrahim and some other religious leaders as well as Tadika teachers (*cikgu*). These religious leaders and teachers always use religious institutions such as mosques, *pondoks* and Tadikas, and religious activities such as sermons and teachings, to disseminate their thoughts. Second are the operatives, who are mostly young men who are highly motivated. They are recruited and trained at secret locations and then tasked with carrying out a wide range of violent activities in their local area and farther afield. Third are the propagandists, who comprise many male adults. These propagandists usually use public spaces, especially teashops, to spread their version of the news and arouse local people. Talib added that, although the ideologues and operatives are no longer very active because they are closely monitored by soldiers and many of them, mostly southern Guba residents, have fled, the propagandists are still quite active. They continue to use Talib's teashop to disseminate information; Talib and his customers therefore must exercise great caution when discussing the insurgency in public.

Some residents, especially male teenagers, are approached by the insurgents in their recruitment of new members.[15] Farouk, a young man from central Guba, said that in 2009 some friends of his had begun acting strangely. They talked to him a couple of times about Patani history, focusing on how Malays and Islam had been mistreated by the Siamese kingdom and (later) the Thai state. Then they invited him to join them, but he declined on the grounds that what he was doing was already helping boost Islam. He said that his friends neither cajoled nor threatened him after he turned them down. They just left him and never talked to him about it again. Farouk said that if he had accepted their invitation, they would have taken him somewhere to take an oath that he would keep all their activities secret and not betray those involved. Then they would take him somewhere else for weapon training. And when he had finished training, they would task him with missions, starting with distributing leaflets and scattering metal spikes on roadways and ultimately conducting arson and shootings. Likewise, Nazri, a teenager from southern Guba, said that he and his younger brother had once been approached by a friend who wanted them to join him. Thai maltreatment of Islam and Malays was invoked; when Nazri and his brother demurred, the recruiter friend simply left. Nazri confirmed other similar comments about the insurgents' recruitment strategy: "There is no force or coercion in the recruitment. They want only those who are willing, who voluntarily join them."

Despite widespread stories about Okhrae Dalae in Guba, I never witnessed their operations in the field. Nor did I ever talk to anyone who admitted being Okhrae Dalae. Importantly, despite being the only Thai Buddhist in the area, I never felt any threat to my personal safety. Farouk told me that the reason why I was "spared" was that "they know you don't think badly of them. They think you are harmless. So they let you stay here doing your research." Rather than through direct encounters, I was made aware of Okhrae Dalae in Guba through the stories told about them, through the consequences of their operations, and through the broad effects — fear and distrust — they created in the area.

2.4. A Moment of Fear and Distrust

I woke up one morning to find that Maeh and Wae (the mother and father of the family I stayed with) were returning home from tapping rubber very early. With surprise, I asked them about the early hour, and Maeh replied:

> A couple was killed and beheaded in a rubber plantation. They both were Thais from Sayo village. They came to tap rubber in Ba Roh village as usual. But early this morning they were killed and beheaded. It's very scary. I didn't see their bodies or their heads, although their rubber plantation is next to ours, because soldiers blocked the road and did not allow anyone to pass.

Like other violent incidents in the area, this killing and beheading took place anonymously. And, as a result, it led to various speculation about the killers and their aims. Some said it was done by Okhrae Dalae in their attempt to force Thais to flee the region. This speculation is in line with that of state authorities. However, many others suspected that the atrocity may have been committed by paramilitary rangers in their effort to discredit Okhrae Dalae and to generate anger against Malay Muslims among Thai Buddhists in the area.

No matter who was behind it, the killing and beheading of a Thai Buddhist couple created fear among the residents. Neither Maeh and Wae nor many of their neighbours in Guba went out to tap rubber in Ba Roh for three days, although soldiers had secured the area since the afternoon of the day the incident took place. They were still frightened by the incident's sheer atrocity. On the first day of their return to work, Maeh and Wae went in group in a pick-up truck, rather than individually on motorcycles as usual, to collect rubber scrap, rather than tapping rubber, although the amount of rubber scrap was not sufficient for collection. They were still haunted by fear of the perpetrators. Asked whom she feared, Maeh said she did not know. Asked who she thought did this, Maeh said she had no idea either. The only thing she knew was that the killers are so daunting that they could kill anyone, including her if they wanted to. Some residents not only feared the perpetrators but were also afraid that they might be attacked by Thai Buddhists in retaliation against Malay Muslims, whom they thought to be the killers. It took Maeh, Wae and others about a week to shed their fear and resume their normal life.

The case of armed strangers is also revealing. Shortly after his usual lateness in getting up one morning, Najmudin, my roommate, told me that the previous night he had seen a group of armed strangers walking by in the riverside forest. He said that, at the time, he and his friends, one of them an off-duty soldier from Pahong Gayu military camp, were drinking *kratom* cocktails as usual. Suddenly, a group of men emerged from one end of the forest and continued along the riverbank. There were four of them, all armed with machine guns. When they walked past nearby, Najmudin and others in the group greeted them in Malay and asked what they were up to and where they were going. But the strangers did not respond, and Najmudin and his friends did not dare to ask anything further, as only one of them — the soldier — had a weapon, and it was only a handgun. All they could do was watch the strangers walk past and disappear at the other end of the forest.

Asked whether the strangers were Thais or Malays, Najmudin said they were Malays, as he had heard their voices from a distance. Asked who he guessed they were — Okhrae Hitae or Okhrae Dalae — Najmudin said "Okhrae Dalae". Asked if he feared them, Najmudin said, "Absolutely". Najmudin and his friends then felt compelled to move their regular *kratom* cocktail drinking spot to a different location to avoid dangerous encounters with these mysterious armed strangers.

The news about the armed strangers spread across Guba rapidly. After talking with Najmudin for awhile, I left the house and walked to the roadside pavilion to discuss the issue with Ishak, who was sitting there alone. I told him what I had learned from Najmudin about the armed strangers. However, not only did Ishak already know the whole story but he had also developed his own theory about it. He said that the armed strangers were not Okhrae Dalae as Najmudin had surmised but that they were "troops on their duty". Then he provided relevant information to support his theory. He said: "They are new troops recently sent here to perform specific tasks, as we saw in the TV news. People in other areas have also seen these troops and this kind of military operation."

Ishak's speculation is in line with that of Talib, who said that the armed strangers Najmudin and his *kratom* cocktail gang had encountered may be soldiers on duty, but in no way were they Okhrae Dalae. This is because, he added, "today's Okhrae Dalae don't operate in such a way. That's how those of past decades operated — secretly moving through the forest. But Okhrae Dalae now operate primarily in the villages, and they would not disclose themselves like this. That's the old style, operations in clandestine movements."[16] Talib added that that was not how Okhrae Dalae threatened people either. "If they want to kill you, they just kill you. And that's it," he said bluntly.

As with similar incidents, although it is still unclear who these armed strangers were and what purpose they had, their mysterious appearances, which had lasted for about two weeks with the number increasing to seven persons, created fear among Guba residents. Many became more vigilant and watchful, some even changing their daily routines.

Distributed leaflets, especially those threatening deadly force, also created fear among the residents. As discussed above, there were rumours of leaflets forbidding Muslims from working on Friday..Although no one had ever seen the leaflets, most residents followed the instruction. And although there were other reasons such as Islamic observance behind such a decision, the main reason for not working on Friday was fear of those behind the leaflets. And even though there were later leaflets that people did see that clarified that it was permitted to work on Friday, many residents still did not go to work on that day. This is due largely to confusion and uncertainty. It took people about six weeks to decide to go back to work on Friday mornings again. Some people took the incident as an opportunity to quit working on Friday mornings for good. In addition to getting the day off, they came to think that not working on Friday mornings was in line with Islamic practice.

Fear is particularly acute if a threatening leaflet targets specific individuals or groups. Najmudin said that he used to be a member of the village security team. But he quit because there were leaflets forbidding people from cooperating with the Thai government, and the village security teams were specifically targeted. "They said they would kill all members of the village security team, and I believed they really meant it. So I quit," said Najmudin. Likewise, Talib, as mentioned earlier, said that his older brother, a policeman in Satun Province, stopped his regular holiday home visits after his relatives found a leaflet and a plastic bag with rice grains and eggs on the wall of his older sister's teashop. "They wanted my older brother to quit his job; otherwise, he would be killed. But my older brother insisted that he would not quit his job. Our family tried to figure out how to get out of this tough situation. Then we came up with the idea that my older brother should not visit home during weekends for awhile. We don't want him to get killed," said Talib. It took almost a year for Talib's older brother to resume his holiday home visits, and they were not on a regular basis as before.

If fear is the head, then distrust is the tail of the same coin. This is because the anonymity of those who perpetrate violence has rendered almost everyone a suspect in one sense or another. And, given that it is almost impossible to know who has become involved with the unrest and how, avoiding being targeted by either side is what people attempt to achieve in leading their daily life. The situation recounted below illustrates how the unrest has brought distrust even among villagers themselves.

Late one afternoon in November 2008, due to my intervention, a conversation at a roadside pavilion turned to the topic of the disappearance of Imam Ibrahim of the southern Guba mosque. I asked why a new imam had not yet been appointed, even though Ibrahim had disappeared more than two years earlier. Daud said there was an acting imam who could perform all tasks on behalf of the imam. In addition, almost all the imam's tasks and duties could be performed by his assistants, the *khatib* and *bilal*. So there was no need to appoint a new imam for now, he said. On the other hand, Saifuldin said that "actually" Imam Ibrahim had not gone anywhere and still performed all his tasks and duties at the southern Guba mosque. "Then why do we need to appoint a new imam?" he provocatively asked me back. However, while others were expressing their opinions with reservations, Mohammed was very quiet. Sometimes he seemed to send me a signal to not raise this sensitive issue. At other times it looked like he disagreed with what his companions were saying, but he kept his mouth shut. He sat quiet and listened to the others until the conversation ended. Then he left the pavilion like the others when it was getting dark. Although he did not say anything to me, I noticed that he had something on his mind.

In the late morning of the following day, while I was sitting alone taking notes on a wooden bench, Mohammed rode his motorcycle past. When he saw me, he turned his motorcycle around to where I was sitting, parked it, and walked over to me. I greeted him as usual. He greeted me back and sat beside me. "The reason why I didn't say anything about the imam of the southern Guba mosque yesterday is that there were many people there, and I don't know for sure if and how they might be involved with the unrest," he said. Then he added: "As you know, the reason why the imam had to leave home is that he is suspected of being involved. Except for his immediate relatives, especially his dad Babo, no one knows how and where he is. And as you know, besides the imam, there are many other villagers who are involved with the unrest. They may be operatives, supporters or sympathizers. And they are all around here." Mohammed said that he could not trust anyone, even his close friends. He also warned me about the sensitivity of the issue I had raised the day before, given Babo's influence in the settlement.

While having to be careful when talking with their neighbours, Guba residents at the same time have to be watchful about strangers. They have to keep an eye on the vehicles that drive past, especially pick-up trucks they have never seen. This is particularly the case if a vehicle drives back and forth several times, or if it is parked nearby and the windows remain raised.

In one such instance, it was getting dark and the rain was pouring down when two friends and I, sitting and chatting on a marble bench in front of a nearby house, noticed a black pick-up truck pulled over around the entrance of an alley leading to the inner part of central Guba. We stared at the pick-up with suspicion, as we had never seen it before and had no idea why it was parked there. My friends were tense, as five minutes had passed but no one got out the pick-up and the windows were rolled up. They put their hands on the pistols they carried at their waists, ready to pull them out if needed. Luckily, there was no incident, as a few minutes later the pick-up left in darkness. One of my companions, Saifuldin, said: "They should not have done like this. At least they should have lowered down the windows so that we can see their faces. We cannot trust anyone, especially the strangers. I was ready to shoot if anything irregular happened."

However, given the unrest in the area, not many strangers came to Guba. Except for young *kratom* cocktail customers, most visitors were either relatives or guests coming for various occasions, especially religious events. And when kinship and religious ties were connected, these visitors were no longer strangers. However, the soldiers and police around Guba were always considered "strangers", regardless of how often they showed up on operations in the area. State authorities were also primary persons of distrust.

The following encounter illustrates how soldiers were regarded and distrusted by Guba residents. At the very beginning of their operations in Guba, troops from Pahong Gayu military camp collected data on the village and its residents. They walked throughout the whole area and talked to people at their houses. They had questionnaires, which they asked some family members to fill out, mostly fathers and sons. They also took pictures of the houses and of people they interviewed. One day, they came to the roadside pavilion in front of the house where I stayed, where I was sitting and chatting with a group of local acquaintances as usual. They smiled and greeted us in Thai. One of them explained what they were up to and asked for our cooperation. The soldiers chose to interview Wae and Aiman, two family members. However, Wae does not speak Thai, so Najib volunteered to do the translation for him. Aiman did not need this kind of assistance, because he is fluent in Thai. The interview took about ten minutes. After completing the interview, the soldiers took pictures of Wae and Aiman and their houses, which were nearby, before saying thank you and leaving.

On the surface, the interviews went smoothly and seemed to be successful. The soldiers got all answers they wanted. However, there were feelings of uneasiness, frustration, and distrust among the residents throughout the whole interview. Due to his friendly personality, Wae always answered questions with a smile. But when it came to questions about his sons, he felt uneasy. A soldier asked him how many children he had; he said seven, which is true. But when a soldier asked him about his sons' lives and occupations, he felt nervous and sometimes provided false information so as to protect his sons from getting in trouble. Wae did this even though, to my knowledge, none of his sons are involved in the unrest. Aiman, on the other hand, consistently provided the soldiers with false information. For example, when asked about his occupation, Aiman said that he tapped rubber like the other villagers although he had never done that. When asked about his income, he said about 3,000 baht a month, which, based on my observation, is very much lower than the amount he really earns. He did not tell the soldiers about a wide range of work that he is actually engaged in. Importantly, he continued to carve a *kris* blade throughout the interview,[17] looking frustrated and annoyed all the while. The soldiers noticed these things but did not say anything about them.

I did not ask Wae or Aiman why they had lied to the soldiers. But, shortly after the soldiers left, Aiman complained about why they wanted his personal information such as education, occupation, income, and properties, even though he had done nothing wrong. "What will they do with the data?" he asked with frustration. One person at the pavilion said, "Perhaps they want to keep an eye on us," while another added, "They want our details because it makes things easier for them if they want to get us." No one thought that the soldiers' gathering of personal data benefited them, the local residents.

Fear and distrust, two sides of the same coin, have various effects. In addition to the effects of the incidents related above, some local people simply move out. Many southern Guba males have left their home because they were suspected of being involved with the insurgency. I asked some people if these suspicions were true. They said for some, yes, but for many, no. Then I asked why innocent residents felt compelled to run away if they had not done anything wrong. I was told: "Because they don't trust state authorities. They were afraid that they might be tortured for a confession. They have heard a lot about this. So they ran away rather than turning themselves in, even though they have nothing to do with the insurgency." I never talked to or even saw these runaway villagers, and the rumours about them were confusing and could not be confirmed. Some said that they had fled and never returned, while others claimed that some of them might visit their homes at night.

Most people who have moved away from the Deep South are Thai and Chinese Buddhists, although this was not the case in Guba. However, there is one case from a nearby village that is noteworthy. During a 2009 election for SAO chief executive and members, I met a policeman at a polling station at Pahong Gayu school. He was assigned to team up with other security personnel such as soldiers, territorial defence volunteers and village security teams to provide security for the election. He greeted me and said that he recognized me. He then recalled the situation in which we had first met. He told me that he had not returned to his home in Laboh Luwah village, where we had met, for more than four months. Now, during workdays, he stayed with his friend in a police flat in Raman, and he spent his weekends with his wife and children in their newly purchased house in downtown Yala city. He said that the reason why he decided to move out and stay with his family in the city is that, apart from familial ties, he felt insecure while staying in the village, even though he'd grown up there. He said that these days he couldn't trust anyone, even his close friends he had known since childhood, because "you never know if and how they might have gotten involved with the unrest. They will not let you know, especially if you are a state authority like me. I am afraid that I might be targeted and get attacked one day. So I decided to move out and stay in town, which I think is safer."

Fear and distrust notwithstanding, Guba is one of a few places in the Deep South that is still vibrant. Besides the residents feeling free to carry on with their daily lives, relatives and friends continuing to arrive for cultural and religious festivals as well as *kratom* cocktail customers fill the settlement with liveliness. When night falls, roadside teashops are packed with adults, teenagers and children, drinking beverages, chatting, watching satellite television, playing chess and, for some, conducting illegal businesses. The unrest has not totally transformed Guba.

Importantly, the unrest is just a symptom of a "disease" that has long infected the southernmost part of Thailand. It is the disease of subjectivity in relation to sovereignty, which over the past decade has become more severe. Okhrae Dalae have invoked the history of Malays who inhabited the region long before Siam's invasion to justify their course of action and to recruit new members and attract sympathizers. They also point out how badly Islam has been treated by Siam for the past few hundred years to legitimize their fight against the Thai state. The Thai state, for its part, has employed various apparatuses — schools, the military draft, royal projects and more — to ensure that it still has the residents under some modicum of control. Guba residents have thus found themselves caught up in the convergence of these forms of sovereignty imposing subjectivities on them — the issue I examine in the next chapter.

Notes
1. Okhrae Dalae (or Orang Dalam in standard Malay, which means "insider") is the term that Guba residents use to refer to the insurgents. However, the term does not refer to any movement or organization in particular; it simply refers to insurgent Malays. And there is no opposite term as Okhrae Luar (or Orang Luar in standard Malay, which means "outsider"). The "outsider" the residents face most often in their everyday lives are soldiers, whom they call Okhrae Hitae (or Orang Hitam in standard Malay, which literally means "black man" and refers to paramilitary rangers, whose uniforms are black) and Okhrae Hijau (or Orang Hijau in standard Malay, which literally means "green man" and refers to army soldiers, whose uniforms are green).
2. Although the anonymity of the perpetrators of the recent unrest begs the question of what it is about and who is behind it, there is a tendency to attribute it to local Malay Muslims. Duncan McCargo (2008, p. xii), for example, submitted that about

70–80 per cent of incidents were carried out by militants, about 10–20 per cent were linked to the authorities, and about 10 per cent were criminal. Likewise, although once arguing that the recent violence is largely a "conspiracy theory" staged by vested interest groups and crime rings (Askew 2007, pp. 5–37), Marc Askew in a later collaboration with Sascha Helbardt refers to it as "insurgent-driven" (Askew and Helbardt 2012, p. 779) and examined (1) the structure and recruitment pattern of BRN-Coordinate, which is allegedly responsible for most of the violence, and (2) the lives and motivations of six individual insurgents. This tendency to attribute the violence to Okhrae Dalae is reflected in Guba from the perspectives of both the authorities and the majority of residents.

3. Although BRN-Coordinate, after the peace talks of 28 February 2013, emerged as the organization that is behind most of the recent violence (Helbardt 2015, pp. 1–3), none of the leaflets distributed around the region have ever borne its name. This is also true for the other established insurgent organizations such as PULO, the BRN, and Bersatu, which are only peripheral to the violence that erupted after 2004 and which have produced no leaflets in the current violence, like they did during their earlier periods of activity. As will be seen later, leaflets tend to be signed by various groups that are likely to be ad hoc names rather than actual organizations.

4. McCargo (2009, p. 165) classified the insurgents' leaflets into three groups — warning leaflets, propaganda leaflets and satirical leaflets — and he particularly examines the propaganda ones. He maintains that the underlying discourse of the propaganda leaflets is the glorious history of Patani as a centre of Malay culture and Islamic learning, and the colonization of Patani by Siam/Thailand, thus employing history as a weapon of war and for an immediate political purpose (2009, p. 166). Their primary purpose is to fuel resentment against the security forces, the central government, and the Thai state (2009, p. 178). However, as I discuss later, the leaflets I found are more wide-ranging and aimed to achieve broader goals than simply fueling resentment against the Thai state.

5. General Sonthi Boonyaratglin was the commander in chief of the Royal Thai Army during 2005–07. On 19 September 2006, he, as head of the Council for Democratic Reform, staged a military coup against the Thaksin Shinawatra government and replaced it with the government of General Surayud Chulanont. In 2007, he resigned as commander in chief and as chairman of the Council for National Security (the former Council for Democratic Reform) to serve the Surayud government as deputy prime minister in charge of security affairs. During his tenure as commander in chief, Sonthi, as the first Muslim to hold the position, said that he would take a new approach to the unrest in the Deep South, meaning that he would end it soon. However, rather than ending, the violence escalated, leading Malay Muslims in southern Thailand to criticize Sonthi. The doubts about Sonthi's word expressed in the leaflet are an example of such criticism.

6. A *tok imam* is a mosque leader. The phrase consists of two words. *Tok* has two different meanings in local usage; first, it is an unofficial honorable title used for

people with important status such as a *pondok* headmaster (*tok guru*), village headman (*tok naebae*), and midwife (*tok bidan*). Second, *tok* is a kinship term, usually referring to a grandmother. However, sometimes it means an elder, which can be a man, such as *tok laki*, which means "husband". An imam is a mosque leader, who has two assistants: the *khatib* (who preaches the sermon) and the *bilal* (who announces the call to prayer at designated times). The imam's roles primarily include leading worship services, providing religious guidance, and in some cases serving as a community leader. Given the respectability of the position, the imam is usually an elderly man, and the word *imam* is usually prefaced by the word *tok*, which implies seniority as well as serving as an honorific. For a discussion of imams in the recent unrest, see McCargo 2008, pp. 28–33.

7. An *ustaz* (or *ustad* in Arabic) is a male religious teacher.
8. Imam Nawawi is an alias of Abu Zakaria Yahya Ibn Sharaf al-Nawawi, who is a highly respected Islamic scholar and jurist. He was born in 1233 in Nawa village, which is south of Damascus. His name — al-Nawawi — means "people of Nawa". He is known for having devoted himself to the study of Islam, and he wrote many books particularly on the Hadith and jurisprudence, which are still widely used in Muslim countries. He is also known as a simple person who bravely fought the unjust rulers of his time in accordance with Islamic principles. Given that the unrest in Thailand's Deep South is conceived by the insurgents as a war against an unjust Thai state, Imam Nawawi's life and teachings are often invoked in their operations; this leaflet is one example. (For his life and works in the English language, see Halim 2014.)
9. Although the Srisunthorn forces, which operate in local communities, include personnel from various units — army, marines, border patrol police, paramilitary rangers, and militia (McCargo 2008, p. 99) — local residents encounter army soldiers and paramilitary rangers more than others. And although the militias such as the village security teams or Chor Ror Bor are part of the Srisunthorn forces and considered part of the overall security forces (McCargo 2008, pp. 121–26), they are not regarded as such by the residents. My account of security forces operations in Guba is therefore focused primarily on army soldiers and paramilitary rangers.
10. "Babo" is a local Malay pronunciation of an Arabic word *baba*, which means "father". However, it is used as an honorific term for those learned in Islam, especially *pondok* owners, because the relationship between a *pondok* owner and his students is similar to that between a father and his children. The person who founded the first *pondok* in Guba is highly revered and respected following this tradition, and he was then called "Babo". His life and contribution to the revival of Islam in Guba is discussed in Chapter 3.
11. The army soldiers at the Pahong Gayu school military camp are part of the Srisunthorn forces. According to Duncan McCargo (2008, pp. 100–101), these units were often billeted at government schools because they could use the surplus facilities resulting from falling student enrolments. Their duties included

escorting teachers to and from schools, patrolling communities, talking to residents and community leaders, and gathering information. At the Pahong Gayu camp, the soldiers also perform special tasks such as providing medical services and implementing development projects, although with limited success, as I will show later.

12. The SAO (องค์การบริหารส่วนตำบล, อบต.) is a new form of local government created under the Subdistrict Councils and Subdistrict Administrative Organizations Act of 1994 (พระราชบัญญัติสภาตำบลและองค์การบริหารส่วนตำบล พ.ศ. 2537). It consists of the SAO Council and the SAO Executive Committee. The SAO Council includes members from each village who vote for the council chairman. The SAO Executive Committee is led by the chief executive of the SAO, who has two deputies and one secretary. The chief executive, in principle, formulates policy and relies on a chief administrator and a staff of government officials to implement it. The chief executive and members of the SAO are elected by local residents and serve a four-year term. The emergence of the SAO in a sense was conceived as part of the decentralization and democratization process in Thailand in the 1990s before the country was "turned upside down" by the military coup of 2006. (For a study of decentralization and democratization in provincial Thailand in the 1990s, part of which involves the emergence of the SAO, see Arghiros 2016.)

13. Private Islamic schools are a type of school in southern Thailand that are converted from older *pondok* schools following the Sarit Thanarat government's national integration policy discussed earlier. These schools are increasingly popular among southern Muslims. In 2016, there were 122 private Islamic schools in Yala, Pattani and Narathiwat Provinces. Although there are a greater number of government schools in the region, at 219, the Islamic schools are more popular. The ratio of secondary-level students enrolled in private Islamic schools versus government schools in 2016 is 69:31 (Regional Education Office no. 8, 2016, pp. 16, 26–28, 36–37). Private Islamic schools are more popular among the Muslim population because they offer regular, vocational and religious curricula that meet the demands of parents who want their children to study Islam along with secular subjects. Since the recent round of unrest began in 2004, security agencies have regarded them as places for indoctrination and the germination of many insurgents, and Thamavitya Mulniti School, where Ibrahim taught, is the leading such school (Askew and Helbardt 2012, p. 795).

14. BRN-Coordinate's military wing has a chain of command structure. Below the military council, the three provinces of Yala, Pattani and Narathiwat are divided into three military areas, with each area under the control of an area commander. Each area commands four to six battalions, with one battalion comprising two to three companies (*kompi*), each of which consists of three or more platoons (*platong*). Below the platoon is the *regu*, and below the *regu* is the RKK, which are the operational levels. One *regu* is composed of two to three RKK squads, each of which consists of six fighters tasked with specific functions. RKK squads

might be thought of as small group patrols. An RKK squad is BRN-Coordinate's smallest tactical unit through which independent military action is sustained and operations are planned and performed (Helbardt 2015, pp. 39, 50–53; see also Askew and Helbardt 2012, p. 784; McCargo 2008, pp. 163–75).

15. Sascha Helbardt (2015, p. 90) argues that explanations for the outbreak of the southern insurgency, such as the crisis of legitimacy and popular discontent, are problematic because rebellious attitudes are unlikely to translate into collective action without the recruitment of insurgents who are willing to take the risk that they may have to fight. He therefore examines how BRN-Coordinate recruited and trained insurgents, finding that the organization adopted a strategy of selective recruitment based more on recruits' identification with hostile Islamo-nationalism and an imagined Patani nation and less on the desire for short-term material benefits or coercion. BRN-Coordinate developed a regime of combined physical and psychological methods that fosters the resocialization of those selected as members into subjects who are no longer afraid of death and who maintain the secrecy of the organization (Helbardt 2015, pp. 90–134). In addition, Askew and Helbardt (2012, p. 782) argue that "interpreters of violence" tend to make reference to history, nationalism, religion, ethnicity, or elements of state repression that appear self-explanatory. This is mainly because not only are the socioeconomic and educational backgrounds of insurgents different, but also their motives, routes of involvement, and functions within the organization. Askew and Helbardt then examine the structure of BRN-Coordinate and its recruitment pattern with respect to the lives and motivations of six "Patani Warriors", finding that the motivations are varied — ranging from religious conviction and ethnic loyalty to personal excitement and specific grievances — and dynamic. In other words, there is no single "insurgent type" among "Patani Warriors" (Askew and Helbardt 2012, pp. 779–809; see also Helbardt 2015, pp. 140–76; McCargo 2008, pp. 147–52). The stories of Okhrae Dalae in Guba are not sufficiently numerous to make observations about their diversity, but my interviews with potential recruits are in line with Askew and Helbardt's argument about BRN-Coordinate's recruitment pattern.

16. Sascha Helbardt (2015, p. 233) argues that instead of full-time guerrillas hiding in the jungle, as with separatist movements in the past, the current insurgency is based on a part-time guerrilla-cum-terrorist force that hides in the villages and takes advantage of the state's limited control at the local level. Talib's observation is therefore in line with Helbardt's argument.

17. As a local Malay artist, Aiman earns supplementary income from producing artistic works. These include various items, most significantly the *kris* (dagger), and he is a member of a group of artisans from Burong Kueteetae subdistrict who make these daggers. When he has free time, he always carves *kris* blades and hilts and then sends them to the group, which markets them for sale. Aiman happened to have free time on the day when the soldier interviewed him, and thus he was carving a *kris* blade as usual.

3

Subjectivities on the Rise

During the month of Ramadan on 30 August 2009, a female reporter interviewed the Fourth Region army commander for the evening TV news about the unrest in the Deep South, a region that fell under his jurisdiction. She asked him why the number of violent incidents had dramatically increased during the month, and he replied that it was mainly because the insurgents had distorted Islam to serve their cause. He explained:

> They [the insurgents] claim that according to Islamic teachings, any deeds done for Islam during the month of Ramadan will bring double merits to the doers. And they claim that violence done on behalf of or for Islam during the month of Ramadan will bring the perpetrators double merits. Their claim is a distortion of Islamic teachings, but some local Muslims believe it and acted accordingly. That's why the number of violent incidents is increasing dramatically during this month.

The commander's explanation was supported by prominent state-appointed Islamic religious leaders and scholars. They gave interviews clarifying that Islam neither encourages nor condones any violence or killing, which in fact is a sin in Islam. Importantly, during the month of Ramadan, they said, Muslims are specifically required to refrain from committing any sin. Rather than double merits, to commit violence, especially killing, during the month of Ramadan would burden Muslims with double sins instead.[1]

Whether or not killing for Islam during the month of Ramadan brings Muslim perpetrators double merits is a question Guba residents find difficult to answer. Saifuldin said that while watching the news, he was uncertain about the insurgents' claim because his knowledge about Islam is just rudimentary. Aiman did not say anything but hinted that this is a serious question in need of thorough pondering and strong reference. Daessa felt uncomfortable when I addressed the issue to her and suggested that I seek the "correct" answer from knowledgeable persons. In general, the residents felt they had been put on the spot when I asked them this question. This is not only because the question is difficult for some of them to answer or because it is the first time they have had to answer the question, but also because how they answer it reflects what kind of Muslims they are and the extent to which they feel obliged to Islam. It is a question of subjectivity in relation to Islam vis-à-vis the Thai state, which has only intensified during the recent unrest.[2]

This chapter examines different subjectivities that have become more pressing to Guba residents in the wake of the recent unrest. It is divided into two parts. The first part explores how formal subjectivities including Muslims, Thai citizens, and royal subjects were created. The second part explores how informal subjectivities including subordinates and *kratom* kids were made. The chapter ends with a recounting of a state ceremony in which different subjectivities converge and tension emerges.

PART 1: FORMAL SUBJECTIVITIES

3.1. MUSLIMS

One evening, a group of male teenagers gathered at a table in front of a roadside teashop in Guba that had not opened yet. They chatted and laughed with their usual merriment. However, the atmosphere changed when a group of men in white robes (*thawb*) walked in a row towards them. They stopped chatting and stood up so as to show respect to these persons. Then an elder who led the row talked to the teenagers, primarily to remind them to perform their prayers five times daily and especially to attend the mosque on Fridays at noon to perform prayers. The teenagers listened to the elder solemnly and nodded to show that they agreed with him. After about five minutes of preaching, the men left the teenagers for other spots to repeat their advice to other residents. Then the teenagers resumed with their chatting and laughter.

Such "portable" preaching is a recognized religious activity the residents call *dakwah*, although it is in fact an activity of a religious movement called Jemaat Tabligh.[3] Dakwah as a movement was first introduced to Guba around 1990 and has grown in the area. In addition to Dakwah, Guba since the 1970s has also witnessed other Islamic strands that have transformed the practice of Islam in the area with respect to preaching, pilgrimage, the use of women's headscarves, evening religious classes, Koran reading classes and other practices. However, such changes cannot be attributed to the advent of these Islamic strands alone. Rather, they have much to do with Guba's specificity, which in turn has shaped the way in which these Islamic strands have played out in the area. Any account of changes in Islam in Guba since the 1970s needs to take into consideration the settlement's specificity, especially the activities of its highly revered religious leader, Babo.

3.1.1. The Return of Babo and the Advent of Islamic Strands

People in Guba always said that, in the past, Islam was practised only casually in their village. Not many people performed prayers five times a day, the mosques were poorly attended even at Friday noon, many did not fast during the month of Ramadan, and there were no public evening religious classes either at the mosques or in private homes. Many women did not wear headscarves, and they greeted men by touching hands. Many men wore short pants that revealed their knees and dispensed with religious caps altogether. Importantly, the village tolerated a variety of activities considered sinful ranging from gambling and opium smoking to popular entertainment and even prostitution.

This state of affairs is generally attributed to the villagers' ignorance of Islam. Jamal said that the people of that period, including religious leaders, had only vague knowledge about Islam. They did not know what was right or wrong, or what was allowed or not in Islam. They may have realized that some of their activities were considered sinful, but they had no idea how sinful they really were. So they felt free to behave as they chose. Yaakob had a very strong opinion on this. He said that Guba residents of the past "behaved like those having no religion. Women didn't wear headscarves and they greeted men by shaking hands. Men wore short pants, not sarongs as in these days. They committed adultery and drank palm wine. They lived their lives like animals."

While most Guba residents tended to subscribe to this line of thinking, Ishak, who had once engaged in a wide range of "sinful" activities, has his own explanation. He said that he had gambled at bullfighting and cockfighting, played dice games, performed in musical shows, and indulged in various cultural performances. He even raised dogs to help him in hunting wild animals. He said he knew by heart that these activities were sinful and not allowed in Islam, because he had attended a *pondok* in Balor subdistrict and learned about Islam there. But he continued to indulge in lax behavior because, he said, "I just wanted to have fun. I knew that I committed sin more than merit. But it's fun."

Different explanations notwithstanding, most Gubo residents agree that a major reason for the renewed focus on Islam was Babo's return to the village. Babo was born and grew up in southern Guba. At the age of fourteen, he left the village to attend a *pondok* in Balor subdistrict. He studied Islam and other subjects such as Arabic language there for six years. After completing his study at the *pondok*, he married a woman from Yula village and then left for Saudi Arabia with her to continue his religious study, with funding from some religious institutes. He and his wife lived in Saudi Arabia for fourteen years, studying religion and other subjects, before returning to Guba in the late 1960s.[4] Upon his return as the first person from Guba to have studied Islam in the Middle East, local residents raised funds to build him a house on land that he owned. He, in return, taught an evening religious class at southern Guba mosque on Tuesday and Friday nights, a religious mission he has carried out to the present day. He also founded a *pondok* near his home in 1975. The *pondok* drew some fifty students, mostly from outside Guba, before being closed after one year of operation due to, according to his students, damage by flooding. Then in 1979 he opened a Tadika near his house, which has remained in operation to the present day. His Tadika draws dozens of students, mostly from southern and central Guba. In addition, he habitually visits Guba residents at their homes and preaches to them about what Islam considers to be right and wrong, and what is allowed and what not.

Babo's activities are said to have boosted Islam in Guba. More residents began performing prayers five times daily and attending the mosques, especially at Friday noon. Fasting during Ramadan is more widely and strictly practised than before, and more people attend evening religious classes at the southern Guba mosque. Activities considered sinful in Islam such as bullfights and cockfights, dice games, outdoor movies and musical shows have been discontinued. Guba residents were said to have turned over a new leaf, becoming pious and devout Muslims, primarily through Babo's religious mission. Babo has therefore earned stature as a highly revered religious leader in Guba and nearby villages.

However, Babo's success story is not fully endorsed by all residents, especially the elders. Some elders have reservations about and even criticisms of Babo's religious enterprises. For example, Ishak, who is a little bit older than Babo and has witnessed and participated in all the changes, agreed that Babo had played a crucial role in boosting Islam in Guba but refused to attribute all "positive" changes in Islam to Babo alone. He said that, prior to Babo's return, the residents already had knowledge about Islam and were well aware of what is right and wrong, what are sins and what are merits in Islam. One reason why they were lax and committed sins is that no one led them to do the right things. In addition, Babo simply taught what practices and activities are sinful but did not specifically tell anyone to quit such activities. Importantly, the residents did not feel obliged to observe his preaching much. The main reason why they quit their sinful activities is that they felt personally ashamed, especially when Babo "caught them in the act". Ishak said:

> The reason why I quit sinful activities has nothing to do with Babo. I quit playing Dike Hulu [a traditional Malay musical performance] because I felt I was getting old and I was also shy of kids. These days a lot of kids play Dike Hulu and now it's become a kids' performance. In addition, I am now a Haji [a Muslim who has performed the hajj]. I should not do any sinful things. So I quit them all.

Ishak added that the disappearance of gambling in Guba hardly had anything to do with Babo. As discussed earlier, two Chinese brothers who had operated a gambling den left Guba for Raman primarily because they found better economic opportunities there; and a new gambling den was opened by the village 1 headman even after Babo had returned to the village. Although no one opened any new gambling establishments after the village headman closed his gambling den, Ishak, who had been appointed the new village 1 headman, was paid to turn a blind eye when Khru Razak's subordinates hosted gambling parties. Likewise, Ishak said that bullfights and cockfights were discontinued primarily because the operators tended to lose money, and the games were more strictly regulated by state authorities. Other people I talked to corroborated this.

Importantly, Ishak commented about how Babo carried out his religious enterprises, especially the *pondok*. While Babo's students attributed the school's closure to flooding, Ishak said that it was due largely to Babo's teaching techniques and even his personality. As he put it:

> Babo closed his *pondok* because there were no students. This is because he didn't have a fun teaching technique to attract students. He is also stingy and small-hearted. He didn't pay attention to students' lives, and his teaching method wasn't fun or lively; it was vapid.... Many students quit, and no new students came. So he eventually had to close his *pondok*.

In addition, although acknowledging Babo's contribution, some residents said that there were other factors contributing to changes in Islam in Guba. Yaakob said that Babo returned home and carried out religious activities at a time when other contributing factors were already at work. Internally, many children, especially from southern Guba, were completing their schooling in other locales, focused primarily on Islamic studies, and returning home. These children, now entering early adulthood, were not only practising "correct" Islam but encouraging their relatives to do the same. Externally, some Islamic sects were already spreading into Guba when Babo returned home. The "New Group" (Kaum Muda in Malay, Khana Mai or คณะใหม่ in Thai) and Dakwah are the significant ones.

According to Yaakob, the New Group is part of an Islamic sect called Wahhabism, which originated in Saudi Arabia. Wahhabism was brought to southern Thailand in the 1980s by some local residents who were involved with it while in Saudi Arabia. However, when it was introduced to southern Thailand, Wahhabism was modified in terms of its focus so as to take into account specific local issues and concerns. On the one hand, in line with its central tenets, Wahhabism as practised in southern Thailand is aimed to "correct" Islam by referring to the authentic teachings of the Prophet Muhammad rather than the opinions or interpretations of religious scholars or ulama. On the other hand, Thai-style Wahhabism emphasizes the purification of Islam by stripping away the local Malay beliefs and customs that predated Islam and that, over the centuries, had become intertwined with it. It is therefore locally called the New Group to mark its difference from traditional Islam, or the Old Group, which is strongly associated with Malay culture.[5]

Yaakob said that the New Group spread to Guba via local people who had lived in Saudi Arabia, primarily himself and his close friend Abidin. However, Yaakob added that although he had heard about Wahhabism when he was in Saudi Arabia, he did not get involved with it or pay attention to it while he was there. It is not until he returned to Thailand in the 1980s and paid more attention to religious study that he found himself attracted to the New Group. This is mainly because, he explained, it provided him "with the right teaching of Islam. It's not like village Islam that is severely implicated with local beliefs. The more I study it, the more I find it right." Given his conviction in the correctness of the New Group, Yaakob renounced the practice of "village Islam" or adjusted older practices to New Group methods, for instance in how he performed prayer.

However, the New Group is not vibrant in Guba; not many residents subscribe to it. This is partly because many residents believe that the traditional Islam they have long practised is already "correct". It is the New Group that is misled. As Ishak put it: "[The New Group] is fake. What we have is real. The old is real. So people didn't accept it. And they [the New Group practitioners] knew that they could not expand their base here. So they left for other places." The New Group also failed to catch hold in Guba because of the residents' low level of Islamic education. New Group practitioners tend to have acquired higher education in Islam from abroad, whereas Guba residents, especially in the central and northern parts of the settlement, generally have completed only an intermediate level of high school; only a few have attended traditional *pondoks*, not to mention universities abroad. As Dahari, a northern Guba resident, put it: "Guba people don't have high education. Most of them have completed grade 6 for secular education and class 6 or 8 in *pondoks*. Most people who became New Group members pursued higher education in foreign countries such as Saudi Arabia and Egypt with a focus on Islam." In addition, the New Group was prohibited by Mana, the village 1 headman at the time, who deemed it too radical and thought that traditional Islam was already sufficient and beneficial for the people in his village. He said: "I didn't allow them [the New Group practitioners] to spread their beliefs here, because the old one we have is already good. I have the right to do so because I am the village headman, and this area is under my supervision."

Given the resistance, indifference, and prohibition, New Group practitioners in Guba keep a low profile. Except Yaakob, who confessed to me that he is a New Group practitioner, no one disclosed to me that they were New Group members. According to Yaakob, these low-profile New Group advocates just practise what they deem to be right without trying to convince others, as no one, including himself, wishes to create conflict with their neighbours. In addition, Yaakob said that the New Group does not have a formal organization, a physical centre, or regular collective activities among its practitioners. Yala Islamic College (now Fatoni University) is run as a normal Thai university with a focus on Islam, not as the New Group's institute or centre. Taken together, these circumstances have led to the virtual absence of the New Group in Guba, unlike in other parts of the Deep South where the New Group is vibrant and has generated conflicts among residents.[6]

While the New Group is not prosperous, Dakwah (Jemaat Tabligh) has proven otherwise. This is mainly because, unlike the New Group, Dakwah neither proposes new ideas and practices nor forbids existing beliefs and customs. Mana said that he allowed Dakwah to carry out its activities in his area because "it invites Muslims to follow the path of the Prophet". Jamal said that Dakwah is acceptable because "it invites us to pray five times a day and go to the mosque for Friday noon prayer".

The first Dakwah practitioner in Guba was Shazrin, who propagated Dakwah alone in the early 1980s for five years before he died. The second practitioner also died after a few years of work in late 1980s. Then, after the Markaz Dakwah Jemaat was built in Yala in 1993, seven new Dakwah practitioners emerged, mostly male adults and elders, led by Tok Zaki, who explains:

> I teach villagers about how the Prophet lived his life — how he ate — and tell them to do accordingly. No new belief is involved. The main activity of Dakwah is to invite Muslims to study religion and perform prayer at the mosque. It is like following the path of the Prophet as Allah wants. Every Wednesday evening we have a meeting at the northern Guba mosque and walk through the village to talk with villagers about Islam and what they should do. Every Thursday night I attend a weekly meeting at the Markaz in Yala. I perform a three-day Dakwah missionary programme every month and attend Dakwah annual gatherings every year.

After about thirty years of perseverance, Dakwah now has a firm ground in Guba. In addition to core members who carry out religious activities on a regular basis, both northern and southern Guba mosques are routinely used as shelters for Dakwah groups on their missions. Importantly, participation in Dakwah's annual gatherings around Bangkok in 2005–10 was financially supported by the Arzeulee SAO. Participants, a quota of eight from each of the six villages making up Guba, were provided with an air-conditioned bus plus food and water for free. Moreover, during 9–11 May 2009, again supported by the Arzeulee SAO, Guba for the first time hosted a large Dakwah gathering. About one hundred Dakwah members from different places, led by a Malay Muslim police colonel, stayed at the southern Guba mosque and performed religious duties. Many residents joined these activities.

Some Guba residents joined Dakwah because they believed it would guide them to what they perceived would be the correct path. A male teenager said that he joined Dakwah because he wanted to be a good person. A middle-aged man said that Dakwah gives him advice on how to behave with good manners, which he thinks is the core of Islam. Given its perceived capacity to lead Muslims in the right direction, many who turned to Dakwah have skeletons in their closets. For example, Tok Zaki, Guba's Dakwah leader, joined the group after being released from a year in prison, where he had been detained for the killing of three people — even though he was never pronounced guilty. Likewise, Umar joined Dakwah after spending years in prison for attempting to murder Ishak. Indeed, one of Dakwah's missions is to help "the lost" find the right way. For example, all the male teenagers who attended Dakwah's annual gathering in Pathum Thani in 2008 are *kratom* cocktail addicts and school drop-outs, and two of them had been expelled from school for drinking *kratom* cocktails there. Worried about these teenagers' future, Guba adults hope that Dakwah will help guide them to a better way. Their hope is not groundless, as some juvenile delinquents have indeed turned over a new leaf because of Dakwah. The case of Zaidi is cited most often.

Zaidi is a committed member of Dakwah. When young, he was widely known as a delinquent. He dropped out of school at grade 9 and stopped attending Tadika when he was ten years old. He did not work, either to help out his family or to support himself, and spent most of his time playing around in the village. He always got into fights with other teenagers and was arrested and detained at the police station quite often, costing his family considerable money in paying the fines. The situation deteriorated when he became addicted to drugs, specifically methamphetamines. He was always asking his relatives for money to buy drugs, and he would become angry and go on a rampage if denied. When high on meth, he sometimes hurt other people and other times wanted to commit suicide. However, his life came to a turning point after his maternal grandmother died. Raised by his grandmother after his mother passed away (his father had earlier abandoned the family), he was deeply depressed by his grandmother's death and swore that he would quit all drugs and other misconduct and join Dakwah to compensate for all the bad things he had done to his grandmother. And he did what he had sworn.

Zaidi now turned over a new leaf. After joining Dakwah, he has lived his life strictly according to Islam. Following popular images of the Prophet Muhammad, he wears a long beard and white robes (*thawb*) almost all the time. He performs three-day Dakwah missions to different places every month, occasionally joins forty-day Dakwah missions, and attends the annual Dakwah gatherings each year. He has married a pious woman from another village who is always in black robes (*abaya*) with a piece of black cloth (*niqab*) covering her face. He said this about his new life:

> Dakwah gives me a new life. It teaches me how to live my life in the right way according to Islam. There are no other teachings. We just live our life like the Prophet Muhammad. We follow the path of the Prophet. And that's all. I was once led astray, and Dakwah helps me find the right way.

The return of Babo, the provision of formal religious education to the younger generation, and the advent of Dakwah and the New Group combined to create conditions that have made Guba residents increasingly aware of the need to practise "correct" Islam. More women now wear headscarves, and mosques are fully attended for Friday noon prayers. Praying five times a day has become common practice, and religious classes and Koran reading classes are now popular among the residents. Rather than only casually following Islam and engaging in what are thought to be "sinful" activities, Guba residents have now begun to lead their lives in accordance with what they deem right in Islam. A formal Islamic way of life has been established and is being pursued.

3.1.2. A Formal Islamic Way of Life

No longer something vague and distant, Islam is now made vivid and is embedded in all aspects of the lives of Guba residents. Shortly after being born, a female baby is circumcised by having a tiny part of her clitoris cut bleeding,[7] while a boy needs to wait until he turns seven or older to be eligible for the circumcision rite. When they are first able to read and write, both boys and girls are required to attend evening religious classes either at the mosques or at private homes. These classes focus on an accurate vocal reading of the Koran in Arabic, without having to understand its meaning. Children also attend Tadika on weekends, where they learn not only Islam (as they do in evening religious classes) but also subjects such as the Arabic and Malay languages. In addition, Islam is taught at the government elementary schools as part of the local curriculum. Taken together, Guba children aged five to twelve have classes in Islam and related subjects every day, two times a day on weekdays and once a day (but for a longer time) during weekends.

After finishing primary schooling (which corresponds to religious study at Tadika), children who want to continue their education at the secondary level attend private Islamic schools in town. Apart from Islam and related subjects, the schools offer secular subjects such as the sciences, mathematics and English language. However, those who want to focus their study primarily on Islam attend a traditional *pondok*. While the study period at a secondary school is fixed, that of a *pondok* is not, depending on how much one wants to learn about Islam as well as on the instructor's opinion. Some may spend a couple of years at a *pondok*, whereas others may devote up to ten years to Islamic study there.

Postsecondary education, however, is varied and not as closely tied to Islam as study at the secondary level. Some may go to vocational colleges, whereas others may go to universities either in southern Thailand or in Bangkok. These colleges and universities offer regular curricula and do not focus specifically on Islam. However, as discussed above, Yala Islamic College (now Fatoni University) is Thailand's first Islamic higher education institute, offering curricular courses and activities in accordance with Islamic principles. Although the university has admitted students from different countries including China and Cambodia, so far it has not admitted any student from Guba.

While the study of Islam at formal educational institutes in Thailand always ends at the secondary level, one can study Islam at any time at various social institutions. Adults who want to study Islam have at least three options to choose from. First are evening religious classes that focus primarily on accurate, vocal readings of the Koran in Arabic. These classes are offered at mosques, and there is usually one catering specifically to children. Second are private Koran reading classes taught by people at their homes. These classes are offered in the afternoon, usually two days a week. Like those at the mosques, they focus on an accurate reading of the Koran in Arabic. But they differ from reading classes at the mosques in that students must pay a tuition fee, although there is no fixed amount and payment often depends on a student's willingness and capacity to pay. Third are Babo's religious classes, which are specifically offered on Tuesday and Thursday nights at the southern Guba mosque and on Friday mornings at his home. Babo's classes, rather than Koran readings, are basically his own preaching of Islam.

In addition to being able to avail themselves of a lifelong study of Islam, Gubo residents observe a wide range of religious duties. These begin with the circumcision rites as mentioned earlier. Around the time that boys turn thirteen, and girls menstruate for the first time, they begin to perform prayers five times daily, both at their homes and at the mosques. Males also perform prayers and other religious duties at the mosque for the Friday noon service. Many residents do not work on Friday mornings, in keeping with their notion of Islamic practice. During the month of Ramadan, all Guba residents from teenagers on up fast during the day. They also make a donation or *zakat* at the end of Ramadan. And whoever can afford to travel to Saudi Arabia performs the hajj. Taken together, people in Guba fully observe the Five Pillars of Islam: the profession of faith, prayer, the giving of alms, fasting, and performing the hajj.

3.1.3. Diverse Muslims
Guba residents' religious life is not monolithic. This is primarily because, although similarly exposed to the various processes of "crafting" a Muslim,

each resident makes sense of and engages with these processes differently. This results in diversity among Muslims in Guba.

At one end of the spectrum, and in line with popular portrayals and perceptions, lie devout and pious Muslims. These residents fully and strictly observe religious duties. They perform prayers five times a day and never fail to do so regardless of the situation they are in at the time, whether travelling, attending official meetings or seminars, and the like. Likewise, these pious Muslims fast not only every day during the month of Ramadan but also for an additional six days after the month as well as on other days throughout the year. In addition, they habitually attend Babo's preaching sessions and Koran reading classes both at the mosques and at private teachers' houses. Their primary wish is to perform the hajj at least once in their lifetime, and some participate regularly in the various religious activities of Dakwah.

Tok Zaki is an example of such a pious Muslim in Guba. Not only does he perform prayers five times a day but he also routinely prays at the mosque and recites an extra prayer, taking about thirty minutes altogether. Likewise, not only does he fast every day during the month of Ramadan but he also always breaks his fast at a mosque, especially the Markaz in Yala, where a series of services are jointly performed after the breaking of fast. In addition, as Guba's Dakwah leader, Tok Zaki spends most of his time engaged in Dakwah's numerous religious activities. For example, every Thursday night he goes to the Markaz to attend the Dakwah committee's weekly meeting. He also regularly participates in Dakwah missions to different places, sometimes for three days and sometimes for two to four weeks. Generally, he is appointed leader of these missionary groups, which consist of Muslims from different places in southern Thailand. And when other Dakwah missionary groups visit Guba, he is the person who coordinates between local mosques and the visiting groups and takes care of related matters. Guba residents are quite used to seeing Tok Zaki around the village in his white robes, on one religious task or another.

It is not only men or members of Dakwah, like Tok Zaki, who are pious. Some women in Guba with no appointments or affiliations are equally committed to the faith. Maeh is one of them. Maeh is a wife and a mother of seven who has worked very hard throughout her life to support her family. But what distinguishes her from most other women in Guba is how she practises Islam. Not only does she strictly perform prayers five times a day, but her prayers are also longer than normal, as she chooses long chapters from the Koran for the optional segment of each prayer.

In addition, she always recites an extra prayer after the regular one. People who tap rubber in her family's rubber plantations know that she is not available for any kind of business during the time in the evening customary for reciting two prayers. This is because, after her longer-than-normal evening prayer, or *maghrib*, she performs an extra prayer, which takes about half an hour. Then she takes a short break before performing the night prayer, or *isha*, which is also followed by an extra prayer. This whole process takes about two and a half hours. She always recites the Koran in white robes at home, day and night, and often fasts throughout the year. In addition, she regularly attends a Koran class on Tuesday and Sunday afternoons. She also always attends Babo's religious preaching at the mosque on Tuesday and Thursday nights and at his home on Friday mornings, as well as religious teachings conducted by noted religious scholars at the mosque. Altogether, Maeh is regarded as an example a good Muslim.

While Tok Zaki and Maeh represent one end of the spectrum, at the other end is a person like Taha, a middle-aged father of two. People know Taha to have a casual attitude towards religion. He hardly performs any prayers and always stays at home on Friday at noon, when most men go to the mosques. Likewise, when it comes to the month of Ramadan, not only does he hardly ever fast but he also continues to drink *kratom* cocktails with his friends during the day. He even drinks alcohol in town and has taken methamphetamines for some time. Needless to say, he has never been to Mecca for the hajj and shows no sign of eagerness to do so. Nor has he ever engaged with Dakwah. The satellite television in his teashop always plays popular music, dramas and movies, and it is common to hear loud, popular Thai songs emitting from his teashop even late at night. He wears short pants that show his knees — which is deemed improper for Muslim men.

Taha's female counterpart is Laila, a divorced young woman aged about twenty. Unlike most Guba women, she always wears fitted blue jeans with a tight T-shirt and does not wear a headscarf while outside her home. She doesn't pray five times a day, and she hardly fasts at all during the month of Ramadan. She indulges in various drugs, ranging from *kratom* cocktails and marijuana to methamphetamines. She does not work on a regular basis, either to support herself or her family, nor has she remarried, although she has dated a few men. People know her to ride back and forth on her motorcycle, sometimes alone and sometimes with her male friends, and to hang out with her male friends near roadside teashops.

These individuals representing the two ends of the religious spectrum, however, cannot exemplify Guba residents in general with regard to Islam.

In making sense of and engaging with Islamic trends since the 1970s, most residents find themselves somewhere between the two extremes. Some are closer to the pious end, whereas others are closer to the casual. Jamal is an example of the former. Like most Guba residents, he is committed to performing prayers five times a day, but he often fails to do so for various reasons, for example getting up too late to perform the dawn prayer (*fajr*) or taking too long a nap to do a noon prayer (*zuhr*). In addition, his prayers are short, comprising only the compulsory part. Likewise, although he fasts every day during Ramadan and breaks fast at the mosque, he is always the first to leave the mosque, while others stay behind to pray after breaking fast. On one occasion, when I had arranged to meet him after prayers at the mosque and he left the mosque early, he explained: "I didn't want to keep you waiting long. So I did only the prayer, not including the blessing-wishing part." Likewise, he is among the first to finish the Friday noon prayer at the mosque because, he said, "I'm lazy to do so." He tends to ask for my opinion whether or not he should go to the mosque at night for the special prayer (*tarawih*) recited during the month of Ramadan, despite the fact that I am a Thai Buddhist with no authoritative idea about Islamic practice. One night, while we were watching a religious television programme from Malaysia, he asked me if I really want to watch that channel. When I said it was up to him, he switched to a Hollywood movie channel, Filmax, right away. In addition, he is one of a few adults who attends an evening Koran class at the mosque to compensate for what he missed during his childhood. But he quietly confesses to missing classes sometimes for days, and he sometimes asked me if he should attend a given class. While these behaviours lead many to dub him as "Jamal the Reluctant", they at the same time illustrate how Jamal has attempted assiduously to be a "good" Muslim.

Daessa, a mother of three, is another resident who places achieving the status of "good" Muslim as her first priority. She regularly prays five times a day, and fasting during the month of Ramadan is her annual commitment. She always wears a headscarf outside her home regardless of what else she happens to be wearing. However, there are some circumstances in which she does not feel obliged to observe some religious duties. For example, on one afternoon while helping Maeh prepare food in the kitchen, she heard Maeh talk to the other women there that it was time to perform the noon prayer. But while the others joined Maeh in performing the prayer, Daessa played with her four-year-old son nearby. She rejoined the others after they'd finished the prayer. Importantly, sometimes she finds certain religious precepts too difficult to observe, especially the prohibition against working on Friday mornings. She said that she was once asked by Saifuldin, Maeh's oldest son, not to tap rubber in his family's rubber plantation on Friday mornings, reasoning that working on Friday mornings is not in line with Islam. At first she followed his suggestion, but later she changed her mind, because she saw other employees tap rubber in the family's plantations on Friday mornings, and she also saw people tapping rubber elsewhere during this period. Importantly, she does not think that working on Friday mornings is forbidden in Islam. "I have never seen anywhere in the Koran forbidding work on Friday mornings", she reasoned. This is not to mention her family's need of cash for household expenses. Daessa told me that she has tried her best to be a good Muslim. It is totally up to Allah to judge her on the Judgement Day, she told me.

While Jamal and Daessa exemplify those wanting to get closer to being a devout and pious Muslim, most of those in the Red-Whiskered Bulbul singing contest circle, all males, do not explicitly express such a wish. Rather, their daily activities are often on what is considered the margins of proper Islamic behaviour. For example, they held bird-singing contests on Friday mornings despite the fact that, according to one interpretation of Islamic teachings, not only work but also recreational activities are forbidden on Friday morning. When asked if he knew that holding bird-singing contests on Friday mornings may not be in line with Islam, Azlan, president of the village 1 Red-Whiskered Bulbul Club, said, "Yes". But the reason why the club still did so is that other nearby villages have taken all the other time slots, and Friday morning is the only time slot that was left for Guba. Azlan also claimed that, while holding a bird-singing contest during this period may be sinful, the magnitude of the sin was very small. So the club decided that it was acceptable to go with Friday mornings to hold the contests.

These Muslim subjectivities are not static but subject to continual shifting. In certain circumstances, those regarded as devout and pious Muslims fail to observe religious duties, resulting in the reshaping of their "Muslimness". For example, Maeh once missed her Koran class two times in a row because she was too tired from work, leading some to comment on her commitment to Islam. Likewise, a casual Muslim like Taha always participates in corpse-bathing rituals, which many are reluctant to volunteer for even though the practice is thought to yield a great deal of merit, leading many to praise Taha for his courage and religious commitment. Importantly, differences in how people behave as Muslims do not lead to the formation of exclusive groups from which certain Muslims are excluded. Guba residents always get together, regardless of their differences in how they perform religious duties. They chat and laugh, with no one, pious or otherwise, acting as "moral police" and commenting on those exhibiting lax or sinful behavior. Lax Muslims have never been excluded from any group. On the contrary, their participation is always welcomed, and their stories are of special interest because they sometimes include extraordinary experiences that more pious residents would have no inkling of. Guba is therefore one place where Muslims can coexist in all their diversity, and extremists find it difficult to succeed.

3.2. Thai Citizens

"I love the king, love the nation, sir", Basir, a Guba teenager, impetuously shouted in Thai, with one hand in salute, while chatting with his friends beside the main road one afternoon. He wore a pair of military trousers, a military cap and a dark T-shirt. But he is not a soldier of any kind. He is a school drop-out with no regular job who indulges in a variety of drugs. Villagers note that he habitually rides his motorcycle up and down the streets, and some know that he has occasionally lost control while on drugs and tried to kill both himself and others. However, his life took a new turn when he was tasked by a soldier at Pahong Gayu camp to recruit unschooled and jobless male teenagers in village 1 to participate in a military-sponsored vocational training programme.

Although it is unclear to what extent Basir observed his duty and how successful he was at it, that he was approached by the military in the first place exemplifies the extent to which Guba residents, and Malay Muslims throughout the Deep South, since 2004 have been increasingly drawn into the Thai state. Male teenagers are particularly targeted, because security agencies believe that they are most vulnerable to the recruitment or, to use the security agencies' word, "inducement" (*chakchung*, ชักจูง) of the insurgents. A series of programmes were launched to prevent such recruitments and to forge young Muslims in the south into Thai citizens loyal to the nation. Most such programmes were carried out by the military, including the vocational training programme Basir was tasked with.

3.2.1. Disciplining the Children

In an old, worn-out schoolbag belonging to Shaari, a sixth grader of Guba school, lay three textbooks, one exercise book, one pen, one pencil and one eraser. The textbooks are for mathematics, English and social studies, with some notes and scribbled marks on the pages and some pages torn or missing. The exercise book has not been used much, and, like the textbooks, has some pages torn and missing. When asked about textbooks for his other subjects, Shaari said that he kept them in his desk at school and that the three I had found in his schoolbag are for subjects he had studied that day. Wondering about their contents, I took a closer look at the three textbooks, with particular attention to the one on social studies. Like Thai social studies textbooks in general, Shaari's seemed to be part of the state's effort to make loyal Thai citizens. It describes how Thai society is held together by three institutions: the nation, the religion, and the monarch. At the same time, it prescribes how citizens, regardless of their differences (i.e., ethnicity and religion), should behave in order to keep Thai society functioning properly.

I asked Shaari if he understood what the social studies textbook said; Shaari, who ranked behind most others in his class, said, "Not quite". He was uncertain what the three institutions, especially "the nation", really meant. So I changed the topic and asked him what he did in school that day. Below is a summary of his reply.

9:00 a.m.	Form lines in front of the flagpole and sing the national anthem along with the raising of the national flag
9:10 a.m.	Swear an oath of allegiance to the nation, the religion, and the king
9:12 a.m.	Praise Allah (in Arabic)
9:13 a.m.	Sing *Sadudi Maharaja*, a song praising the king and queen
9:16 a.m.	Sing *The Great Artist*, a song praising the king with regard to art
9:20 a.m.	A teacher gives a homily
9:25 a.m.	Go to the classroom
9:30 a.m.	Mathematics class
10:30 a.m.	English class
11:30 a.m.	Lunch break (but having none, as students fast during the month of Ramadan)
12:30 p.m.	Perform a noon prayer at a small mosque near the school
12:50 p.m.	Form lines in front of the classroom
1:00 p.m.	Social studies class
2:00 p.m.	Physical education class
3:00 p.m.	Class ends; form lines in front of the classroom, then go back home

Shaari's activities in school illustrate three major characteristics of primary education in southern Thailand during the recent unrest. First are short school hours. While generally school is in session eight hours a day, school days in Guba last only six hours, for all study and other activities. This is primarily because, given that schoolteachers are a primary target of the insurgency, the school day starts later and ends earlier than normal. In the morning, teachers gather at a designated meeting point and then commute to school protected by a military escort team. But teachers always arrive at the meeting point at different times due to various personal reasons, or sometimes teachers need to wait until the escort team is ready. As a result, they habitually arrive at school later than expected. On some days the national flag raising and national anthem singing start at 10:00 a.m., with only one or two teachers who came on their own present. The school day also needs to end earlier than normal for safety reasons. Teachers gather together and go back home along with the escort team. In addition to the shortened hours, Guba school, like other schools in the southern region, is not always in session, as teachers often attend special activities and meetings, many of them related to security issues. Altogether, students in the Deep South spend less time at school than students elsewhere in Thailand.

Second are the religious observances. As part of an ethics class, fourth- to sixth-grade schoolboys are required to perform noon prayers in a small mosque nearby, while schoolgirls are free during noon break. A schoolboy named Ajib is tasked with writing down in a report book the names of his friends who come to the mosque to perform noon prayers, and then handing the report book over to the teacher, every day. Schoolchildren who fail to attend mosque will have points deducted in the ethics class. In addition, during the month of Ramadan, fourth- to sixth-grade schoolchildren, male and female alike, along with their teachers, are required to fast during the day. The school does not provide free lunch for children during Ramadan like it does during the rest of the school year. If some children do not want to fast, they have to find food on their own, whether going home for lunch or buying some snacks in school or nearby. These religious observances are not required by the central government or the Ministry of Education. Rather, they are consequences of the "Islamic reform" enacted in the southern region since the 1970s.

The third major characteristic of primary education in the Deep South is the performance of Thai citizenship. Like schoolchildren in general, Guba schoolchildren start the school day by singing the national anthem along with raising the national flag. Below is an English translation of Thai national anthem.

> Thailand unites the flesh and blood of Thais.
> Nation of the people, belonging to the Thais in every respect.
> Long maintained [has been] independence.
> Because Thais seek, and love, unity.

Thais are peace loving;
But at war we are no cowards.
Sovereignty will not be threatened.
Sacrificing every drop of blood for the nation.
Hail the nation of Thailand, long last the victory, *chai yo*! [Hurrah!]

The national anthem is not simply a spirited retelling of how the Thai nation was built, maintained and protected, and how Thais have sacrificed for her. Rather, it is primarily a prescription about what Thai citizens should do with regard to the nation. To have students sing the song while raising the national flag is to embed this great duty in the hearts and minds of Thai citizens.

Performing Thai citizenship includes swearing an oath of allegiance:

> We will be loyal to the nation, the religion, the monarch. We will be good children of parents. We will be good students of teachers. We will be good citizens of the country.

The oath of allegiance emphasizes schoolchildren's loyalty to state ideology predicated on the nation, the religion and the monarch. It also details how to put such loyalty into practice, namely by being good students, good children and good citizens.

In addition, the school holds special activities on a regular basis to reinforce the loyalty of schoolchildren as Thai citizens. These special activities have been given great emphasis in the southern provinces since 2004, when the residents' allegiance to the nation was in desperate need. The Guba school's Children's Day fair in 2009 is a case at hand.

On 9 January 2009, I visited the Guba school to observe the Children's Day fair. Activities included games, shows, lot-drawing for gifts, food and trinket giveaways, and an award- and certificate-giving ceremony, all of which exemplified the process of crafting loyal citizens out of children. The first order of business is the prime minister's Children's Day motto. Since 1956, during Field Marshal Phibun's administration and in the second year of Children's Day,[8] the prime minister has traditionally produced a motto for the event. These mottoes centre on children's duties with regard to the nation. For example, the 1973 motto, delivered by Field Marshal Thanom Kittikachorn, advises: "Good children are the blessing of the nation; smart children lead the nation to prosperity." In 2009, the motto, given by Prime Minister Abhisit Vejjajiva, was: "Smart thinking, pure mind, lighting the dream, bond, love, harmony." The motto was crafted with Styrofoam, painted, and affixed to the backdrop of the stage; it was recited by all schoolchildren who were asked by their teachers to do so. Although abstract, the motto addresses Thai children, prescribing for them expected roles and duties with regard to the nation.

After the participation of the prime minister in delivering a motto is the involvement of other government agencies. Like in previous years, there were plenty of gifts donated by different government agencies for schoolchildren at the event I attended. This is primarily because, due to the unrest in the region, many government agencies have been allocated with increased budgets for their operations in the South, part of which is to be used for this kind of activity. This is particularly the case for the military. After the Children's Day fair I attended had been underway for awhile, an APC and a military pickup from the Pahong Gayu military camp arrived at the school gate. A group of soldiers emerged from the vehicles with gifts and an ice-cream container. They walked over to the fair and gave these items to the teachers, to add to already existing mountains of gifts. The teachers were excited about the soldiers' arrival. One of them thanked the soldiers for their kindness on behalf of the school via the loudspeakers and asked the schoolchildren to give the soldiers a big hand. Another teacher took pictures of the soldiers while they were handing gifts and containers of ice cream to his colleague, who acted as a school representative. Soldiers hung around the fair for awhile, talking and teasing with the schoolchildren and taking pictures of the activities, before leaving for other schools in their operational area to repeat the same mission. Although not accompanied by any official statement, military contributions to the Children's Day fair are aimed primarily to win the "hearts and minds" of schoolchildren, in a period of general unrest.

Finally, the students themselves participate by staging shows. In the fair I attended, most of the skits consisted of singing. Some sang popular Thai songs, whereas others sang karaoke English songs they had learned in class. Interestingly enough, fifth-grade schoolchildren sang the national anthem as their show on the stage. Despite singing the anthem almost every morning in front of the flagpole, they nevertheless felt so excited, as performers often are — their hands and voices were shaking. Some could not remember some parts of the lyrics, while others found it difficult to pronounce the lyrics in Thai.

I returned the textbooks to Shaari and thanked him for his cooperation. He put the books back into his schoolbag with a smile on his face as always. I asked him how he felt about school that day, and he said that there was nothing special about it. He just went to school, attended classes, and played with his friends. He had a good time at school. Then I asked him how he felt about singing the national anthem and raising the national flag, and he said he felt nothing — he just did what he was instructed to do and did not pay much attention to it. I asked him to sing the national anthem for me, and as it turns out he had not memorized all the lyrics, even though he is now in grade 5. He had not memorized all the lyrics of the two other compulsory songs (the royal anthem and *Sadudi Maharaja*), either. However, when I asked him if he considered himself a Thai citizen, he said, "Yes". And he also answered in the affirmative when I asked if he thought the duties of the citizen he swore to in front of the flagpole were correct. He wanted to be a good child to his parents and a good student to his teachers — this attitude helps explain why he had won the outstanding public service student award at the school's Children's Day fair that year.

His willingness to be a good child and a good student notwithstanding, Shaari finds it difficult to observe all the duties and obligations of Thai citizens, especially conscription (which, given his young age, Shaari had not yet had direct experience with). I asked him if he wanted to serve the country by being a soldier, and he said, "No". When asked why, he said, "I don't want to get killed. Also, it is very hard being a conscript. I heard that they [Thai Buddhist senior soldiers] torture and beat us. So I don't want to be a soldier or a conscript." Shaari added that his friends do not want to get conscripted either because they do not want to get killed or face hardship. For these children, the military draft is something they don't want to face when they turn twenty-one.

3.2.2. Training the Men

Primary education is compulsory for all Thai children, and registering for conscription is an obligation for all Thai males aged twenty-one. As Thai citizens, Guba men have to participate in the conscription process. And given the hardship and danger involved in serving in the military as well as the deprivation of the family's crucial labour force, the military draft affects not only every man's life but also that of his family. In the past, conscription was a major event in Guba, as it was in other rural areas of the country. With no cars and no paved roads, draftees together with their families, relatives, and friends left home early on foot with food, water and other necessities for their journey, heading for the Raman district office, where conscription was conducted. They spent a whole day there, as conscription started at 9:00 a.m. and ended at 5:00 p.m. Given that men from many subdistricts were to be conscripted on the same day, the conscription site and nearby areas were always extremely crowded. This led to the establishment of the only annual fair of Raman district, where various consumer goods, local food and beverages, clothes, shoes and other items were sold.

Conscription is still a major event for people in Guba, although there is no longer any difficulty travelling. Draftees are still anxious, and so are their families, relatives and friends. The conscription site and nearby areas are still crowded, and the fair, still Raman's only annual fair, still draws thousands of residents. However, the insurgency has significantly reshaped the conscription process. Anxiety levels among draftees have increased at a time when loyalty and devotion to the nation, expressed crucially through conscription, are in more urgent need than ever before. The military draft of 2009 is a case in point.

One evening while my friends and I were sitting and chatting at a roadside pavilion as usual, Nazri, a son of the imam of the northern Guba mosque at the time, stopped by on his motorcycle. He said that his family was going to hold a Ya Sin chanting ceremony at his home the following night, and he invited us to come. One of us asked him for whom and for what purpose the chanting was to be held, and Nazri said, "For me". He said that the following week he was going to be conscripted, and his family thought that they should hold a Ya Sin chanting ceremony for him. After Nazri left, I asked my friends at the pavilion what Ya Sin chanting was and what meaning it had with regard to the military draft. They said that Ya Sin is a sura or chapter of the Koran, known as "the heart of the Koran", and is always chanted to bless those facing risks or dangers such as a long journey, a severe illness, death — or military conscription.[9] However, they added that although the chanting of Ya Sin for those going to participate in the military draft had long been a common practice in Guba, during the previous five years, as the insurgency had intensified, the practice had taken on new urgency. This is mainly because new conscripts are almost always stationed in the Deep South, where soldiers are a prime target of the insurgents regardless of their religion or ethnicity. Families then try to prevent their sons from being conscripted, and Ya Sin chanting is seen as a means of facilitating this desire. This was confirmed by Nazri when he talked to me two days later. He said, "I don't want to get conscripted because I don't want to get killed or crippled for the rest of my life. The chanting of Ya Sin will help me out with this."

I did not attend the Ya Sin chanting at Nazri's house as I had promised because Saifuldin was not at home at the time to take me there. But I attended the conscription event, which was held on 10 April 2009 on the ground floor of the Raman district building. At first I planned to ride a motorcycle to the building. But later I changed my mind, as Saifuldin told me that his younger brother Ali, who was enrolled at college, needed to attend the conscription event to submit his postponement petition, and Saifuldin was planning to drive Ali there. So I went to the district building with the two brothers. We arrived in Raman at about 8:15 a.m. Saifuldin dropped us off on the main street, part of which had been transformed into the annual fair. Then we walked past a security checkpoint and entered the conscription site, which by now was packed by recruits, even though it was still about half an hour before the conscription process began. Military officers were busy preparing documents and other materials on the ground floor of the building, while recruits looked around with curiosity. On the front wall hung a banner with a picture of an Olympic gold medal–winning Thai boxer (who is also a soldier), with words urging Thai men to register for the military draft.

At about 8:30 a.m., a military officer spoke on a microphone, telling conscription participants to form rows on the lawn by their respective subdistricts and explaining to them the procedures they would undergo. Men formed the rows, and the conscription process began. I walked around the area observing and talking with people I knew, both draftees and their relatives. An hour later I saw a middle-aged senior government official walking around, talking to people. He was accompanied by two heavily armed security guards and five subordinates. He was the Raman district chief. He greeted and talked to the draftees and their relatives for awhile before heading to a nearby building of the district office to perform other duties. But he did not visit the conscription station, which was overseen by soldiers.

Things would have gone normally had a high-ranking military officer not shown up. It was about half an hour after the district chief retreated to his office that a convoy of a black sport utility vehicles (SUVs) and three military pick-up trucks arrived at the conscription site. The process was halted, and most of the soldiers ran to the SUV to salute the arriving officer. He was the commander of the Fourth Region Army, which oversees the southern region. While an officer was saluting the commander, another person hurriedly rushed behind me in a panic towards the arriving soldiers. It was the district chief. He joined the others in saluting and reporting to the commander, whose arrival he apparently had not been forewarned about. Then the commander, followed by a cluster of officers, walked around the processing area greeting, talking and taking pictures with draftees and their relatives and friends, most of whom felt ambivalent, reluctant, or even embarrassed by his attention. The commander spent about half an hour on his public relations mission before leaving for other conscription stations in the region. The conscription process resumed, and the district chief returned to his office.

Such sudden visits by the highest-ranking officers had begun happening only recently. Prior to 2004, conscription was left primarily up to the district military registrar in cooperation with other agencies such as the local government hospital and the district office. There was no tradition of a high-ranking military officer, especially the commander himself, paying a visit to the conscription station. However, after the insurgency picked up steam after 2004, conscription has assumed greater military significance. Doctors from Raman hospital who once examined draftees have been replaced by military doctors, and jobs once performed by district officials are now carried out by soldiers. And the commander started paying visits to conscription stations. These changes have taken place only in the southernmost region, while the conscription process in the rest of the country remains the same as before.

The climax of the conscription process is the participants' drawing of red and black cards from a box. If the drawn card is red, the participant gets conscripted and will be stationed at a military camp for two years. But if the card is black, the participant is free to go without obligation to serve. However, if a participant wishes to perform military service for the two-year period, he can simply apply at the conscription station without having to go through the normal conscription procedures. In the past, sometimes there was no need for prospective conscripts to draw red and black cards, as there were a sufficient number of volunteers to meet the required number of soldiers from a given conscription station. On the day I attended, 495 men from eight subdistricts of Raman district participated in the conscription process. (Men from Raman's remaining eight subdistricts attended the conscription process on the following day.) Nearly 250 of them petitioned for postponement, and almost 150 failed to meet the criteria, being too short, too thin, handicapped, or suffering from some other physical deficiency. Only 105 young men therefore participated in the card drawing, and the military wanted 89 conscripts from the Raman station on that day. However, 33 participants volunteered for military service. Thus, there were 56 red cards in the box, with the remaining 49 black.

At about 3:30 p.m., a military officer spoke on a microphone, telling qualified participants to gather together on the ground floor of the district building for the card drawing. The participants walked into the conscription station, formed their rows, and sat, while their relatives and friends swarmed the building trying to provide moral support. Once everything was set, a soldier explained the drawing process to the participants as well as the remaining procedures for those who would be conscripted. Then he lifted an empty box and showed it to the participants and spectators to assure them that there was nothing inside. He put the cards into the box and called the participants by name, one by one. Most did not want to get conscripted. Those drawing a black card openly expressed their delight, whereas those drawing red cards looked disappointed and sad. This critical moment was shared by hundreds of spectators, some of whom shouted with satisfaction when a red card was drawn by an unknown participant, because that lowered the odds that their relative, drawing later, would also be conscripted. The drawing took about one and a half hours, and the crowd dispersed as soon as it was done.

Nazri came to the roadside pavilion on his motorcycle at dusk later that day with a smile on his face. He had not been conscripted. Nor did he go through the entire procedure. I saw him when he was at the physical examination stage and noticed that something irregular had happened to him but was unclear what it was at the time. Then he was separated from the other participants and guided through a special procedure. As he put it:

> When I was in the physical examination stage, a doctor's assistant told me there was an irregularity with my right ring finger. He then separated me from the rest and had me join the line of those waiting to meet with the doctor. Then the doctor touched my finger and asked if it hurts, and I said yes. So the doctor said I didn't have to participate in the conscription, as my right ring finger was crippled and it would prevent me from shooting a gun.... Lucky me, I don't have to be a soldier and get stationed in the South. I don't want to get shot and die.

Nazri ended his story with a smile and rode his motorcycle back home in darkness.

I did not ask Nazri if he thought that this result could be attributed to the Ya Sin chanting. To my knowledge, no Guba men were conscripted that year. Nor did any volunteer for military service. Those who were at the conscription centre were tremendously relieved when they drew black cards. Some even jumped and shouted loudly in excitement in front of the soldier who held the box with the cards. These men adamantly did not wish for conscription, despite the state's massive campaign promoting the military draft. This unwillingness to serve the country via conscription is not limited to men of conscription age but significantly includes young boys not yet eligible. Bahari, a fifteen-year-old boy who often travels to Malaysia to tap rubber, said that he was afraid of getting conscripted because, he thought, he would be humiliated by higher ranking Thai Buddhist soldiers. He was also afraid of getting killed while stationed in the southern region. He said that he would participate in the conscription process when the time comes, but added: "I will flee if I get conscripted." When I asked where he would flee to, he mentioned Malaysia as a possible hiding place.

Although some Guba residents said that they wanted to join the military or wanted their children to do so, it is not because they want to serve the country as they are expected to. Daessa said that she was so worried about her son Faizal, because he had quit school against her and his father's will. She had no idea about what to do with Faizal at present, but when he turns twenty-one she will have him apply for military service. This is because, she said, "I want him to get trained and disciplined so he will know what difficulty and hardship are." Asked whether she was afraid he might get killed while serving, she said, "No. Whatever he is, he will die anyway. It is totally up to Allah when he will die. If Allah does not want him to die while serving in the military, he will not die." With this in mind, I asked Faizal himself when I met him that evening if he wanted to join the military, as his mother wanted him to. Interestingly enough, he said "Yes". However, when I asked if he wanted to do so in order to serve the country, he said "No". He gave his reason why he wanted to join: "I want to get a monthly salary." Asked if he was not afraid of getting killed, he said "No. I am going to die one day anyway, whether or not I am a soldier." This family's thoughts about serving in the Thai military then have nothing to do with the state's increasing need of loyalty and devotion from residents of the southernmost region during the current unrest.

It is also important to note that, although more Malay men from the Deep South have volunteered for military service over the past few years than before, it is not because they want to "serve the nation" as they are expected to. The conscription in Raman district on 4–5 April 2013 is a case in point. There was no drawing of red and black cards on the first day of the conscription because the number of volunteers met the demand. And although there was a card drawing on the second day, only three participants were needed to meet the demand of twenty. The main reason why more participants are volunteering for military service is that the monthly salary plus "danger pay" is relatively high and, in the estimation of many recruits from poor families, worth risking life and limb. But there are also other reasons. Loh, a young man from Guba, said that he actually had applied for the military in advance. But his documents were lost when the military truck carrying them was ambushed by a roadside bomb a few days before conscription day, and he did not ask the soldiers about them when he participated in the conscription process. He said that he wanted to be a soldier because he "want[ed] to carry a gun legally because I was once caught for carrying a gun illegally. I am not afraid of clashes because I have a gun. They shoot, I shoot. Today I am still carrying a gun."

In addition to conscription, the military since 2004 has launched various programmes primarily targeting young men from the Deep South. On the surface, these programmes are aimed at assisting young men in terms of providing an occupation, and preventing or rehabilitating from drug use. But the underlying rationale of these programmes is to invoke loyalty to the nation from these young men and prevent them from getting involved with the insurgency. Eysa said that during one week on an army base, as part of the Jalanan Baru project,[10] which focuses on drug prevention and vocational training, he took part in many activities. In addition to a series of anti-drug video screenings and vocational workshops during the days, he attended and participated in various shows and performances in the evenings. These shows were centred around the theme of "cultural diversity", with the Thai state as the guardian and supporter. They emphasized the ways in which Malay culture and Islam had enjoyed freedom of expression in Thailand, and even been promoted and protected by the state. Eysa and his companions were then encouraged to appreciate the state's benevolence with regard to their ethnicity and religion. After the week-long event, Eysa was appointed an anti-drug volunteer tasked with preventing his fellow teenagers in the village from getting involved with drugs and also from being recruited or "induced" by the insurgents.

These military aid programmes are in line with state policy regarding the Deep South in general. Since the eruption of the recent unrest in 2004, the Thai state, in its attempt to win the "hearts and minds" of Malay Muslims and turn them against the insurgents, has launched numerous programmes to provide assistance to them in addition to conducting full military operations against the insurgency. These programmes have been implemented not only by the military but also by several government agencies whose regular responsibilities may not be directly related to public welfare.

3.2.3. Taking Care of the Population

One result of the recent unrest in the Deep South has been a dramatic increase in budget for government agencies with responsibilities in the region. The situation has spawned a special budgetary category for "Programmes for Solving Problems in and Developing the Southern Border Provinces", which has significantly changed the ways in which government agencies carry out their work. On the one hand, security agencies are specifically tasked with development projects, many of which would normally be implemented by non-security-related agencies. On the other hand, several non-security-related agencies are now required to add security agendas to their regular responsibilities. Take for example the 2010 fiscal year budget (Table 3.1).

As shown in Table 3.1, the government agency allocated with the biggest budget for these special activities is the Internal Security Operations Command (ISOC); the programme accounted for 92 per cent of ISOC's total budget for the year of some 8.24 billion baht.[11] As a result, nearly all of ISOC's annual budget is earmarked for the Deep South, leaving very little to be spent nationwide. ISOC's Region 4 Forward Section, which oversees the southern unrest, is in charge of allocating this large amount of budget.

TABLE 3.1
Thailand's 2010 Fiscal Year Budget for the Programme for Solving Problems in and Developing the Southern Border Provinces

Government Agency	Budgeted Amount (in Thai baht)
Ministry of Defense	(total allocated budget: 154,032,478,600)
Royal Thai Armed Forces Headquarters	50,000,000
Royal Thai Army	2,106,557,200
Royal Thai Navy	919,624,000
Royal Thai Air Force	502,900,000
Total	3,579,081,200
Ministry of Interior	(total allocated budget: 187,998,707,100)
Office of the Permanent Secretary	27,672,400
Department of Provincial Administration	1,753,961,700
Department of Public Works and Town and Country Planning	32,353,200
Total	1,813,987,300
Royal Thai Police	(total allocated budget: 66,594,572,400)
	1,046,634,200
Internal Security Operations Command	(total allocated budget: 8,240,272,500)
	7,587,604,200

National Intelligence Agency	(total allocated budget: 655,568,300)
	48,000,000
Ministry of Justice	(total budget: 15,168,159,000)
	51,888,600
Ministry of Education	(total allocated budget: 346,713,093,300
Office of the Permanent Secretary	611,088,700
Office of the Basic Education Commission	302,851,700
Office of the Vocational Education Commission	138,000,000
Office of the Higher Education Commission	130,709,600
Prince of Songkla University	58,546,000
Princess of Naradhiwas University	14,520,000
Total	1,255,716,000
Ministry of Culture	(total allocated budget: 4,347,816,600
Department of Religious Affairs	14,387,000
Office of the National Culture Commission	118,260,000
Total	132,647,000
Ministry of Agriculture and Cooperatives	(total allocated budget: 54,357,849,400)
Office of the Permanent Secretary	70,000,000
Rice Department	5,272,000
Department of Fisheries	38,500,000
Department of Livestock	40,930,000
Land Development Department	108,869,600
Department of Agriculture	28,636,000
Department of Agricultural Extension	20,153,600
Cooperative Promotion Department	66,274,900
Total	378,636,100
Office of the Rubber Replanting Aid Fund	(total allocated budget: 977,435,000)
	7,846,900
Total	**15,902,041,500 (from 1,700,000,000,000)**

Source: Adapted from *Phraratchabanyat Raichai Pracham Pi Ngoppraman B.E 2553*.

The Ministry of Defense was allocated with the second-largest share of this special budget (3.58 billion baht), with the army receiving the most (2.10 billion baht, or 58.86 per cent of the amount). This special budget constitutes 2.32 per cent of the total budget allocated for the Ministry of Defense. Importantly, the total budget the Ministry of Defense received in this fiscal year is double the amount it was allocated in fiscal year 2004.[12]

The Ministry of Interior ranked third in terms of budget allocation for the border provinces, with the Department of Provincial Administration receiving the most. The two other security-related agencies that were allocated funding under this special budget are the National Intelligence Agency (NIA) and the Ministry of Justice. However, these two agencies received only a small share of the special budget. This is because the NIA is a civilian-dominated agency, whereas the southern insurgency is overseen by the military, which has its own intelligence agencies; and the Ministry of Justice does not get involved in field operations.

The agency that was allocated the fourth-largest amount of the special budget is the Ministry of Education, which is not directly involved in security issues, although one of its major tasks is to reinforce state ideology. Although the two major universities in the Deep South were allocated relatively small amounts of the special budget, they received funding under a different budget category, called "Programme for Promoting and Developing Religion, Art, and Culture" (58,546,000 baht for Prince of Songkla University, and 14,520,000 baht for Princess of Naradhiwas University), earmarked for anti-insurgency initiatives.

Other non-security agencies that were allocated funding from this special budget are the Ministry of Agriculture and Cooperatives, the Ministry of Culture, and the Office of the Rubber Replanting Aid Fund. The small amount of budget notwithstanding, as many as eight agencies under the Ministry of Agriculture and Cooperatives carried out special programmes in the southern border provinces under the budget initiative; some of them, such as the Rice Department and the Department of Agriculture, normally have nothing to do with security issues at all. This also holds true for Office of the Rubber Replanting Aid Fund, whose primary function is to support the agricultural economy. As for the Ministry of Culture, the small amount of the special budget it received is intended to be utilized alongside the ministry's regular budget and programmes, which are in line with state policy on the Deep South.[13]

With the large amount of special budget allocated to various government agencies, Thailand's southern border provinces since the turn of the twenty-first century have witnessed numerous programmes providing assistance and care to local residents. Guba is no exception to this.

Every morning and evening, Guba residents see a convoy of military vehicles pass by on the main road, either to patrol the area or to escort schoolteachers. They also often witness these soldiers searching the village on foot and sometimes conducting surveys. These are military operations they are familiar with and expect to see. However, sometimes soldiers conduct operations that villagers are not accustomed to and do not expect at all. The provision of medical service is one example.

Late one morning in January 2011 while busy with their daily activities, people in Guba heard something from a distance. It was a voice from a loudspeaker on a military pick-up truck informing them that on that day, at 10:30 a.m., free medical service would be provided at the northern Guba mosque, and all residents were invited to come. Ishak said, when the pick-up passed by, that he had never seen soldiers on this kind of mission before. When I asked if he would go for the service, he said, "Of course. It's free." Then he left for his wife's home to prepare himself, and I told him I would go too to observe the proceedings.

Alone, I walked to the mosque, arriving about 11:00 a.m. A medical service station had been temporarily set up in the Tadika's open-air classroom, located in the front part of the mosque compound. About thirty soldiers, fully armed, scattered across the area, but only four of them, all young, were administering the service; a civilian medical caregiver was stationed at an adjacent desk. Two soldiers conducted a primary health check and the other two issued prescribed medicines to recipients who had undergone a more thorough medical check-up by the civilian caregiver. However, only few residents had come for the free service at the time. Three of them had just finished, and in fact no one was being examined by the caregivers when I was there. Noticing me, one of the caregiver soldiers asked me if I wanted a check-up. I asked him if I was eligible. He, thinking that I lived in Guba, said yes. So I stepped up to the service station and had him check my blood pressure; he asked me some personal and health-related questions. Then I was sent to the civilian caregiver at a nearby desk for a "full" check-up. After asking me a couple of questions over the course of about a minute, the civilian caregiver prescribed some common medicines. I took the prescription back to the soldiers' desk and gave it to a soldier seated there. He gave me the prescribed medicines, and the process ended. After having availed myself of the free service, I walked around the mosque compound talking to some residents, including Ishak, who joined me while I was undergoing the check-up and observing the activity. I left the mosque at about 12:30 p.m., and the medical service ended about an hour later.

It is noteworthy that, although free of charge, the military's medical service did not draw much attention from people in Guba. Only some fifty adults and elders showed up, and none of them had serious health problems or severe illnesses. Although some teens and children were around the mosque compound, none of them entered the service station to get check-ups. I asked Ishak, who frequently visits private clinics given his good economic standing, why, and he said that people now have many ways to get medical treatment for free, and they were suspicious of the quality of the service provided by the military. He said that he had come just to get common medicines such as cream and ointment for muscle stiffness and pain and a bottle of syrup to ease an upset stomach, but he did not expect to receive the more specialized medicines prescribed by private clinics. A woman I talked to said she had come to get paracetamol and other common medicines she usually bought at drugstores in Raman that she was running out of. Both Ishak and the woman were well aware that this free medical service was part of the military's effort to win their "hearts and minds" amid the ongoing unrest. And they also knew that they could not expect professional treatment or quality medical care from the military's special service. As Ishak put it, "I know they try to please us because they don't want us to take sides with the insurgents. And I know they are not good at this kind of thing at all. But I came here just to get what they can afford. And there is no harm. That's it." Ishak added that some residents were so afraid of the soldiers that they avoided any interaction with them, and as such they did not come, even to get free medicine.

In addition to special medical services, the military has vigorously initiated many agricultural projects to improve the livelihood of local residents. Suhana, a middle-aged central Guba woman, said that soldiers came to ask her if she was interested in participating in their "sufficiency economy" project. She said yes, and they had her sign her name and then attend a one-day workshop at a military camp in Narathiwat Province. After the workshop, in which the king's sufficiency economy[14] was explained and demonstrated, she was provided with a small pond, some fish, and five hens for free so she could practise self-sufficiency at home. She added that now she was participating in another project implemented by the Centre for Sufficiency Economy of Arzeulee Subdistrict, which is also supported by the military. She invited me to visit the centre someday, and I accepted her invitation.

The centre is located on land owned by Suhana, about 200 square metres being temporarily used for the project. Four women were sitting in a pavilion when my wife and I arrived. We greeted them, and then one of them, Sophia, a fourth-year university student and one of the project participants, explained the project to us. She said this project originated when a woman who worked at the Arzeulee Subdistrict Government Agency Centre told a friend of hers that a project was going to be implemented in Arzeulee subdistrict and asked her friend to find fifteen people to form a group to run the project. Her friend, a young northern Guba woman, spread the news in her circle and eventually recruited fifteen people, most of them central Guba women. Then her friend submitted a project proposal to a local military unit, and after it was approved all group members attended a two-day workshop on the sufficiency economy at a military camp in Narathiwat Province. After the workshop, each group member received 3 hens, 3 ducks, and 500 catfish, all to be raised at the centre as a group project. In addition, the group received materials to build a structure in which to grow mushrooms, and soldiers of the Pahong Gayu military camp came to dig three medium-size ponds and build a fence around the centre. Sophia said that the group now has daily income from selling eggs, and they are waiting for the first batch of mushrooms to be ready for sale. I took a picture of the group members and my wife with the project's banner before leaving with thirty eggs we had bought from the centre.

Despite the benefits provided free of charge, however, these military agricultural projects do not enjoy popularity among the residents. Jamal said that he did not sign his name to participate in the sufficiency economy project because he did not have enough time to devote to it. Effendi said that the reason why he declined the soldiers' invitation was that he did not have time to attend the workshop at the military camp. Only a few residents participated in these projects, and even then they did not pay much attention to them. In addition, although the Centre for Sufficiency Economy of Arzeulee Subdistrict is a subdistrict-level project, the fact that it is implemented in Guba and has only fifteen Guba residents as beneficiaries does not speak well for benefit distribution among other Guba residents, to say nothing about the residents of the five other villages in Arzeulee subdistrict. People in Guba and the subdistrict in general consider the military's agricultural projects as trivial to their livelihood.

Besides agricultural projects, the military also provides help and support for special events using special budgetary allocations. For example, it distributes gifts and ice cream to schools in its operational areas at Children's Day fairs. When village 5 residents held a football tournament, the military gave not only money but also medals and trophies for the winners. It also helps residents when they are in need of certain items. For example, water was running short at the wedding ceremony of Yaakob's niece. Those in charge of the water supply tried to figure out how to solve the problem and came up with the idea of requesting the military's special water service. They called the village 2 headman, who has a good relationship with the soldiers at the Pahong Gayu military camp, and asked him to coordinate with the soldiers to deliver water to the wedding. About thirty minutes later, a military water truck arrived. Yaakob thanked the soldiers and offered them food and drinks after they finished their mission. The soldiers in return donated 1,000 baht for the wedding.

In addition to the military, several non-security agencies vigorously provide assistance for the residents amid the unrest. A prominent example is Raman hospital. The hospital staff routinely travels around the villages in a hospital van, parking at roadside pavilions to distribute medicines and provide medical service. In general, their outreach service is similar to that provided by the military — starting with a primary medical check-up done by a junior nurse, followed by a full check-up by a senior nurse, and ending with free prescription medicines. However, this service differs from the military's in two ways. First is the amount and quality of the medicines provided. In addition to distributing packets of basic medicines to all who come for check-ups, the nurses provide, as needed, particular medicines for treating individual patients' ailments, and some of these medicines can otherwise be expensive. Second is the number of villagers who gather for the service. On one occasion, 112 residents arrived for check-ups, and the service went on for three hours. Although most recipients were adults and elders, many teenagers came for the service as well. These recipients also hung around the pavilion and chatted with each other for awhile after they had gotten their check-ups. This differs from the military's medical service, where not many residents showed up and those who did were exclusively adults and elders.

What lies beneath these different levels of attendance is worth mentioning. For one thing, obviously, people know that trained medical personnel can provide better care than soldiers. However, the reasons for the disparity in attendance are more complex. Villagers' relationships with nurses and doctors from the district hospital are not stressful or filled with distrust and fear as their relationships with the military. They hung around the pavilion for awhile after receiving their medicines rather than leaving abruptly, as they had done at the mosque. In addition, advance work done by village health volunteers makes a huge contribution to bolstering attendance. Before the hospital team arrived, the volunteers visited houses in their designated zones of responsibility and informed the residents about the impending free medical service. And when the team arrived, the volunteers led them to the designated pavilion and helped them transform the place into a temporary medical service station.

It is noteworthy that, although the Ministry of Agriculture and Cooperatives was allocated with a special budget for the southernmost region, none of the agencies under its supervision came to implement special projects in Guba. Prior to the eruption of the recent unrest, many development projects such as irrigation systems and reservoirs were implemented in Guba and nearby villages. But since 2004, no agricultural development projects have been conducted in the area. The subdistrict agricultural agent was removed and stationed at the Raman district office, leaving the subdistrict office under his assistant's supervision. He goes to his office only once in awhile; his primary task is to collect data rather than to initiate or conduct agricultural development projects, as before.

While no agricultural development projects have been carried out in Guba in recent years, one specific "help and care" project under the Ministry of Agriculture and Cooperatives has been vigorously conducted and enjoys popularity among the residents, namely the disaster relief programme of the Department of Livestock. Under this programme, farmers register their crops and farm animals with the department. The registration is aimed to achieve many objectives, but the most important one to the residents is that they can claim compensation money if their registered animals or crops are damaged, lost, or die because of natural disasters, especially flooding, which occurs every year. The flood relief programme in 2009 is a case in point.

In the late afternoon of 26 February 2009, I began to notice that the villagers were up to something uncommon. I saw many of them carrying photos but had no idea what they were about. Aryani, whose husband had allegedly been killed by the insurgents, came up and asked me if I had taken any pictures of dead cows. I said no and could not guess why she had asked me such a question. Then I saw Wae with a digital camera walking to his motorcycle. I asked him where he was going, and he said to the mountain forest to take pictures of his two dead cows. He invited me to come along, but Maeh advised that the forest was too far and too hard for me to get to. After Wae left, I asked Jamal why he needed to take pictures of his dead cows. Jamal said that the cows had died because of the recent flooding. And because Wae had registered these cows, he was entitled to get compensation money for them. However, apart from the registration document, Wae also needed to provide proof that the cows had died because of the flood. So he first had to take pictures of his dead cows, and then submit the photographs to the subdistrict livestock office along with other documents in his request for compensation money.

Wae returned home in the late evening with the required pictures. He told me that he would use these pictures along with other documents to request compensation. The next day, he went to meet with the subdistrict livestock officers and submitted the materials. It took him about a week to get an official letter informing that he was entitled to compensation money of 12,000 baht for his two dead cows and designating the day he could pick up his check. Wae was very happy about the news, although the amount of compensation is smaller than the cows' actual worth. The night before Wae went to the provincial office to pick up the check, Saifuldin came to me and asked if I was free the next day. I said yes, as I had no plans yet. He said that was good, because the next day he would be very busy and could not accompany Wae, who does not speak Thai, to the provincial office to get his check for the dead cows. He suggested that perhaps I could accompany Wae and help him with this chore. I said no problem; I would take care of Wae the next day.

Wae and I left Guba the next morning in a pick-up truck with Najmudin driving and also with Farid, who, like many other Guba farmers who had sustained a loss, was also scheduled to pick up his check on this day. We arrived at Yala's Provincial Office of Livestock at about 9:00 a.m. People, many of whom were from Guba and nearby villages, packed the ground floor of one building, although the check distribution had not begun yet. I helped Wae put the letter he had received into a plastic tray and told him to wait for his turn. Then five government officials entered the room, got seated, and started the process. While waiting for Wae's turn, I walked around and talked to some other Guba residents. Most of them were pleased with the compensation money they were receiving, although it was usually less than the actual value of their dead animals. Importantly, although there were inconsistencies and even unfairness in the compensation — for instance, Wae was getting 12,000 baht for two dead cows whereas Farid was getting 11,000 baht for only one dead cow — no one complained or raised the issue with the government officials. The people I talked to were happy with their compensation, indicating the popularity of the disaster relief programme.

In addition to material assistance, the Thai government has programmes to provide people in the Deep South with cultural facilities. As indicated in

Table 3.1, the Ministry of Culture was allocated a special budget to develop programmes in response to the southern unrest. Guba is one of the places where agencies under the Ministry of Culture vigorously performed this duty, with emphasis on residents' ethno-religious identity. The example of Aiman illustrates this well.

Aiman is one of few residents who obtained a bachelor's degree from a major university (Prince of Songkla University, Pattani Campus). His major — performing arts — entailed the study not only of traditional Thai performing arts but also Malay arts. Rather than seeking a job in an urban setting, like university graduates in general, he chose to return home after graduation and work in the local art and culture scene, as well as taking care of his family's business. He also oversees a *silat* (traditional Malay performing arts) troupe in Guba and holds important positions in local arts groups like the *kris*-making group in Burong Kueteetae subdistrict. The front part of the ground floor of his house is arranged as a local museum, where Malay arts and antiques are displayed and which is occasionally visited by various groups of people.

Aiman is widely known as a local artist and cultural specialist and has frequently been sought out by state authorities in charge of cultural affairs. In addition to delivering lectures and providing guidance and information for several schools and outreach classes, he was elected chairman of the Arzeulee Subdistrict Cultural Promotion Committee set up by Yala's Provincial Office of Culture. His local museum was one of two in Yala Province to be selected by the Department of Cultural Promotion to be a Chaloemrat Cultural Centre, as part of a celebration for King Bhumibol. He is also increasingly sought out by culture-related state authorities to participate in various cultural events such as parades, performances, exhibitions, and fairs, including Yala Province's Red Cross annual fair.

Late one morning, my wife and I saw Aiman and other residents preparing something in his house. Curious, we walked over and asked them what they were up to. Aiman said that they were preparing materials for a *bungo sireh* (a footed tray for a floral arrangement), for a contest to be held at Yala's Red Cross fair[15] that night. He said that officials from Yala's Provincial Office of Culture invited him to participate in the contest and that he had accepted their invitation, as he thought it was aimed at promoting Malay culture. He asked us if we wanted to come along, and we said yes.

We left Guba about 2:00 p.m. in the family's pick-up truck, with Najmudin as driver as always. The pick-up was densely packed with many of us — six contest participants, five male teens and adults who wanted to visit the fair, and my wife and I who wanted to observe the contest and the fair — and materials for making the trays. We arrived at the fair about an hour later; it had not started yet. A government official at Yala's Provincial Office of Culture called Aiman on the phone and told him to wait for her. She soon arrived and led us to a building, where she disappeared upstairs and we waited again, for an hour, as it started to rain. At about 5:00 p.m. when the rain had stopped, she came back downstairs and led us to her agency's booth at the fair, where the tray-making contest would be held.

The Office of Culture's booth was intentionally decorated to represent the ministry's commitment to cultural diversity. Although more than half the booth area was devoted to displays of Buddhist culture, the de facto state religion, the remaining part was spared for the expression of other ethnic identities such as Chinese and Malay (*kris* making) and other religions such as Islam (headscarf making). Importantly, in addition to representing Thai and Chinese ethnic identities, one of the three gables of the booth was designed to architecturally represent Islam. The Ministry of Culture's message was that, despite their differences, these ethnic and religious identities peacefully coexist in Thailand's Deep South.

When we arrived at the booth, the government official arranged spaces for Aiman and his team, which was now split into two groups, to make the flower trays. She told us that in addition to us, two other teams, which had not yet arrived, would participate in the contest. One team, from Yalor village, arrived fifteen minutes later, all adults and elder women. They were split into two groups, like us. The third team was made up of schoolchildren from Yala Female School, and they did not participate in the contest. They made a flower tray just for demonstration and display. So there were only four teams participating in the contest, two being ours and the other two from Yalor village. It took about two and a half hours for our teams to finish their trays. Our competitors finished shortly after us, while it took an additional hour for the schoolgirls to complete theirs. Once completed, all the trays were put on display, awaiting judgement. At about 9:30 p.m., three judges — all government officials, two Thai Buddhists and one Malay Muslim — arrived, and the contest began. Each judge took a close look at the trays and jotted down their marks on pieces of paper. It took them about fifteen minutes to finish their job, and then they gave the slips of paper to our host, the head of the Office of Culture. The results were announced: Aiman's team was the winner, while our second team took third place. Each team received a certificate and money, and posed for a picture with the provincial cultural head while receiving the award from him. We left the fair at about 10:00 p.m.

The *bungo sireh* contest was aimed primarily to promote Malay culture. Aiman said that *bungo sireh* is a Malay equivalent of the Thai *bai si*, commonly used in the processions of important ceremonies such as weddings, circumcisions, welcoming important guests, and the like. It is primarily made of male betel leaves and has tiers ranging from three and five to seven and nine, which represent Mount Meru in Hinduism. As such, it was not Islamic but Malay culture influenced by Hinduism that was on display.

Malay culture has variously been promoted by government agencies in other ways as well. Schoolchildren are encouraged to wear traditional Malay dress to school on Fridays. There is a Malay language option on a state-owned television channel. Every sign at Raman hospital has Malay in the Yawi script along with the Thai language. An academic institute in Bangkok conducted a government-funded research project on transcribing Malay into the Thai alphabet, to further help conserve the Malay language in Thailand. After the eruption of the recent unrest in 2004, the list of projects and activities initiated by the government to promote Malay culture became exhaustive.

Islam has also been widely promoted. The wearing of headscarves by Muslim women is no longer opposed but encouraged, and Malay Muslims wishing to make a hajj pilgrimage receive a wide range of support from government agencies, especially those related to security. In addition, many mosques have been built or renovated with financial support from government agencies, which also provide regular funding for *pondoks* and Tadikas. In the southern provinces, a state-owned television channel airs prayers five times a day, along with chanted readings from the Koran. During the month of Ramadan, various television programmes on Islam are aired on many television channels, especially those owned by the state and the military. These are the Thai state's messages to Muslims in the country, directed especially at those in the south, that the state fully supports Islam.

In addition to various programmes implemented by government agencies, the Thai government has also provided "help and care" for people in the Deep South in many other ways. For example, the Thaksin government, regardless of its alleged heavy-handed policy with respect to the southern unrest, provided scholarships for about 3,000 students in the three southernmost provinces to study nursing in colleges and universities, guaranteeing them jobs in state hospitals after graduation. In recent years, many government positions in the southernmost region have been especially designated for local Malays. The military in particular has provided a wide range of jobs for those who are interested, hiring ten to fifteen men in each village to work for them. Those who wish to join the military in a salaried capacity can apply either for a two-year stint in military service, or to become a paramilitary ranger. Government positions are now more available to Malay Muslims of southern Thailand than ever before.

These government programmes and activities are in large part aimed to win the "hearts and minds" of Malay Muslims amid the recent unrest. Although most residents criticize and distrust the military's "help and care" programmes, some of them appreciate these special services. Suhana said that the Centre for Sufficiency Economy of Arzeulee Subdistrict is good because it provides her with additional daily income. She also thanked the soldiers of the Pahong Gayu military camp for digging the fish ponds, building the structure for growing mushrooms, and installing the fence at the centre for free. Aiman, although criticizing the ways in which the idea was put into practice, agreed with the Provincial Office of Culture in holding the *bungo sireh* contest, as he thinks it helps conserve Malay culture. Likewise, Mohammed, whose daughter was awarded a government nursing scholarship, said: "I am really thankful for the programme. It is really helpful to us. Without that support, our kids could not have made it, because they cannot compete with Thai kids in the towns." Criticism, distrust, and reservations notwithstanding, the purpose of these "help and care" programmes has been achieved to a certain degree. Many residents feel that their concerns have been addressed and their citizenship acknowledged. This is particularly the case when it comes to royal projects, which specifically address certain problems faced by the residents.

3.3. Royal Subjects

According to Guba residents, the Thai state is neither monolithic nor homogeneous. Rather, it is diverse and at times self-contradictory. They think that the civilian governments[16] and the military have always taken a different stance when it comes to the southern unrest, and the latter tends to overrule the former. As such, they do not believe government statements about the unrest claiming that "politics leads the military". The residents also distinguish among the different military units, with the paramilitary rangers the worst of all. The police are always considered wicked. However, southern Muslims have never regarded the monarchy, especially King Bhumibol, as part of the Thai state or government. Many Muslims, like Thais in general, regard King Bhumibol as a person whose life and works were above the messy, and at times dirty, political infighting and corrupt bureaucracy. They always make comparisons between King Bhumibol and the government, with the former benevolent and the latter malicious. As one of them put it: "The king is really good to us in the three southern border provinces, but the government is not." Royal initiatives are a case in point.

3.3.1. Royal Initiatives
Royal initiatives in the southernmost region have been associated with politics from the very beginning. They were born out of three related power struggles in the political arena. First is the revival of the Thai monarchy. The Thai monarchy had been waning since the reign of King Vajiravudh and was formally stripped of political power in 1932 during the reign of his successor, King Prajadhipok, when the country's polity changed from absolute monarchy to democracy. Royal influence continued to deteriorate when Field Marshal Plaek Phibunsongkhram held power during 1938–44 and 1948–57, as he proclaimed himself the country's leader at the expense of two successive young monarchs — King Ananda Mahidol was thirteen years old in 1938 and King Bhumibol was twenty-one years old in 1948. A number of state ceremonies were inaugurated to celebrate the nation under the guidance of the non-royal leader, Phibun, while several royal rituals were discarded or trivialized. This created resentment among many royalists, who bided their time awaiting the revival of their revered institution (Nattapoll 2013; Thongchai 2013).

Second is the legitimization of Field Marshal Sarit Thanarat's coup d'état in 1957 and his subsequent tenure as prime minister. During his years in power, Phibun firmly established himself as the country's leader, which made it difficult for anyone to succeed him. With almost no comparable base of legitimacy, Sarit resorted to the monarchy as a means to validate his coming to power via the coup. Many discarded or ignored royal rituals were revived, and the tradition of the royal family's visits upcountry was resumed. The monarchy, now embodied by King Bhumibol, began to regain its strength and established a tradition of cordial relations with the military (Thak 2007).

Third is the use of socio-economic development programmes as a means to gain loyalty and allegiance from Malays in southern Thailand and discourage separatism. Bureaucrats and technocrats have held that one of the reasons why some Malays are sympathetic to Malay separatists is that they have felt economically forsaken, especially when they compare themselves with fellow Malays in Malaysia. From the early 1960s onward, a number of socio-economic development programmes were launched in the region, in part to prevent Malays from being drawn to Malay separatism, and to create a sense of national unity and belonging among Malays (Che Man 1990; Nantawan 1977; Uthai 1988; Yegar 2002).

Given that the revival of the monarchy was partly effected by assigning the monarch with a new role — taking care of his subjects through development projects — royal initiatives are therefore the arena where the three objectives met and were put into practice.

In 1959, one year after Sarit came to power, the royal family made its first visit to the Deep South, meeting with Malay Muslims and learning directly about their problems and needs. Initially, they provided Malay Muslims with small gestures of assistance, such as mobile medical units. However, after the completion of Thaksin Ratchaniwet Palace in Narathiwat Province in 1974, not only did the royal family begin to visit the Deep South on an annual basis, staying about a month each time, but it also shifted its focus from providing occasional help to conducting development projects in which King Bhumibol's role was highlighted. For instance, during his first stay at the southern palace, the king found that most of the peat swamps in the region were unsuitable for agriculture and that those who lived adjacent to them were faced with flash floods after heavy rains, damaging 60,000 *rai* (9,600 hectares) a year. He then suggested that a drainage canal be built alongside the peat swamps, and it was the Royal Irrigation Department that implemented his suggestion. It was officially reported that, due to the royal-initiated drainage canal, the heavy monsoons of 1975 did not cause flooding, and for the first time in five years those living alongside the peat swamps were able to grow rice with the yields increasing up to 100 per cent. This project became a model for water management around other peat swamps of the southern region (Chalita 2013, pp. 49–50).

Royal initiatives were well established after the Office of the Royal Development Projects Board (RDPB) was founded in 1981 under the government of General Prem Tinsulanonda, who became known as "the King's Man" (Handley 2006, pp. 276–98). The RDPB was intended to mediate between King Bhumibol and government agencies, eliminating bureaucratic hassles such as lack of cooperation between agencies, budget delays, and the like. Its primary task is to supervise and ensure that all royal projects are carried out in accordance with the king's wish. The RDPB also founded Royal Development Study Centre with an office in every region to carry out royal initiatives. These centres draw together government officials from different agencies and academics to conduct research and development projects. They also provide training courses for local residents to improve their quality of life. In the Deep South, the RDPB founded the Pikulthong Royal Development Study Centre in 1991 in Narathiwat Province. The Pikulthong Centre is focused primarily on peat swamp management and development. In addition to coordinating several development projects involving peat swamps being implemented by different government agencies, the centre disseminates research findings on peat swamps among local residents, especially farmers. Of some 3,000 royal initiatives across the country in 2012, 398 have been carried out in the Deep South under the supervision of the Pikulthong Centre (Chalita 2013, pp. 51–53). Below is an account of my visit to the centre to see how royal initiatives are implemented.

In October 2012, my wife, Saifuldin, a local NGO worker, and myself made a visit to the Pikulthong Centre. On arriving at the centre, a young female staff member greeted us with a smile, led us to a meeting room, and told us to wait for the director and a staff member in charge. Then a middle-aged male staff member, who is a senior government official of the Department of Forestry, came in and briefed us on the goals and missions of the centre. When the briefing was almost over, the director came in with a young male staff member and began his session. Once he finished, both the director and the forestry official allowed us to interview them. After a friendly, thirty-minute interview, the director said that his staff member would now show us around the centre. We thanked the director and the forestry official and followed the staff member to the entrance of the main building. Initially, the staff member planned to have us ride in the centre's trolley for the tour. But there were two groups of guests at the time, and they fully occupied the trolley. So we decided to tour the centre in our own pick-up truck, with the centre's staff member as a guide.

He took us to many stations. The first was a plot demonstrating King Bhumibol's technique for changing the peat swamp's acidic soil into a soil that could be used for agricultural production. The technique is called "teasing the soil". He led us across the plot and briefed us on the technique, using revering language whenever referring to the king. Then he brought us to another plot demonstrating the king's "New Theory on Agriculture", which since the 1990s has been vigorously promoted across the country by government agencies, agricultural and non-agricultural alike. Likewise, he walked us across the plot and briefed us on the theory, showing great veneration. Then he quickly showed us a few more stations that were not directly related to any of the king's ideas, as our time was running short. We thanked him when we were done with the tour and then left the centre in our pick-up, which now was loaded with a variety of saplings the centre had given us for free.

I asked Saifuldin while we were driving if there were any royal initiatives in Guba or nearby villages, and he said, "No". This is understandable, as most royal initiatives in the South involve the large peat swamps, none of which are around Guba. Although Baroh Tok Nae Wae in northern Guba is in fact a peat swamp, it is small and has undergone development projects in general not connected to any royal initiatives. Neither Saifuldin (until now) nor any other Guba residents, to my knowledge, have ever been to the Pikulthong Centre. Their only experience with royal initiatives was their protest against the government's plan to build a dam across the Saiburi River in the midst of their village in the 1990s.

It was widely said among the residents that the Saiburi Dam construction project was initiated by King Bhumibol in his attempt to dilute the salty water in Bacho peat swamp, which ironically was a result of another of his initiatives. At the very beginning of the campaign against the dam project, one resident said that government officials of the Royal Irrigation Department, which was in charge of the project, threatened: "This is a royal project. How dare you protest it?"[17] The residents did not stop but continued their protest in cooperation with their supporters, namely NGO workers and specialists in the field, until the project was cancelled. However, it is highly possible that the cancellation was also the result of the intervention of an official who works for Princess Sirindhorn. Some residents said that while they were conducting their own research on the impact of the dam, a man from Bangkok came claiming that he worked for Princess Sirindhorn and that, in accordance with the princess's wish, he wanted to learn about the residents' attitudes towards the planned dam. They told the man that they opposed the dam, and he said that he would report their comments to the princess. Although the residents could never confirm whether the Bangkok visitor was genuine, and he has never made contact with them since, what they experienced in a negotiation with a Bangkok minister a few months later proved that the earlier visitor's claims were likely to be reliable. It took only about fifteen minutes for the minister to pronounce that the dam construction project across Saiburi River was to be cancelled; he did not even have to listen to the research findings the residents had painstakingly prepared. One resident who attended the negotiation speculated: "It must have been because of the palace that the dam construction project was eventually cancelled. We know that they [the palace] want to please us." The residents were aware that their "hearts and minds" were what the monarchy wanted to win, and this even before the insurgency resumed in 2004.

3.3.2. Royal Recognition

In addition to a large number of royal initiatives, the monarchy expresses concerns for its Malay Muslim subjects in other ways, one being royal recognition. Royal recognition entails a ceremony in which members of the royal family grant various kinds of awards to citizens who have an outstanding talent, who achieve success, who win a contest, and so on, so as to officially pronounce that such talent, success, or victory has been recognized by royal family members. Given the wide range of such accomplishments to be recognized, royal recognition becomes a principal way through which Thais (and sometimes foreigners) are granted a rare or once-in-a-lifetime opportunity to meet with and receive a blessing from a royal family member. Such opportunities range from large-scale events, such as when a member of the royal family hands out diplomas to thousands of university graduates in a single day, to more exclusive circles, such as the S.E.A. Write Award ceremonies where award-winning writers from across Southeast Asia are gathered in a more intimate setting. It is through these ceremonies that many Thais, particularly from rural areas that have perhaps never benefited from a royal initiative, have the opportunity to receive a personal blessing from a member of the royal family. Maeh's receipt of an "outstanding mother" award from Princess Soamsawali (former wife of then Crown Prince Vajiralongkorn), in an event honouring many selected mothers, is a case in point.

In general, Maeh does not differ from other mothers who work hard to earn income and take care of their family. However, what distinguishes her is that she is so strongly committed to her children's education. Of only a handful of Guba children attending college and earning college degrees, five are her children. When asked why she so emphasizes education, she told me:

> [It's] because I have never had the chance to go to school when I was young, although I really wanted to do so, because my parents were poor. My life is difficult because I have no knowledge. I cannot find a well-paid and easy job because I have no education. Wae and I have to work hard in rubber plantations to support our family, and I don't want my kids to face hardship and difficulty as we do. So I want them to get an education, as high as they want and I can afford. Life is hard for those having no education.

Although Maeh's strong commitment to her children's education is widely known in Guba, it was not until Somphon, a secondary school teacher in Kanchanaburi Province northwest of Bangkok, learned about it that her life began to change. In addition to teaching, Somphon was involved with various activities, including the Western Region Community Forestry Network, where she is a cofounder and coordinator. She heard about Maeh through Maeh's sons, Aiman and Saifuldin, whom she worked with on environmental and socio-cultural issues. After visiting the family a couple of times and learning about Maeh's life and her commitment to her children's education, Somphon set out to get Maeh's "goodness" recognized publicly. She came up with the idea of nominating Maeh for the Outstanding Environment Conservation Mother Award, which is granted every year by Princess Soamsawali as part of the celebration of the queen's birthday. It was Somphon's responsibility, as the nominating person, to travel to Guba and collect data about Maeh herself, but given the unrest in the Deep South Saifuldin was put in charge of the task. After receiving Maeh's profile from Saifuldin, Somphon nominated her for the award, and about four months later she learned that Maeh had won out over forty-two other nominees that year.

Maeh then had to attend the award ceremony in Bangkok, a city she had never visited in her life. She, together with Aiman and a female relative, travelled to Bangkok by train but stayed at Somphon's house in Kanchanaburi during the period. The ceremony was held on 5 August 2008 at Mahidol University, where Maeh and outstanding mothers of other fields were given the awards by Princess Soamsawali. When the princess arrived at the ceremony, the royal anthem was played, and Maeh as well as all other participants stood still to pay respects to the princess and the king. Then Maeh and the other award winners were called by name to receive their trophies along with a sum of money from the princess. Although feeling extremely excited, Maeh performed her role quite well. She and her companions spent two more days at Somphon's house after the ceremony, visiting several tourist attractions in Kanchanaburi and nearby provinces with Somphon's facilitation.

The winning of the award brought Maeh nationwide fame. Three days after returning home, journalists from the *Daily News*, one of the country's leading newspapers, came to interview her. On 10 August 2008, her story as the winner of the 2008 Outstanding Environment Conservation Mother Award appeared on the newspaper's environment page. The story tells about how Maeh leads her life in accordance with nature and how she raised her children, especially Saifuldin, who now is a leading environmental activist in the southern region, to follow her example. At the same time, the *Journal of the Environment*, published by the Faculty of Environmental and Resource

Studies at Mahidol University, which hosted the ceremony, published Maeh's story with a focus on how her life and deeds have helped conserve the environment. Even three months after the ceremony, reporters, journalists and writers were still coming to interview Maeh. It took her some time to get used to her new fame, resulting from the ceremony. Although it was not her wish in the first place, this rare experience reminded her of how significant and authoritative royal recognition can be.

3.3.3. Royal Involvement with the Recent Unrest

The insurgency in the South has been a matter of grave concern to royal family members, particularly Queen Sirikit. Worried about the almost daily violent incidents that began in January 2004, the queen decided to extend her annual visit to Thaksin Ratchaniwet Palace from one month to two months (September–October) that year so that she could meet with and listen to more local people about their losses, sufferings and hardship from the unrest and determine how she could best help them. When she returned to Bangkok on 16 November 2004, she granted a special audience to about a thousand people, including Prime Minister Thaksin, cabinet members, senior government officials and Village Scouts[10] to deliver an address on what she learned during her two-month stay in the South. Below is part of her address:

> I thank you all for coming to meet with me following my invitation. I think you all know well what drove me to this want — the unrest in the southern border provinces. As such, I could not stay there [Thaksin Ratchaniwet Palace] for only one month as usual. I had to stay there for two months because I am so worried about the people there. In particular, I have witnessed their livelihoods and realized that now they, whether Buddhist Thais or Muslim Thais, are suffering severely. Innocent Buddhist Thais were killed every day and the killings are still going on even now. I talked to the subjects [*rasadorn*] in the provinces of Pattani, Yala, and Narathiwat, and all of them said they have lived there peacefully since their grandparent's time.
>
> [...] I have accompanied His Majesty the King for more than thirty years but have never seen anything cruel and brutal like this before. Sometimes they [the insurgents] posted leaflets on rubber trees forbidding villagers from tapping rubber, otherwise they would get killed. They acted as if the land were lawless. The villagers told me that in Tanyong Limo village,[19] if Buddhist Thais go to tap rubber in the area, they will get beheaded and their heads will be thrown away somewhere else. Then there will be strangers coming to ask if you want to sell your rubber plantations and *rambutan* and *longkong* orchards. If you say no, late at night

someone will come and destroy your fruit orchards and rubber plantations. [...] When I paid a visit to Tanyong Limo village, the villagers, mostly women,[20] told me it was good that I went there that day, because they wanted to hear just one word from my mouth, whether or not they had the right to stay there. Or did I want them to leave? I told them of course they must stay there because the fruit and rubber trees are all grown up. We should stay and help each other figure out how. These subjects said they had been living there since their grandparents' time, hundreds of years. And where should they go? "We have not done anything wrong," they said. "Why do we have to let someone expel us from our land?" These subjects asked me to tell the government and the prime minister, please do not withdraw the troops from the three southern border provinces, because if the troops stay here, they will survive. But if the troops are withdrawn, they may die. Then I told them I will have the marines train them at shooting long guns.

[...] I have witnessed the situation for two months and have reflected on whether or not we should let the daily killing go on endlessly. I am a queen aged seventy-two years and saw the incidents but kept sitting quiet, having no idea how to speak out to help such helpless Thai people. So I told myself, no. I'd better speak to you and ask if it is appropriate to let someone kill others with impunity. The country has laws but they cannot be enforced in the three southern border provinces. I don't know why. But it is so scary.

[...] Thank you all for coming to listen today. And thanks to the prime minister and the government for painstakingly helping to solve the problem. And I promise that I, at the age of seventy-two, will practise shooting a gun again without wearing glasses. I will shoot with my bare eyes. Thank you. Thank you very much. (*Khaosod*, 18 November 2005)

Two major points can be drawn from the queen's address. First is the ethno-nationalistic element. The queen generally referred to people of the South as members of an ethnic category — Thai. However, she meant Thai as an ethnic category in a "supra" sense that transgresses, covers or subsumes all other ethnic categories such as Malay and Chinese. Regardless of their ethnic origins, those living in the southernmost region, like their counterparts across the country, are considered Thai. In addition, while subsuming or concealing ethnic differences, the Thai ethnic category allows other kinds of difference and identity to surface alongside. The major one is religion. As such, when the queen referred to people in southern Thailand with regard to their differences, she used such ethno-religious terms as "Buddhist Thai" and "Muslim Thai". Likewise, any ethno-religious term that implies ethnic categories other than Thai are not allowed. The queen chose not to use such terms as "Malay Muslims" or "Muslim Malays" in referring to the people of southernmost Thailand. Importantly, Thai ethnicity is strongly associated with the nation. Because the residents of the Deep South, especially the Buddhists, are all Thais, they all have the right to live there regardless of any "foreign" attempt to expel them. Likewise, because the queen considered herself a Thai with obligations to the Thai nation, she, at the age of seventy-two, strongly felt she had to "practise shooting a gun again without wearing glasses" so as to protect that nation.

The second point raised by the queen's address concerns the aid programmes specifically designed for those affected by the unrest. The queen said that she used donations from her seventy-second birthday anniversary to buy 600 *rai* of land in Narathiwat Province and allocated it to the families of those killed on duty, especially low-ranking police officers and soldiers. In addition to two *rai*, each family received a house to stay in and agricultural training in such areas as raising fish and growing plants, so they could earn their living on this land. The queen added more details about this project in her seventy-third birthday anniversary address. In the address, she said that she regarded the project as a "sufficiency economy village project", following King Bhumibol's initiative. She said that she used the donations to buy an additional 707 *rai* of land in Narathiwat Province and asked the military to help build 150 houses for the families of those killed on duty. She received help from the Pikulthong Centre to provide the families with agricultural training. In addition, she implemented the king's initiative to establish rice banks, from which families could borrow rice for household consumption when they run out of rice. The residents were also provided with security by the military while living on this land. The queen said that the project was intended to benefit both Buddhist Thais and Muslim Thais who had suffered from the unrest. She added that she learned from a newspaper report that a delegation from the Organization of the Islamic Conference (OIC) had travelled to Thailand and visited this village, and were impressed by how the Muslims of southern Thailand were being treated. The queen said: "They [the OIC] said they admired and were so pleased with the sufficiency economy village project. They even talked to Muslim families who had been chosen to stay in the village. An international Islamic committee praised us, which pleased me the most. They said that Thailand takes care of Muslim families very well" (*Khaosod*, 13 August 2006).

In addition to the sufficiency economy village project, the queen in her address also mentioned a demonstration farm project — another project through which she provided those suffering from the unrest with special assistance. Although the project was implemented primarily because of a request by Thai Buddhists and as a result is basically aimed to ease their sufferings, it also provides help and support for Malay Muslims.

There are twenty-one demonstration farm projects in the Deep South. The closest one to Guba is the Wang Phaya–Tha Thong Demonstration Farm Project located in Tha Thong subdistrict. According to the farm supervisor, the only government official at the site, the farm was founded primarily to relieve hardship and difficulties caused by the unrest by offering the residents employment — 220 positions with a daily wage of 150 baht — close to home and safe. Initially, the farm targeted residents of Wang Phaya and Tha Thong subdistricts, many of them Thai Buddhists. But later it expanded its service area to cover other nearby subdistricts including Arzuelee subdistrict, because many people working at the farm quit for better jobs elsewhere. About thirty people have worked at the farm since the beginning, all of them Thai Buddhists who said that the reason why they wanted to work there was that it is a royally initiated project specifically promoted by the queen. Of the current 220 employees, about 40 per cent are Thai Buddhists. These daily wage earners work on a variety of jobs on the farm from 8:30 a.m. to 4:30 p.m. But in reality they work for fewer hours. In addition to various farm plots and stations, there is a military regiment at the farm in charge of escorting some farm employees to and from their homes. The farm is a project of the Foundation for the Promotion of Supplementary Occupations and Related Techniques under the Royal Patronage of Her Majesty the Queen. However, all funding allocated to the farm is from the Internal Security Operations Command, the state agency that was allocated the biggest budget for coping with the southern insurgency.

Another royal initiative related to the recent unrest that some residents have benefited from is Ratprachanukroh School 41. The school is part of the Ratprachanukroh school network, run by the Ratprachanukroh Foundation under royal patronage, founded and supported by King Bhumibol. Initially, both the foundation and the schools were aimed to help those suffering from natural disasters such as storms and flooding. Later, they expanded their scope of mission to cover other forms of disaster, including man-made calamities like the unrest. On 5 December 2005, stone-laying ceremonies for Ratprachanukroh school buildings were simultaneously held in five southern provinces: Satun, Songkhla, Yala, Pattani and Narathiwat. These ceremonies were intended both to celebrate King Bhumibol's sixty years on the throne and to help local children who are orphaned or otherwise prevented from attending school on a regular basis by the insurgency. The schools were built by army engineers.

Ratprachanukroh School 41 is aimed to support children of Yala Province. It is located on a 288-*rai* plot in Tha Thong subdistrict, about 1 kilometre away from the Wang Phaya–Tha Thong Demonstration Farm Project. Like Ratprachanukroh schools in general, it offers grades 1–12, is coeducational, and has both boarders and commuters. Students are provided with everything they need for free, ranging from tuition, books, and other classroom materials to food, housing and medical care. One of the schoolteachers said: "This school is the best. Students don't have to pay for anything. They just come empty-handed and get everything for free." However, the school admits only a small number of children despite its vast physical area and carrying capacity. In 2011, it had only 253 students (11 were Thai Buddhists), 57 teachers (2 were Thai Buddhists), and an administrative staff. Given the highly competitive admissions procedure and the excellent facilities provided (compared to those of other government schools in the region), study at Ratprachanukroh School 41 is mostly reserved for those with connections, as in the case of Effendi.

Effendi is a native of Tanyong Mat subdistrict of Narathiwat's Ra-ngae district and has a house in Bukae Kuejee. However, his "house registration", a document that indicates residency, is in Pahong Gayu, and he spends most of his free time in Guba, either at the teashops or at the roadside pavilions. He has taken part in various community activities that involve the Thai bureaucracy since he was young. He used to be a member of a young farmer's club in Narathiwat Province, and he performed so well in the club's activities that he was granted an Outstanding Young Farmer award when he was seventeen years old. The award was presented to him by Princess Sirindhorn, and a framed picture of the ceremony hangs on the wall in his house. After being granted the award, he was given an offer by a government agency to visit Japan as part of a delegation, but he declined because he wanted to go to Mecca to perform the hajj at the time. Upon his return from Mecca, where he spent three years illegally working in a garment factory, he worked at the Centre for Community Justice at the Raman district office, in charge of four subdistricts including Arzeulee. He worked there for about one year and then quit, finding that the centre was not capable of solving problems as he had expected. Then he worked for Raman District Probation Office for almost one year and quit that, too, because he saw no progress being made. Although now he is a rubber trader, an occupation he started fifteen years ago, he still gets involved with the Thai bureaucracy in various ways and knows many government officials at the Raman district office and other government agencies. In sum, he is a man with many wide-ranging connections.

Effendi uses his connections with government officials and other influential figures for various purposes, one of which was to enrol his children in Ratprachanukroh School 41. According to the school's criteria, his children are not eligible because they have and live with their parents, whose economic standing is average or better, and they have never been directly affected by the unrest. But, given excellent facilities the school provides to students for free, Effendi asked people he knew who have influence at the school to enrol his children there. His two sons study and stay at Ratprachanukroh School 41 during weekdays and go home during weekends. Effendi also plans to put his youngest daughter in the school when she turns seven. "I want my daughter to get a PhD," he told me, and Ratprachanukroh School 41 is the foundation of this ultimate dream.

Another way the king got involved with the recent unrest is to provide quick advice on tackling the problem, namely "to understand, to access, to develop" (*khaochai, khaotheung, phattana*, เข้าใจ เข้าถึง พัฒนา). Like his other pieces of advice, this phrase has been publicly embraced by all state agencies, especially the military. For example, the Southern Border Provinces Peace Building Command instructed all units to pursue a nonviolent approach — "politics leads the military". In particular, it ordered military units to "win over villages" using the king's advice. While it is still unclear to what extent and in what way such advice is put into practice, it conveys a message that the residents of the Deep South are the king's subjects whose well-being must be looked after.

The king's involvement with the unrest also significantly includes ceremonies for government officials and other state employees who die in the line of duty. If the fallen is a Thai Buddhist, he or she receives royal corpse-bathing water before being put into a coffin. Some, especially high-ranking officers, may also receive royal cremation fire for their cremation ceremony. But if the fallen is a Malay Muslim, he or she receives royal grave soil to be laid on the grave. These gestures, along with the government's monetary compensation and other forms of assistance for the families, are aimed to acknowledge the bravery and devotion of the fallen to the country and to bless their death in accordance with their faith. I witnessed one such ceremony as it played out in Pahong Gayu.

About a month after the killing of three village 1 security team members in Pahong Gayu, a royal grave-soil ceremony was held in Pahong Gayu cemetery. Four tents were pitched at the cemetery, and about forty Pahong Gayu residents, mostly women, along with official leaders such as the subdistrict headman and the village headmen as well as village security team members, attended the ceremony. Two SAO members also joined the ceremony, according to an official invitation letter. Around noon, a convoy made up of the Yala governor's black SUV and accompanying vehicles arrived. Everyone in the tents stood upright when the governor got out the SUV to pay him respect. Then three men in white royal uniforms got out a van; two of them carried the royal grave soil wrapped in pieces of black and white cloth in their hands. The governor led the two men and other attendees to the graves of two of the slain security team members. At the graves, the two men unwrapped the cloth, and the governor put ten lumps of grave soil on one grave and nine on the other (one lump was missing for some unknown reason), while the imam of Pahong Gayu mosque and other religious leaders were praying *dua* around the graves. Once finished with the ceremony, the governor walked back to the tents and talked to some residents, especially religious leaders and official leaders, before travelling to another cemetery, where the third slain security team member was to be buried, to conduct the same ceremony. These ceremonies are intended to bestow the king's blessing on those who have died in the line of duty, protecting the country.

Royal projects are notable in that they transcend much of the red tape of the bureaucracy. In particular, they operate using resources, budgets and personnel drawn from several government agencies that normally work together only rarely. As a result, they produce satisfactory results across the country, including in the Deep South. A female resident of Bacho district of Narathiwat Province who had participated in the queen's handicraft production project smiled when I asked how she felt about the project. She said that the project was good as it provided her with supplementary income, and because there were authorities and agencies to take care of all details ranging from raw materials and pattern designs to markets. Likewise, a Guba woman I met at the queen's demonstration farm told me that she felt good about the farm, as it provided her with supplementary income whenever she wanted, and there was no comparable source of employment in the area. Another Guba woman felt grateful for the special medical service she received under royal patronage, because without it, it would have been almost impossible for her to treat an illness that she had been suffering from. Effendi said that Ratprachanukroh School 41 is a real blessing for people in the area. Without it, it would have been impossible for them to access such an excellent educational facility. In this regard, the aim of royal projects and other royal initiatives to win the "hearts and minds" of people in the Deep South had been achieved to some degree.

In addition to government programmes and royal projects, people in the South also seek help, support, and especially protection from influential figures. This is particularly the case when considering the incidents of "fear and distrust" the recent unrest has brought to the area. To live in such an environment, where life can be taken anytime at someone's will with impunity, people have found it increasingly necessary not only to stay away from conflicts when they erupt but also to seek protection from local strongmen, especially when they themselves fall under suspicion or accusation of involvement in the insurgency.

PART 2: LOCAL SUBJECTIVITIES
3.4. The Subordinates

One night while watching Bakhtiar, a southern Guba resident, working on a malfunctioning fixture for a fluorescent bulb, I asked him where he had obtained his skill at such tasks. He replied, "When I served in the military." He said further that he had served in the military twice, first on his elder brother's behalf due to a mistake in the official documents and second when his turn came. What is interesting is that although he went through the card-drawing procedure during the first conscription process, he volunteered for military service the second time. I asked him why he had decided to do so despite the fact that he had already served. He said: "Because I wanted to get protected. Being a soldier and knowing people in the military can help protect you from being bullied, especially by influential figures." Although the recent unrest renders the military no longer a desirable source of protection, at the same time the need to be protected is more pressing than ever before. Mohammed, a northern Guba resident, said: "You don't know who doesn't like you and wants to get you. They may take an opportunity to kill you and make it part of the situation. But if you have someone powerful to back you, they will not dare to mess with you." To be protected by someone powerful and influential is therefore a necessity for some people amid the unrest.

3.4.1. Khru Razak and His Legacy
Around the 1960s and 1970s, Guba was under the influence of a powerful figure called Khru Razak, a descendant of Raman rulers who held a diploma in teaching from Yala Teacher Training School (now Yala Rajabhat

University). After graduation, he taught at a government school in Balor subdistrict before moving to another school in Raman district. Then he moved to Laboh Luwah village, where he used the downstairs part of the village headman's house for teaching, as there was no school building there at the time. He also lived at the village headman's house and eventually married the headman's daughter. After his wife died during a miscarriage, he married her niece and had several children with her.

Khru Razak also accompanied the village headman in his travels to provide him with protection. Given that he was the only person in the village who was fluent in Thai, residents always asked him for help when they had to deal with the bureaucracy. In addition, he led the villagers in doing various community development activities. For example, given the difficulty travelling from Laboh Luwah to other places because of the lack of roads, he, in cooperation with the villagers, managed to cut a road to Raman and Mayo districts, which, after some improvement done by the state, has become the Raman-Mayo road today. And because there was no school building in the village, he, as the school principal, managed to raise sufficient funds from local residents to build a school building without using any government funds.

Given his hospitable and respectful nature, Khru Razak was also frequently consulted by those having problems with the law. Many of these villagers thought that their cases were being handled unfairly and were afraid that they might be bullied or killed by the authorities. Khru Razak's house was therefore frequented by fugitives from the law, and, as a result, he himself was targeted by state authorities.

There was one fugitive who had asked him for help and ended up staying at his home. Khru Razak then held a feast to raise funds to help him fight his legal case. The feast was huge, and the decorations consisted of mock-ups of such military equipment as helicopters, airplanes, and artillery pieces. However, such decorations were seen by the authorities as symbolic of weapons accumulation, for instance for separatist activity. Police came and searched his home and surrounding areas, even amid the thousands of guests attending the feast. Although the police found nothing and left empty handed, they continued to harass Khru Razak.

Tired of this harassment, Khru Razak along with some close subordinates left his home and hid in a nearby forest. In 1967, under suspicion of being involved in separatist activity, he turned himself in to the governor of Satun Province, whom he was on friendly terms with. The governor promised him that he would be detained for only eight to ten days. But in the end he was detained at the Police Special Branch Division in Bangkok for almost two years and then removed to Klong Prem Central Prison, where he was held for four more years. He fought his case successfully and was eventually released.

Khru Razak was still harassed after returning home. One influential figure asked the district chief to get rid of him on some charge, and the district chief in response told a territorial defence volunteer to work on it. But the volunteer did nothing, because he was Khru Razak's relative; he disclosed the plan to Khru Razak instead. Khru Razak then decided to leave again, after having been home for two years.

His second period of time underground differs from the first in that, in addition to close subordinates, many other villagers joined him. Some had been treated unfairly by the authorities, some sought separation from the Thai state, and others were simply bandits. Some of these bandits continued to commit crimes, such as kidnapping for ransom, leading some authorities to pin this same crime on Khru Razak. However, his son, who is now a subdistrict headman, denied such accusations, saying:

> Outsiders, media, and state authorities called the teacher a "ransom-seeking bandit", but it is not true. The thing is that many people came to ask him for help. Some of these were indeed ransom seekers. Some kidnapped villagers' daughters and raped them. But the teacher had nothing to do with this. He actually helped people out with this. A Chinese of Bannang Sata district was kidnapped for ransom. He then came to the teacher and asked for help and he got it.

However, his son admitted that Khru Razak, together with his subordinates, attacked state authorities several times, the principal attack being a blockade and shooting at Raman police station. He said: "Khru Razak was angry at the district chief, who had sent someone to arrest him. He responded by surrounding and shooting up the Raman police station, which is next to the district office. He had almost one hundred subordinates with him at the time."

Khru Razak hid away in the forest for around six years before turning himself in along with some 300 subordinates in 1976. This surrender was coordinated by the permanent secretary, who once was a Raman district chief and whom Khru Razak respected and trusted. After being released, Khru Razak spent the rest of his life quietly in the village before passing away in a hospital on 5 May 1989 at the age of seventy-two. A rumour had it that he was put to death by a doctor, who was also the hospital's director and the wife of a senior police officer, thus finally fulfilling the long-standing wish on the part of some to assassinate him.

Khru Razak's life and deeds have been framed differently, depending on the context in which they were told and on the relationship between the tellers and their subject. In so-called civil society, circles that often position the community against the state, Khru Razak is celebrated as a local hero who fought the Thai state because of its injustice and brought progress to the region. Such stories of heroism, which are mostly told by Laboh Luwah residents, emphasize those incidents in which Khru Razak was bullied by state authorities and glorify his reprisals against them, a few of which were related above. His writing on his house's wall, "I am ready, come get me whenever you want", on the day that he decided to fight state authorities is always quoted as a rallying cry to fight the central government's injustice. A photo of Khru Razak on the day he surrendered, with the wall of his house in the background and inspirational verse underneath the photo, can be found hanging in some homes around the Deep South (Figure 3.1). The caption reads: "A fighter for justice for southern society," and the verse reads:

Let's fight although life may be lost   *But the fact is that death is a witness*
In the future we have a chance to win   *Life still has hope if we are*
Let's fight although lose but not die.   *determined. Remember it and fight again.*
A golden chance glitters in the bright sky.   *How can comrades give up even once?*

Stories of Khru Razak as a hero of progress, which are also mostly told by Laboh Luwah residents, emphasize his numerous contributions to community development such as renovating school buildings and building roads. Interestingly enough, many of these community development projects were carried out in cooperation with government agencies. This is because, according to Karim, a Laboh Luwah resident, "Khru Razak did not categorically refuse state development projects, but he was against the injustice of some state authorities." Khru Razak's pursuit of progress alongside and within the state is also reflected in the education and occupations of his own children. He sent all his children to secular schools and colleges rather than religious boarding schools, and now many of them, and their own children as well, are government officials, some with leadership positions; one is even a university professor with a PhD from a British university. When concerns about environmental preservation mounted towards the end of the twentieth century, Khru Razak was looked upon as a role model for environmental protection and management.

While such narratives by Laboh Luwah residents position Khru Razak as a local hero, some Guba residents have a conflicting opinion. Instead of lionizing Khru Razak's brave struggle for justice against the Thai state

FIGURE 3.1
Khru Razak

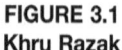

and his contributions to community development, people in Guba point to his crimes and illegal activities committed when he and his subordinates were hiding in the forest near Guba. Many Guba residents will recall seeing dozens of Khru Razak's subordinates walking by their homes with machine guns and hearing stories about the gang's kidnappings and extortion of the owners of large rubber plantations, businessmen and traders, mostly Chinese. Some common people were targeted as well, as the case of Talib's family, below.

Anusorn Unno: Have you ever seen Khru Razak and his subordinates?
Talib: Yes. I saw him in a red car with his subordinates on

	the road in front of my house. And other subordinates accompanied him on their motorcycles. I was about seven years old at the time.
A.U.:	Were you afraid of him?
Talib:	Yes. They had guns.
A.U.:	Is it true that Khru Razak's subordinates extorted money from Chinese and big Thai rubber plantation owners, businessmen, and traders?
Talib:	Yes.
A.U.:	What about local Malays? Were they spared?
Talib:	Not at all. My family was also extorted.
A.U.:	Really?
Talib:	Yes. My family had to give three rubber sheets to Khru Razak's subordinates every month. You know how painful it was. We had only a small rubber plot and we could produce only a few rubber sheets a day. But we had to give some of them to Khru Razak's subordinates. I felt so pained every time I saw my dad give them rubber sheets.
A.U.:	Did they give your family something in return, like protection?
Talib:	No. We got nothing in return from them.
A.U.:	Do you think Khru Razak knew this?
Talib:	Of course. He also benefited from it.
A.U.:	So you don't like him.
Talib:	Not at all. I prayed every day that he dies.
Jamilah [Talib's older sister]:	Life was so hard at the time because there were so many thieves, and many of them were Khru Razak's subordinates. Our cows, which we tied up along the riverbank, were always stolen. And we suspected that Khru Razak's subordinates did it. The elders didn't dare to sleep alone at night for fear that someone might break into their house and steal their belongings or rob and kill them. Life today is very much better. At least we can sleep with no fear or anxiety about thieves and bandits.

However, other Guba residents benefited from Khru Razak and his subordinates. Ishak is one of them. Ishak was the village 1 headman when the influence of Khru Razak spread to Guba. He was not directly subordinate to Khru Razak, but he always helped and supported him when asked. For example, when Khru Razak was working on some construction projects, Ishak, as the village headman, procured government property such as tractors and other materials for Khru Razak to use. Khru Razak in return provided Ishak with assistance when requested. For instance, Ishak once asked Khru Razak to have his subordinates "get" his enemies, and the action succeeded. It was a reciprocal relationship — Ishak used his position to access certain government resources and provide them to Khru Razak, who in return used his influence to help secure Ishak's leadership position in the village.

When his influence was at its peak in the late 1960s through the early 1970s, Khru Razak had about a hundred subordinates. After his second surrender in 1976, these men dispersed. Some joined the Malayan Communist Party (MCP) and other anti-state movements or became full-time criminals, but many resumed their ordinary life. Osman is one of them.

Osman is about eighty years old today. But, despite his age, he is still strong, with a big, tall and tough body. His home is in Ba Roh village, which is adjacent to Laboh Luwah, but he frequently visits Guba partly because his daughter has a house and family here, partly because he is a member of Guba's *silat* troupe, and partly because he, as a local artist, engages in various cultural activities with Aiman. He spends much time sitting and chatting in roadside pavilions in Guba. Judging from how he looks now, one would be surprised to learn that he once was Khru Razak's right-hand man.

Osman said he came to know Khru Razak when his own niece married him. However, the main reason why he joined Khru Razak was not their kin-affiliated relationship. Rather, it was because they shared a hatred of the oppression and injustice of state authorities. As Osman put it,

> I left home with Khru Razak because the authorities mistreated us. Initially I actually didn't get involved much with Khru Razak, as he was a teacher and I was just an ordinary villager. But after he was accused of being associated with the separatist movements, I, as his relative, was included on their list. So I had to leave home and join him in the forest.[21]

Osman added that Khru Razak had about forty subordinates with him at the time, but his network extended to include more than one hundred men. While in the forest with Khru Razak, Osman did not have much to do; he said he just slept and ate. Also, he said he never participated in any robbery or extortion. He said that these illegal activities were carried out by others in the network, and while Khru Razak knew this he was unable to forbid or control them. However, Osman participated in many clashes with state authorities, the most significant one being the attack on the Raman police station mentioned above. He said, in these clashes, that he shot and killed many state officials but did not feel guilty because he considered them his enemies. He had never been shot himself because, he said, "I have good stuff."

Osman said that Khru Razak had nothing to do with the separatist movements at the time. While these movements sought to negotiate with state authorities, Khru Razak made no attempt at such negotiations. He thought that his struggle was legitimate because it was directed at the state's oppression and injustice. And, given that he did not advocate separatism and that his targets were specific individual state officials, Khru Razak had a good relationship with the Raman district chief as well as with some high-ranking policemen. Osman said that he acted as a messenger on a few occasions between Khru Razak and certain officials before Khru Razak decided to surrender, following the officials' advice. He, along with other subordinates, joined Khru Razak in the surrender, ending his years in the forest fighting state authorities without being charged with any illegal activities he had done.

While Osman chose to resume an ordinary life after Khru Razak's surrender, Jasim, another subordinate, chose to join the Malayan National Liberation Army (MNLA), the military arm of the MCP. Jasim spent a few years in the forest with the MNLA before resuming an ordinary life as a "Thai nation development participant."[22] Not only was he granted amnesty upon his return but he was also ascribed with official authority in exchange for a guarantee of "peace" in his territory. This resulted in him being elected Burong Kueteetae subdistrict headman, and he has become a strongman himself with many armed subordinates. Today, he is the most influential figure in Raman and nearby districts, not only among the residents but also among state authorities. For example, after surviving an assassination attempt at a cemetery on 27 September 2009, that same evening his home was crowded with hundreds of well-wishers, including high-profile civilians and high-level government officials such as police superintendants, army commanders, and the governor of Yala Province himself.

Jasim is widely known in Guba. This is partly because he spent part of his childhood with his relatives in the settlement, and partly because he occasionally exerts his influence in the area. For example, when a former village 1 headman implemented a development project at the village's freshwater swamp, the residents, led by Ishak (who held no official position at the time), staged a protest against the project. The protest might have been successful in shutting the project down, had Jasim not intervened. Jasim called many of the protesters to meet with him in person, one by one, and asked them to stop their protest. For fear of Jasim's influence, they all did accordingly. Ishak recalled his meeting with Jasim regarding the protest:

> He had his subordinate tell me that he wanted to meet and talk with me in person about the project. So I went to meet him at his house. He asked me to stop leading the villagers' protest against the project. I told him that I would give it up because of him. If it were not him, I would not have given up; I would have continued to fight.

When asked why Jasim got involved with the project, Ishak said: "Because he had a vested interest in it. The village headman was a kid under his control." However, it is noteworthy that Jasim gave Ishak 20,000 baht in return for his cooperation, and when the project got underway, he had the workers provide Ishak with some soil from the project for free.

In addition to government development projects, Jasim's influence over Guba is significantly exerted through local politics. When the village 2 headman was shot dead (in an act that was officially considered insurgency related, as described earlier) and the position fell vacant, Jasim had his man contest the election. As everyone knew that the candidate was Jasim's man, no one ran against him. As a result, there was no election, and Jasim's man was automatically appointed the new headman. This all occurred with no open resistance or criticism from the residents, despite the new headman's "grey" (undesirable) background. In fact, it is widely believed that, with the exception of the village 3 headman, all the village headmen in Arzeulee subdistrict as well as the subdistrict headman are under Jasim's influence.

The residents' cultural life was also affected by Jasim's influence. For example, only two days before the wedding of Yaakob's niece, Ghalib, who had been assigned to procure a *dangdut* band for the wedding, learned that the deal he had made with a certain band was cancelled because the band was now reserved for the wedding of Lohman Buffalo's daughter. "Lohman Buffalo" is an alias for Burong Kueteetae's SAO chief executive, who himself held some influence in the region. But it was not Lohman Buffalo's influence that had caused the *dangdut* manager to break the promise he had made with Ghalib. Rather, it was because Lohman Buffalo is a close relative of Jasim, Burong Kueteetae subdistrict's headman, that the manager felt obliged to serve his want.[23] Likewise, because they knew that the cancellation had something to do with Jasim, Yaakob and the people planning his niece's wedding neither blamed the manager nor tried to get him to stick to his original deal. The only thing they could do is to accept the result, regardless of their disappointment and discontent. I will specifically discuss this issue in Chapter 5.

Despite frequently running up against the insurmountable influence of Jasim, only a few Guba residents have had a chance to meet him in person. This is because Jasim lives far away and he now has no reason to visit Guba; in fact, in recent years he has hardly ventured outside his house. His grand house in Burong Kueteetae which I visited once is surrounded by a high, strong concrete wall, and he has armed security guards — some his personal contingent and others state employees such as territorial defence volunteers — on duty all time. On the rare occasions when he leaves his home, and only for a short period of time, he is accompanied by at least three fully armed bodyguards. People in Guba mostly learn about Jasim by hearing stories about him. These stories mostly focus on his fierce temperament and cruelty, the frequency with which he is attacked, and his possession of magic, which plays a crucial role in his incredible ability to survive.

One day while chatting with a group of Burong Kueteetae teenagers, who frequently visit Guba for *kratom* cocktails, I raised the issue of Jasim. I asked if any of them had participated or would participate in the military's vocational training camp. One of them said, "Yes, I will." He said that he would join the training in Ayutthaya Province the following month and learn about furniture making. When I asked why he had decided to do so, apart from escaping the boredom of hanging around with nothing to do for two years after completing grade 9, he said that it was because of Jasim's order. He said that Jasim had ordered male teenagers in Burong Kueteetae subdistrict who were not going to school and had no jobs to attend the vocational training camp; otherwise, they would need to seek jobs elsewhere, such as in Malaysia. They were not allowed to hang around in the villages jobless. He said that the reason for this was that Jasim did not want them to be induced by the insurgents. One young man said that Jasim did not like to see teenagers taking drugs and drinking *kratom* cocktails in his area. On one occasion, Jasim learned that a group of teenagers was taking drugs and drinking *kratom* cocktails in a house in his village, so he together with some subordinates went to the house and opened fire on it with AK47s. Luckily, no one got injured. The teenagers added that Jasim was invulnerable because he had survived a car bomb and many other attacks. They said that he was able to make himself invisible. For example, once he was apprehended and sprayed with hundreds of bullets by the police, but all the bullets missed him and hit the police instead. (However, Jasim denied his possession of magic and explained the situation scientifically.) Asked if they were afraid of Jasim, they said, "Definitely, because he's so scary and he's real."

It is noteworthy that Jasim also became significantly involved with combating the insurgency, on the side of the state. Given that he had been ascribed with state authority in exchange for a guarantee of peace in his territory, not only did Jasim openly express his disagreement with the insurgents but he acted as the de facto commander of the village security teams in Raman district. Rajpat, a village 1 security team veteran, said that he, along with other security team members in the district, was once invited to meet with Jasim at his home. He recalled his conversation:

> Jasim asked me if things were all right in Guba, and I said yes. He said I could tell him if I needed some help in doing my job as a village security team member. He actually did not hold any position in the security team administration. But because he has so much influence and can help and protect village security teams, he always acts like he is our supreme commander.

Jasim has mostly been able to keep his promise to the government, as there have only been a few insurgency-related incidents in his subdistrict. But this in turn has brought him more enemies. Of many failed assassination attempts on him in recent years, at least three were thought to be associated with the insurgency. But Jasim has been very quick to retaliate although he denied his involvement. Shortly after each attempt on his life, those he believed to be behind the attempt were anonymously killed or they disappeared, whether voluntarily or not. And these killings, as always, were taken by the government to be insurgency related, with no real effort made to solve them. Jasim is still the most influential figure in Raman, however amid an increasing number of rivals, insurgents and non-insurgents alike.

Although several factors help boost Jasim's influence in Raman, it is his position as an official leader that plays perhaps the most crucial role. In this regard, Jasim shares influence with a network of other officials including subdistrict headmen, village headmen, SAO chief executives, and others. Although the positions these men hold are analogous to local administration across the country, the insurgency has invested local administrators in the Deep South with greater influence. This is particularly the case when individuals are accused of involvement in the insurgency and are in need of help.

3.4.2. Official Leaders

Along a small road to the Saiburi River lies a large, isolated estate surrounded by rubber plantations and fruit orchards. Towards the rear of the estate is a big house and three attached smaller houses, where perhaps half a dozen men nap, or sit around smoking and chatting. A medium-size building that serves as a small factory for making cement bricks, poles, and piping is located in the front part, where two tractors, one backhoe, and one pick-up truck are parked near large piles of sand and rocks. Hundreds of cement bricks and dozens of cement poles and pipes lie scattered across the front part of the estate. The property belongs to Mana, a former village 1 headman and father-in-law of the current headman; he also has another house and a hardware shop nearby, and the six idle men are Burmese migrant workers whom he hired to help with his business.

Mana's reputation is notorious. While in office, he was accused of abusing power by taking advantage of several government projects at the expense of the residents in his jurisdiction. For example, many people said he had the village tap water facility installed at and operated out of his house compound, keeping for himself the money that users paid for water bills, which are higher than what was charged for tap water by the mosque. When the pumping machinery malfunctioned, he told consumers there was no money to fix it but did not disclose where all the money he had collected had gone. Consequently, the tap water project now serves only his house and those of some of his relatives nearby, whereas other people who had previously benefited from the project now must find their own water supply, for instance from wells. Residents said that he always took part of any charitable donations made to the district for himself before distributing the remainder to local villagers, who are the intended recipients. Unable to tolerate his abuse of power any longer, in the mid-1990s a group of village 1 residents, led by people from Pahong Gayu, rallied against him and demanded his resignation (intending to fill the vacancy with a candidate from Pahong Gayu). However, the effort did not succeed, as the Raman district chief, police chief and other senior government officials from the province, who are said to be part of Mana's network, came to settle the issue in the village themselves. Aware of Mana's powerful connections, the villagers made no more attempts to oust him, and they simply awaited his retirement (he retired in 2014).

Despite being despised by many for his self-serving abuse of power, Mana maintains his own clique whose members he provides and shares the benefits with. The northern Guba mosque is a case at hand. Failing to get his younger brother-in-law elected the imam of the southern Guba mosque, Mana, according to many residents, sought to build a new mosque on his own. He submitted a petition to the Provincial Islamic Committee, and, thanks to his personal relationship with some committee members, it got approval. Then, using his connections, he sought funds from various sources to purchase a piece of land to build the mosque on. After the mosque was completed and registered as village 1's official mosque, he managed to get his brother-in-law appointed as the mosque's imam, entirely bypassing the election process. In addition to the mosque, he also managed to build other structures in the mosque compound, including a subdistrict childcare centre, a Tadika, a Community Justice Centre and a Life Quality Development Centre — with the leading administrative positions all to be filled with his relatives and partisans. The childcare centre is managed by one of Mana's daughters, who is the only teacher at the centre and has an assistant from Pa Ou village, and who overseas the budget, allocated by the Arzeulee SAO. Likewise, the Community Justice Centre is managed by another daughter, who receives a monthly salary from the Ministry of Justice under the supervision of the Community Justice Committee, of which Mana is the chairman. The Life Quality Development Centre is overseen by his son-in-law, a husband of a Community Justice Centre staff member and also now the village 1 headman. Moreover, the Tadika is run by three teachers, two of whom are the imam's daughters, who receive monthly salaries from the Ministry of Education. This situation has led many residents to call the northern Guba mosque "Mana's kingdom".

Mana's clique also includes people who are not his relatives. When in office, he had three assistants whom, apart from monthly salary from the Ministry of Interior, he often shares benefits with, primarily aid money sent by the central government. Omar, assistant village headman for peacekeeping, said:

> I had been a village security team member for some two years. But late last year the village headman invited me to be his assistant for peacekeeping. So I quit the village security team and became his assistant. This is very much better, because I get a monthly salary of 5,500 baht and late this year it will increase by 2,000 baht. Sometimes the village headman gave me what he got from the government.

In addition, when the village security team programme was launched in the village, Mana secured the top positions for his acquaintances. He also strengthened and expanded his clique by helping an acquaintance contest an SAO member election; his acquaintance won.

In addition to Mana and his clique, there is another political faction in Guba. This faction, led by Ishak, has competed with Mana's faction since Ishak became the village 1 headman. Ishak said that Mana once hired someone to kill him, because Mana wanted to be a the village headman himself, but he did not succeed. When Ishak retired and a new election was held, Mana registered to run for the position; Ishak promoted his son Jamal to run against Mana. Mana won, due partly to Jamal's reluctance: "I don't want to be a village headman. I don't want to carry a gun all the time like Ishak", he said. After losing this traditional political power base to Mana, Ishak managed to take control over a newly opened one — the Subdistrict Administrative Organization. And it is his grandson Saifuldin whom he tasked this mission with.

Saifuldin said that Ishak and Maeh called him back from a rally with the Assembly of the Poor in Bangkok to contest the first SAO member election to be held in the village, in 1997. He returned, ran, and, with Ishak's support, won the election. When his term ended, he ran for a second term and won again. However, when his second term was nearly up, the SAO chief executive asked him to join his team as his secretary. He accepted the invitation and ran for a third time, but this time as part of the SAO chief executive's team. The team won, and he became the chief executive's secretary. When this term ended, he again entered the election as part of the SAO chief executive's team, and won yet again. However, the designated vice chief executive was not qualified so he had to assume that position instead. In the last SAO election in 2013, he entered as part of the SAO chief executive's team. The chief executive won again, and Saifuldin is now the SAO vice chief executive. While in office, he has managed to strengthen and expand his political base, which often involves heated confrontations with Mana. The fourth Arzeulee SAO election is a case in point.

One night, I was watching television with Wae at Saifuldin's house, when people gradually arrived and walked past us towards the back of the house. I asked Saifuldin, who was busy greeting the guests and preparing tea, coffee and snacks, what was going on, and he said that he and the others were holding a meeting on the upcoming SAO election. He told me I should bring my camera to take pictures of the meeting. There were fourteen participants, all men. Two of them were the *khatib* and *bilal* of the northern Guba mosque. One was the chairman of the village 1 Red-Whiskered Bulbul Club, and four others were core members of the club. Lutfi, an elder who lives in the inner part of central Guba, also attended the meeting. The rest were people who lived in the house, including Jamal, Aiman and Najmudin. They sat on the floor in a circle with sets of tea, coffee and snacks placed in the middle. Saifuldin started the meeting by reminding everyone why they were invited and what the meeting was about. After Saifuldin's opening remarks, the meeting began; it lasted about an hour. In general, it was a friendly meeting with no heated discussion, but a few people dominated the proceedings.

The agenda was to nominate two candidates for the upcoming SAO member election. Many were worried that Yunus, one of two incumbent village 1 SAO members, had not performed well in the job and had abused his power, accruing benefits at the expense of villagers. They felt the need to find someone to replace him in the upcoming election. The other incumbent village 1 SAO member, Mohammed, was present at the meeting at Saifuldin's house; the others considered that his job performance had been satisfactory, and they wanted to support him once again. The meeting was mostly led by Saifuldin, the coordinator, and Lutfi, the father of two prospective candidates. Lutfi sat next to his eldest son, a core member of the village 1 bird-singing contest club. Initially, this eldest son was proposed as a prospective candidate to run along with Mohammed. But, after a brief discussion, and especially after the son himself refused the offer and otherwise sat quietly, Lutfi's youngest son, Yusri, who was not present, became the new choice. It did not take long for the meeting participants to conclude that Yusri and Mohammed would be the two candidates they would support in the upcoming SAO member election.

After all the guests left, Saifuldin proudly said that the meeting was like a *shura*, an Arabic word for "consultation", which is often regarded as a building block of democracy in Islam. He said that elections, which he regards as a device of Western civilization and democracy, always bring conflict to Muslim communities. But conflict can be avoided with *shuras*, as disputes and issues are settled before any election. In this case for instance, he said, there would be no conflict among the residents as they had reached an agreement on which candidates they would support. However, I questioned him about his version of the *shura*. First, I said that no other political factions had been represented at the meeting, specifically Mana's faction, which included Yunus, the incumbent SAO member whom they had roundly condemned as incompetent. So I asked him: "How can you claim that the meeting represents all the different political stances in Guba?" He said that to allow Mana's faction to participate in the meeting was not possible from the very beginning, given the long-standing conflict between him and Mana. Second, I said that I saw no participants from Pahong Gayu and asked him if he had invited them. He said, "No". I asked him why, and he replied that it was hard to do so, and they also have their own circle.

I further asked him that, given that both of the proposed candidates are Guba residents, how could the concerns and interests of people in Pahong Gayu be addressed? His answer was: "We don't discriminate against the villages in observing the SAO members' duties. Village 1 SAO members work for both Guba and Pahong Gayu, regardless of which settlement they are from. Don't you remember how many projects were implemented in Pahong Gayu in recent years, even though both SAO members are from Guba?" So I said, "OK, let's wait and see."

Four residents contested the 2009 village 1 SAO member election. They represented three different political factions in the area. Mohammed and Yusri represented the dominant political faction in central Guba, which was initially led by Ishak and which is now coordinated by Saifuldin in association with Lutfi, who has a large, strong kinship network. Yunus, an incumbent village 1 SAO member, represented a loose political alliance led by Mana, the village headman at the time. Yana, the only woman running and a Pahong Gayu resident, represented an ad hoc political coalition led by the Pahong Gayu mosque committee and members attempting to bring Pahong Gayu's voice directly to the SAO. Their different political factions notwithstanding, however, the four candidates resorted to the same strategy traditionally used to secure victory — money. Three nights before the election, Mohammed and Yusri, together with their promoters and supporters, met in the back of Saifuldin's family's house to discuss their last-days campaign strategy. The meeting was primarily necessitated by hearsay that Yana had started giving money to voters not only in Pahong Gayu but also in Guba. After a short but serious discussion, a conclusion was reached — Mohammed and Yusri had no choice but to fight back with at least the same amount of money if they really want to win the election. The two contestants adopted the strategy which, when combined with other factors, helped them get elected. Mohammed, whose competitive advantage lay largely in the constant hard work he had displayed on the job as an incumbent, won first place with 289 votes, which, he said, "is very much higher than I expected". Yusri, who was advantaged by his father's strong, extensive kinship network, won second place with 190 votes. He was immediately followed by Yana, who took 183 votes. Yunus finished in last place with 149 votes. It was said that Yana, despite her mosque's backing and the huge amount of money she spent, lost the election because of rumours that she had been adulterous among Pahong Gayu residents. As for Yunus, what largely brought him down was his malfeasance on duty. Mohammed and Yusri were elected as planned, and Saifuldin's political faction was given a boost at the expense of Mana's.

The competition between Saifuldin's and Mana's political factions has played out amid a significant change in Thailand's local politics — the re-emergence of the SAO. This administrative organization was first inaugurated by the Subdistrict Official Administration Act of 1956, along with the Subdistrict Council (SC), founded by order of the Ministry of Interior the same year. However, the SAOs were later abolished by a Revolutionary Council Announcement in 1972, whereas the SCs were kept functioning. After the 1992 Black May incident, demands for political reform were on the rise and decentralization was one of the demands. The uncertain political climate led to the promulgation of the Subdistrict Council and Subdistrict Administrative Organization Act of 1994, which was aimed primarily to elevate the SCs that met the necessary criteria into SAOs such that the organization can govern itself in a decentralized fashion, following local needs. The SAOs thus re-emerged in 1994. Now all SCs have been elevated into SAOs, which, due to substantial budget amounts to be administered and the crucial roles to be performed, have become the heart of local politics across the country. The re-emergence of the SAOs has taken place against the retreat of the subdistrict and village headmen from local administration. An integral part of the SC, subdistrict and village headmen are now an inactive, accessory part of the SAO, which is administered mainly by SAO chief executives. Shakib took this political change as an opportunity to enter local politics in Arzeulee subdistrict.

Shakib is a resident of Yula, which forms part of village 2 along with southern Guba. He has been involved in the Thai and Malaysian antique trade since he was seventeen years old. When the first SAO election was held in village 2 in 1997, he ran to become a member. After winning the election, he was selected by the SAO members as the executive chairman of the SAO, which is equivalent to the SAO chief executive now. When the first SAO chief executive election was held in the second SAO election, he ran for it and won; ultimately, he entered three consecutive SAO chief executive elections and won them all. In other words, he has been Arzeulee SAO chief executive from the beginning for five consecutive terms.

Shakib said that, prior to the first SAO election, he had never participated in politics, whether running for village headman or subdistrict headman. The reason why he changed his mind when the first SAO election was held, he said, is that his friends and acquaintances asked him to do it:

> Participating in politics is like burdening yourself. But because I felt pity for the villagers, I entered politics. This is because in the past this area was very much under the influence of subdistrict headmen and village

headmen. If someone wanted to buy or sell land, they had to pay these people. It's like an illegal tax.

Shakib has thus thought of subdistrict and village headmen as competitors from the very start of his career in local politics, and this was clearly seen in the third SAO chief executive election in 2009.

In that election, Shakib ran against Saad, a resident of Pahong Gayu. Saad had run for village 1 SAO member in the first and second SAO elections and won. He had been village 1 SAO member together with Saifuldin for two terms before deciding to run for the chief executive position in the third election, in which he lost to Shakib by about 400 votes. When the fourth SAO election was approaching, Saad once again was the only candidate to throw his hat in the ring and run against Shakib. Confident in his political alliances, Shakib ran his campaign with his usual team (except for one of his assistants, the daughter of a former assistant who was in jail for carrying a gun without a licence). Likewise, feeling that he had learned from his prior defeat and confident that he knew what was needed to win the upcoming one, Saad brought on two new assistants who represented a political faction — subdistrict and village headmen — that was in opposition to Shakib's faction. One of Saad's assistants was a former village headman and the other was a nephew of Jeya, the Arzeulee subdistrict headman at the time. It was believed that, except for the village 3 headman, all the village headmen of Arzeulee subdistrict were under Jeya's influence, and Jeya openly supported Saad in the competition with Shakib. Thus, the third Arzeulee SAO chief executive election became a serious competition between two major political factions in the subdistrict — SAO leadership led by Shakib and subdistrict and village leadership led by Jeya.

Although Shakib was thought to have the advantage, the election result was not so conclusive. Shakib won by only 7 votes; he got 1,108 votes, whereas Saad got 1,101 votes. Although the subdistrict and village leadership who supported Saad were not in favour in Guba, they were in other villages represented in the election, and this made the competition close. Yaakob, who frequently made critical comments about Shakib and openly showed his support for Saad, said that Saad could have won the election if Shakib had fought by the rules. His opinion was echoed even by Mohammed, who has reservations about his alliance with Shakib; he said: "If the competition was fair, Saad might have won. Shakib used the resources of the SAO in his campaigning in the election. But Saad used only his own resources, and he has no one in the election commission to support him either."

Although losing in the SAO election, Mana's faction was still able to hold its ground in the village headman election. After Mana retired as village 1 headman in 2014, an election was held, and two candidates — Mana's son-in-law Meng and Saifuldin's younger brother Aiman — entered it. Although Meng said that he was running because the villagers had asked him to do it, the villagers themselves said that it was rather because Mana wanted him to run. Aware of Mana's wish to continue controlling the village headman position, those in Saifuldin's faction deliberated about who among them could compete best against Meng. Initially, they thought about Saifuldin himself, because he is a long-time politician. However, Aiman, despite having never been involved in politics before, said that he wanted to compete in the election because, he said, "I feel pity for the villagers. They've been taken advantage by the village headman and his clique. I want to help them." Given Aiman's strong determination, Saifuldin as well as others in his faction, although disagreeing, decided to let Aiman run for the position. The result was not far from expected; Meng defeated Aiman by 98 votes.

Meng said that he did not canvass much, and Mana did not use his charisma or influence as former village headman to help him, either. In addition, he said that he spent only about 160,000 baht during the campaign — he gave voters 100 baht each, 500 baht to those who travelled far to cast their ballot. He also received some 300,000 baht from the village 3 headman, who wanted to run for the subdistrict headman position and needed his support. He gave his reason for why he won: "I've been involved with the residents for a long time, especially since I was appointed the assistant village headman for peacekeeping. Villagers like me because they've seen me work and stay with them." Meng's explanation notwithstanding, his victory over Aiman in the election means that Mana's faction is able to defeat Saifuldin's faction in this kind of local politics.

While the rise of the SAO has led to the diminishing role of subdistrict and village headmen in local administration, the upsurge of violence in the insurgency has rendered effective local administration particularly with respect to security more pressing than ever before. As administrators at the lowest and most local level of government, village headmen are a primary target of security agencies, especially the military. They are continually approached by military personnel gathering intelligence, asking them which villagers under their jurisdiction have gotten involved with the insurgency and how, who is behaving suspiciously, who should security agencies keep an eye on, and other questions. They have also been sought out for cooperation by authorities, especially in setting up military camps in their village, mostly on school compounds. They have been asked for other sorts of assistance by the military, ranging from recruiting residents to attending military-held events to facilitating the operations of the military health service unit. These new tasks often put village headmen, as mediators between state authorities and sometimes bristling residents, in difficult situations, sometimes escalating into sharp conflicts between themselves and the military, as vividly exemplified in the case of Mana.

"I don't know what they [the military] wanted from me," Mana said when he recalled his initial encounters with soldiers in relation to the unrest. He said he had already told the soldiers a couple of times that there were no insurgents or insurgent operations in his village, but the soldiers kept visiting and asking him the same questions, as if he were hiding something from them. He said that he helped the authorities set up and oversee the village security team, because he thought the activity would be useful to villagers. But he saw no need to set up a military camp in the village, because insurgents did not operate in the area. He said that soldiers tried in many ways, sometimes underhanded, to prove that his village was not safe from the insurgency and as such needed a military operation.

The military, however, has approached the SAO in different fashion. As a local administrative organization with funding and facilities, the military targets the SAO for support and assistance. Saifuldin complains that soldiers always come asking for money from the SAO when they hold activities for which they have actually already been allocated a budget. He said:

> I don't know where their huge budgets have gone. They keep asking for money from us every time they hold activities. We cannot refuse them; otherwise, we will be suspected of being uncooperative, being against the government, or sympathetic to the insurgents. We have no choice but to slice our budget for them although our budget is already not enough to carry out our own projects and activities.

Likewise, Mahbub, an SAO treasury officer, said that he was worried about being approached by the military to request funding for an upcoming oath-swearing ceremony that would be attended by some 500 residents of village 5. He lamented:

> They came to meet the SAO chief administrator asking for money, and the chief administrator asked me if we had money for that. Actually, there is no money left for anything. But when I told them that, they said if we don't have money, can we support with food or something else? So we asked them to provide us with an official letter, and we will see what

we can provide them with. Then they left, and we have not received their letter yet.

On the other hand, the insurgency renders the influence and charisma of SAO administrators crucial for ordinary residents, especially those suspected or accused of being involved in the unrest. Shakib, who has many powerful connections, said that he is always sought out for help and protection by such people. He said that, one day, five suspects were arrested in Pa Ou village, and while he was running errands in Hat Yai he received a phone call from the owner of the house where the arrests were made. The house owner, a man in his early sixties whom he intimately called "Uncle" told him that now he was hiding in Shakib's house in Yala city. Uncle said that he was genuinely afraid of the developing situation and had no idea where to go or what to do; the only thing he could think about now was to seek shelter and help from the SAO. Shakib then told Uncle to stay at his house in Yala, on the third floor only, and to not let anyone know; Shakib said that he would take care of the matter when he got back. Upon returning home, Shakib made a call to the Fourth Region Army commander informing that, now, the owner of the house where the arrests were made was with him. He told the commander that he did not intend to hand Uncle over to the authorities. Rather, he would take care of the matter himself, as he personally knew the man and could guarantee that he had no involvement in the insurgency. The army commander countered that his sources had reported that Uncle had given shelter to the suspects for four years. Shakib then explained that, due to the strategic location of his house in Pa Ou, Uncle had been approached by the suspects and asked to use his home for their operations, and he had no choice but to accommodate their demand. Shakib told the commander that he would bring Uncle to meet with military authorities for interrogation only with the assurance that he would be released on bail into his, Shakib's, custody afterward. The commander accepted his proposal. The following day, Shakib brought Uncle to meet a gathering of security officials, including police and paramilitary rangers as well as the army commander. Shakib pled Uncle's case and guaranteed his innocence. The commander told the others that, given the SAO chief executive's assurance, "let him take care of the matter, then".

Shakib said that, in addition to Uncle, he has helped more than twenty other villagers in matters related to the insurgency, although his area of responsibility is development, not government. He said that people sought help from him rather than subdistrict or village headmen because they do not trust the headmen, because they work hand-in-hand with state authorities.

Shakib's claim notwithstanding, the headmen are still sought out for help by residents in various matters including those involving the unrest. Mana said that he can use his position to vouch for the innocence of those suspected or accused of involvement. However, so far, he has not done so, partly because, he said, "I told them [the village 1 residents] that I will not help them or bail them out if they get involved with the unrest and get caught. That's why no insurgents operate in village 1." He added that, although he has not yet helped anyone in an insurgency-related matter, he continually helps them in other matters such as bailing out those arrested for petty crimes, returning confiscated driving licences and cancelling fines, and other matters.

Their efficiency in solving problems notwithstanding, the residents' heavy reliance on official leaders is viewed by some as containing shortcomings. Mohammed, village 1 SAO member, said that many residents think they can commit any wrongdoing as long as they have village headmen to help them out. Likewise, Tawhid, a policeman who is now living in Satun Province, said: "People here depend on village and subdistrict headmen instead of the police or judicial procedures." However, he added that now it is no longer sufficient to simply know or have a connection with only one subdistrict headman: "Subdistrict headmen cannot protect you, because now there are many other powers you have to deal with." Multiple sources of help and protection are what the residents need. These include even "grey figures", or those engaged in illegal businesses.

3.4.3. Grey Figures

Like villages of southernmost Thailand in general, Guba is no stranger to illegal businesses. Gasoline that has evaded taxes is available at the groceries and tea shops, and smuggled cigarettes from Malaysia and Indonesia are widely sold. For those who want to buy underground lottery tickets, there is an agent standing by. In case anyone wants to bet on the world's major football matches in England's Premier League, Germany's Bundesliga, or Spain's La Liga, two brokers can provide that service. Although they generate some concerns and comments, these illegal businesses are not the most worrisome in the village. Rather, it is the robust *kratom* cocktail business that residents find the most threatening to their families and community.

Yaakob, a hajj service provider, and Azlan, chairman of the village 1 Red-Whiskered Bulbul Club, have many things in common. They are among the wealthy in Guba, and their big houses are located next to each other along the main road. Importantly, they have sons who are close friends, about whom they share grave worries — namely, the possibility of their involvement with *kratom* cocktails. Yaakob said that he does not want his son, Usama, to hang out with his friends at Aiman's house because he is afraid that Usama will be led astray by his friends, many of whom are primary school drop-outs at risk of becoming addicted to *kratom* cocktails. Likewise, Azlan said that he was worried about his only son, Wadi, because Wadi was very close to his friends; Azlan said: "I'm afraid that his friends will have him try a *kratom* cocktail one day." When their sons, who studied in the same class of the same school, were about to finish grade 6, they discussed with each other where to send them to protect them from harmful local influences. Initially, they thought about a boarding school in Indonesia, where they both have relatives. Later, they changed their mind and thought about a boarding school in Malaysia, where they also have relatives. However, after learning that schools in Malaysia had already begun their semester and that it was too late to enrol their sons there, they decided to send them to boarding schools in Yala Province. They were concerned less about the academic excellence of the boarding schools vis-à-vis district secondary schools, which definitely speaks in favour of the former, than about separating their sons from their friends in Guba, where *kratom* cocktails are a severe threat.

Why are these two fathers, as well as many others in Guba, so desperate about dealing with *kratom* cocktails? Have the community and the families lost their ability to protect their children from such an "evil"? Why are those in the *kratom* cocktail business not arrested or faced with legal action? Why do they still operate freely despite the strong opposition of many residents?

As mentioned in the introduction and in Chapter 1, the sale of *kratom* cocktails is a robust business in Guba. Residents of southern Thailand actually have consumed *kratom* leaves for a long time, primarily as an energy booster. However, since the 1990s, changes have occurred in how *kratom* leaves are consumed in the Deep South. Instead of being eaten fresh, the leaves now undergo a manufacturing process, starting with boiling fresh *kratom* leaves, followed by mixing the filtered *kratom* leaf water with cough syrup, and then mixing that with any brand of cola and ice. This is locally called "4×100" (referring to a 4 × 100 metre relay race), as the drink consists of four components — *kratom* leaf water, cough syrup, cola and ice — and costs 100 baht for a drink. Usually, producers sell a liter of *kratom* leaf water with a bottle of cough syrup for 80 baht, and then customers buy a 15-baht bottle of cola and a 5-baht bag of ice from a grocery shop. Some producers also sell the cola and ice and even provide safe drinking places for their customers.

Kratom cocktails in the region are said to originate from a teashop in Pattani. Initially, the teashop boiled *kratom* leaves for customers to drink mixed with sweet, hot tea. When the concoction became popular among customers, many other teashops in the area followed suit. This new way of *kratom* leaf consumption spread to Guba around the year 2000. It is not clear who was the first to run a *kratom* cocktail business in Guba, but in 2015 there were four producers/sellers, the biggest being Uday. I first met Uday when he returned home for a vacation in 2009, after almost a year-long stint of hard work in a rented, medium-size rubber plantation in Bannang Sata district. He said that renting rubber plantations in Bannang Sata on a yearly basis yielded more profit than tapping rubber in Guba, a statement that many Guba residents disagreed with. But given Uday's conviction that he could earn more outside Guba, I wondered when I noticed that he continued to linger at home. It took me two months to learn that the reason why he did not go back to tapping rubber in Bannang Sata was that he had gotten a better job in Guba — producing and selling *kratom* cocktails. At first, he worked for another *kratom* cocktail producer, and then he started his own business. Each day, he used about ten kilograms of fresh *kratom* leaves, which were delivered from the upper south in pick-up trucks, to produce *kratom* leaf drinks, which he said he sold for a total income of about 30,000 baht per day. He had about ten people working for him, all young men, to help him do business. From a rubber plantation renter with an uncertain income, Uday had become the largest *kratom* cocktail *thao kae* (Chinese for "rich businessman") in Guba.

The prosperity of the *kratom* cocktail business in Guba brought worries to the residents. Some complained that rubber scrap and fruit were being stolen with increasing frequency, and others remarked that burglaries were on the rise. The prime suspects are male teens who do not go to school and have no regular jobs. Parents were concerned about their children. They were afraid that they might get addicted to *kratom* cocktails, and their future prospects would diminish. Although, in Guba, none of these young users had yet committed a deadly crime, some residents were afraid that it was only a matter of time, if preventive action were not taken.

Despite such worries and fears, however, no residents openly commented about those running the *kratom* cocktail rings, let alone taking legal action against them. Mohammed, who sent his only son to Malaysia to protect him from *kratom* cocktail addiction, said that he wished those in the rings would be arrested when he witnessed four technical college students in their uniforms ride their motorcycles into an alley leading to a producer's house. He also complained that the police took no action. However, he never talked about filing a police complaint against *kratom* cocktail producers himself. Nor did he make any comments when in their presence, especially Uday. Likewise, on one occasion, Jamal waited until Uday left the roadside pavilion where they had all been chatting to comment on the business. Religious leaders occasionally addressed the problem at the mosques but never took any action to solve it. Mana did not forbid the producers from working at their business; he just let them know that he would not help them or bail them out if they were arrested. He told young customers that they would not be prevented from buying or drinking *kratom* cocktails as long as they did not commit any crimes in the village. The *kratom* cocktail business is therefore still on the rise, while the residents are struggling to deal with its impact on their own. Many children have been sent to study, work or live away from Guba; fruit orchards are tightly fenced in; fruit and rubber scrap are collected more often; and the doors and windows of private residences are better secured.

The reasons why villagers do not openly confront those in the *kratom* cocktail business are threefold. First, people in general feel that the impacts of *kratom* cocktail consumption are still bearable. Thefts and burglaries are petty and do not occur often. So far, no one has been hurt or killed by a *kratom* cocktail addict. Stronger fences, regular watches and frequent collection have been somewhat effective in preventing thefts of fruit. Rubber scrap can be secured if it is monitored and collected regularly. Would-be burglars are easily put off by a well-secured house. In other words, *kratom* cocktail consumption is something that people can live with as long as it does not lead to deadly crimes.

Second, as the impact is still bearable, to challenge those in the rings, especially the producers, is not worthwhile. It is widely known that, although they are not as influential as elected officials, *kratom* cocktail producers and sellers are people whom ordinary residents should not tangle with. In addition to their intimidating backgrounds and their reputation for violence, almost all *kratom* cocktail producers carry guns, and some of them have young subordinates who are not reluctant to use violence if ordered. A northern Guba male teenager was severely beaten by Uday's subordinates for his alleged theft of Uday's cough syrup, and neither legal action nor personal revenge were taken against Uday or his gang members. In addition, the teenager left home for some other place for many days after the incident for fear of additional punishment. One afternoon after I arrived home, Saifuldin nervously asked me where I had been, as he had received a phone call from a *kratom* cocktail producer asking him what I was around his place for. Even though I had quite accidentally stumbled upon a transaction in progress, the producer told Saifuldin to warn me not to go to that location again. Interfering in the business of *kratom* producers and sellers is an invitation to trouble.

Third, it is almost impossible to bring any legal action against those in the *kratom* cocktail rings. Like other illegal businesses across the country, the *kratom* cocktail business in large part is guaranteed by bribing state authorities. However, it is not the police, who have virtually been absent from the region after the eruption of the insurgency in 2004, who are the primary recipients of bribery. Rather, it is the military who collect bribes from *kratom* cocktail producers to turn their gaze elsewhere. Uday claimed that he had made a contact with a paramilitary ranger camp in Pa Ou village, making a deal with the person in charge there. The deal was easily done, and he subsequently made another deal with soldiers in the Pahong Gayu camp. As a result, despite the Fourth Region Army commander's intensive public campaign against *kratom* cocktail addiction in the southernmost region, Uday has never been arrested. In fact, he was tipped off by soldiers he had bribed when combined forces planned raids on his facilities. One morning, for example, to my surprise, Uday and a male teenager sat chatting at the roadside pavilion in front of the house where I was staying. Curious, I joined them. Then a Thai Buddhist from Ba Roh village who had converted to Islam, sporting extensive tattoos, arrived on his motorcycle and joined us at the pavilion. They chatted about several topics with laughter, as if everything were normal, even as a convoy of military and police vehicles passed by. I later learned why Uday and his men had been laughing: the convoy had in fact come to search his production facility, but they would find nothing because he had cleared the site of evidence after a tip-off. His gaiety was simply his way of ridiculing the futility of the raid. This incident exemplifies why villagers believe that it is useless to try to take legal action against those in the *kratom* cocktail rings.

The relationship between *kratom* cocktail producers and state authorities, especially the military, however, is far more complex than simple bribery. Many low-ranking soldiers, especially young army conscripts, are regular customers themselves. When off duty, they ride the same motorcycles they use while on duty to the houses of *kratom* cocktail producers to buy *kratom* leaf water and cough syrup. After then buying cola and ice, they go either to the forest or back to their camp to drink the cocktails. What is interesting is that, while regular military missions in the Deep South hardly ever lead to good relations between soldiers and residents, *kratom* cocktail consumption provides a crucial channel through which many low-ranking soldiers, Thai Buddhists and Malay Muslims alike, develop personal, intimate relations with village residents, especially young people. My roommate, Najmudin, drinks *kratom* cocktails in the riverside forest with soldiers from the Pahong Gayu camp on a regular basis, and Taha, an unconventional Muslim, often visits the camp to drink *kratom* cocktails with soldiers there. One night, a Pahong Gayu soldier, who had been assigned to provide security for the fourth Arzeulee SAO election vote count at the SAO office building, drank *kratom* cocktails with three teenagers right in front of me, as if there were nothing to hide. He hilariously exclaimed that "now I had survived" after finishing the cocktail, and he then walked back into the SAO compound with his Guba friends. It is quite common to see Pahong Gayu soldiers and young village residents hanging out together in Guba.

Such an intimate connection raises a serious question: Are the troops really addicted to *kratom* cocktails, or do they just pretend as a way to gather intelligence regarding the insurgents? Najmudin said these soldiers are genuine addicts and that they have never asked him about anything at all related to the insurgency. He added that some of them are even addicted to methamphetamines; they took drugs to keep themselves awake and alert all night while on guard for fear that they might be attacked or killed if they fell asleep. Likewise, Wasim, a young *kratom* cocktail addict, insisted that the soldiers did not gather intelligence through this means — "They are really addicted to *kratom* cocktails", he said. However, one addict said that sometimes soldiers asked him about suspected insurgents who had been charged with involvement and then fled. Importantly, considering the case of Basir, the intimate relationship between village teenagers and soldiers via *kratom* cocktail addiction can indeed be seen as part of the military's intelligence and infiltration strategy. As mentioned earlier in this chapter, Basir is severely addicted to *kratom* cocktails as well as methamphetamines, but he was nevertheless assigned by soldiers of the Pahong Gayu camp to play a leading role in recruiting male teenagers to participate in the military vocational training camp programme. Potentially, his close connection with Pahong Gayu soldiers via *kratom* cocktail consumption may have landed him such a crucial appointment, despite the programme's ultimate failure. Basir is also the oldest son of Uday, Guba's largest *kratom* cocktail producer and seller, which complicates the relationship between the *kratom* cocktail business and the military even more.

Whichever is the case, soldiers' involvement in *kratom* cocktails gives the military a bad name. Villagers despise soldiers who are addicted to the cocktails, seeing them as aggravating a problem they are already desperately struggling with. As infiltrators and intelligence operatives, these soldiers are already distrusted by villagers for their deceptive operations and false premises for developing local relationships. When combined with their consumption of *kratom* cocktails and speculation about ulterior motives in their involvement in the business, the military begins to appear morally and politically bankrupt in the eyes of the villagers. Many residents have noticed that *kratom* cocktail consumption has been on the rise since the eruption of the recent unrest in 2004. On the one hand, villagers attribute this phenomenon to the virtual disappearance of police from the Deep South. On the other hand, some regard it as part of a state plot to wipe out Malay Muslims from the region. Many ask how tons of fresh *kratom* leaves from the upper south could pass through hundreds of police and military checkpoints unless the military and the police connived with the smugglers. Some said that such connivance may be about personal gains, but many others have said that the checkpoints have been ordered by the central government to allow passage of the *kratom* leaves as part of a broader plot against Malay Muslims. Jafar, a central Guba resident, observed:

> They [the government] want to destroy us, so they let *kratom* pick-up trucks pass the checkpoints easily. Many of our kids are now not interested in anything. They do not go to school and they do not work. In particular, they do not care about the community, which the government likes, because that means they will not pose any trouble or danger to the government.

Although it is difficult to prove to what extent such speculation might be true, the moral bankruptcy of the military and police is already plainly evident to many villagers with respect to *kratom* consumption.

The prosperity of the *kratom* cocktail business has attracted some male teenagers to become "kids" or subordinates of major producers and sellers, as seen in the case of Waddah. Waddah, a grade 4 drop-out, was one of four boys who were occasionally hired by Aiman to collect rubber scrap and do other chores for the family. But he quit these occasional jobs for a regular gig as a delivery boy for one *kratom* cocktail producer in Guba. Almost every day, he hangs around a pavilion in front of Taha's teashop waiting for customers to come. His duty is to take money from the customers and then ride a motorcycle to the production site to pick up the product for the customers, who wait for him at the pavilion. This job earns him about 200 baht a day. However, the relationship between Waddah and the producer is far more complex than just that between an employee and an employer. In addition to getting better pay than at other jobs he might do, he receives other benefits and protection from his boss; for instance, he does not have to worry about being bullied by other teenagers, given his boss's influence. As a child of poor villagers with no connection with anyone in power,

Waddah knows that his powerful boss is his only choice for protection in a place where the law is poorly reinforced and where "rule" and "order" are imposed largely without recourse to the law.

Of several kinds of "influential figures" or strongmen, however, *kratom* cocktail producers and sellers are sought for help and protection the least of all. This is mainly because, on the one hand, their influence is insecure and unstable, given their involvement with an illegal business, and, on the other hand, they themselves still need to seek help and protection of their own from higher sources of influence, namely high-ranking state officials. In addition, they request loyalty from their subordinates in mundane and straightforward ways, having no ideological basis or deeper cause. They do not impose any identity upon their subordinates to articulate. This is quite different from high-ranking state officials, who request that those under their care and protection express subjectivity and allegiance to the source from which they draw their influence — the state — mostly in a symbolic and ideological manner. The insurgency has made such requests more pressing than ever before.

3.5. Faara: A Girl of Multiple Subjectivities

Faara, a grade 5 schoolchild, got up earlier than usual in the morning of 3 July 2009 in order to prepare to participate in an oath of allegiance-swearing ceremony to be held at the Pa Ou village mosque compound at noon. It took her awhile to select a traditional Malay dress to wear for the ceremony, in accordance with her teacher's instructions. Actually, wearing traditional Malay dress is not unusual for Faara, because every Friday, according to the Ministry of Education's policy on promoting Malay culture, she wears such a dress to school. However, given that this would be the first oath-swearing ceremony to be held in Arzeulee subdistrict in which many high-ranking state authorities, especially the Civilian-Police-Military Taskforce 43 (CPM-43) commander, would be present, she felt excited and wanted to wear the most special dress she owns. Likewise, she carefully chose a headscarf to put on, making sure that it matched the dress and was special enough for such an important event. She left home at about 9:00 a.m. to meet her friends and teachers at the mosque compound.

The compound was already crowded when she arrived. Schoolchildren, all in traditional Malay dress, began to form lines according to their teachers' instructions. The villagers, mostly women and members of state-appointed groups such as housewives' groups, women's groups, and village health volunteer organizations, looked for their friends and the places in the tents where their respective groups were assigned to meet. Meanwhile, religious leaders, all men in formal religious dress, greeted each other while looking for their seats. Government officials were in full uniform, and the subdistrict headman, who was tasked with coordinating the event, was busy checking to ensure that everything was in place. Village security teams gradually arrived with clear signs of embarrassment, as they hardly ever wore a full uniform while in the villages. Added to these civilians, across the mosque compound were paramilitary rangers who were in charge of conducting the ceremony. However, instead of being heavily armed as usual, almost all the rangers carried only a handgun, and many of them, especially those at the booths, were female. In addition, two of them were wearing cute mascot suits, teasing and playing around with the children. This helped Faara, who normally is frightened of paramilitary rangers, feel a bit relaxed. She joined her friends in the lines and listened to her teachers' instructions.

Faara was told that around noon Lieutenant General Kasikorn Khirisri, the CPM-43 commander, would arrive to preside over the ceremony. In the meantime, the paramilitary rangers would give the students paper national flags and T-shirts to wave and wear when the commander came. Schoolchildren were assigned to form lines along two sides of a concrete walkway leading to the ceremony's tents so they could greet and welcome the commander with their flags. Then they were instructed to walk behind the commander to the tents and get seated. After the teacher's explanation, four female paramilitary rangers came and distributed flags and T-shirts to the schoolchildren. Then the children were allowed to mingle about on their own for about thirty minutes before lining up again at the entrance to the mosque compound. Faara left her place in the line and played around with her friends while waiting for the commander's arrival.

At 11:30 a.m., Faara, now wearing a yellow T-shirt over her beautiful traditional Malay dress and with a paper flag in her hand, together with the other schoolchildren, all began to line up along the two sides of the concrete walkway. At the entrance were government officials led by the subdistrict headman, in their own line waiting to greet and welcome the commander. Beside them were other state authorities. Many soldiers, fully armed, were on alert and ready for the commander's arrival. Then a convoy of military vehicles arrived, and the commander emerged from a black SUV; was greeted by the paramilitary ranger commander, the subdistrict headman, the SAO chief executive, and village headmen; and led the officials to the tents, with schoolchildren waving flags on both sides of the walkway. Once the commander was seated in an armchair in a tent together with other high-ranking state authorities including the Raman district chief, the subdistrict headman read a report as a welcoming remark. Then the SAO chief executive gave an address (which had been drafted by state officials) on the background and objectives of the ceremony, focusing on the residents' oath to cooperate with state authorities in bringing peace back to the region. Below is part of the SAO chief's address.

> Religious leaders, local leaders, and residents of village 5 as well as the three mosques of the village and residents of other villages who are all Muslims are uncomfortable with the unrest and violence that have been taking place in the southern border provinces since the year 2004. Arzeulee subdistrict as well as nearby villages are among the areas where the misguided constantly create situations and hide. Religious leaders, local leaders and all residents feel that 99 per cent of the people do not get involved with or know about the incidents. Both leaders and residents of Arzeulee subdistrict therefore have become victims of society, and the image of the villages as peaceful places is ruined. The Civilian-Police-Military Taskforce 43 has set up Peace and Development Unit 41-5 under the supervision of Paramilitary Ranger Special Unit 41 to carry out activities in Pa Ou village from 1 October 2007 onward. Villagers feel that life is more convenient, they feel taken care of and that they have participated in developing the village to achieve peace. Importantly, residents and soldiers have grown close to each other, and mutual suspicion has been reduced. Religious leaders, civic leaders, and residents understand the truth of the situation that has arisen in the region. We have reached the conclusion that, if we are still the victims of a society like this, the reputation of the villages will deteriorate. The leaders and the majority of the residents then think that we should create people's power in our villages by holding today's activity, called "Consolidate Force for Peaceful Villages: No Support for the Instigation of Any Form of the Unrest". This activity has objectives as follows. First, create more harmony in our villages without racial or religious discrimination. Second, leaders and residents must cooperate more with state agencies. Third, leaders and residents must get closer to state authorities to reduce mutual suspicion. Fourth, leaders and residents must be conscious of protecting the reputation of the village and the institution [the monarchy].

After this address, two groups of schoolgirls sang Islamic songs, or *anasyid*, on the elevated stage and received awards from the commander, who, along with the other Thai Buddhist state officials, had no idea what the songs were about. After that, the commander granted certificates and handed out national flags complete with flagpoles to eight civilians who had supported the work of the state, including the SAO chief executive, the subdistrict headman, the village 1 and village 3 headmen, the principal of Pa Ou school, and the imams of three mosques of village 5. Then the commander thanked the participants for their cooperation. In addition to helping combat the insurgency, he asked the participants to help prevent the spread of drugs, especially *kratom* cocktails, among teenagers in the area. Then the subdistrict headman led the swearing of the oath of allegiance. Below is part of the oath, which had been prepared by state officials.

> First, I will be loyal to the nation, the religion, and the king, and will give back to the land by doing good deeds forever. Second, I will safeguard our villages and communities by not supporting or helping those who create hardship for innocent people. Third, I will help and cooperate with religious leaders, local leaders, and government agencies in solving the unrest and developing villages and communities to achieve prosperity. Fourth, I will strongly protect our children from drugs.

After the oath swearing, everybody stood still to pay respect to the national anthem, the royal anthem, and the *Sadudi Maharaja* song (saluting and paying respect to the king and the queen). Then the commander left the tent, greeted some participants, and talked to officials and religious leaders before leaving. Meanwhile, paramilitary rangers held fun activities on the stage such as drawing lots for presents. Then the participants ate lunch, which had been prepared by female villagers, marking the end of the ceremony.

Faara participated in the whole process. She swore the oath of allegiance after the subdistrict headman's lead, although she, like all her friends, did not care much what it is about or what it means. Although she did not take part in a singing show on the stage, she attentively listened to the paramilitary ranger's announcements about the lot numbers with hope that one of them might be the same as that printed on the paper flag she had received, but to her disappointment the numbers did not match. She ate lunch with her friends and went to get ice cream and sweets from female paramilitary rangers at the booths. She left the mosque compound with her friends while paramilitary rangers were clearing up the place. She, wearing a T-shirt over her traditional Malay dress and holding a paper national flag in her hand, had had a lot of fun that day.

The oath-swearing ceremony is one where subjectivities and allegiances are at stake. It was held primarily in response to the state's anxiety over the loyalty of its citizens, which it thought was in jeopardy given the insurgents' "misuse" or "distortion" of Islam and Malay ethnicity. The primary aim of the ceremony was to ensure that any articulation of Islam and Malay ethnicity would not be at the expense of the Thai state. The leading officials were participants who had sacrificed all of their Islamic and Malay subjectivities in the expression of their allegiance to the Thai state. They were in full uniform like government officials elsewhere in Thailand, with nothing associating them with Islam or Malay ethnicity. Religious leaders, on the other hand, are participants who sacrifice nothing about Islam or Malay ethnicity in expressing such loyalty. They were all in traditional and formal Malay dress and wore religious caps; some wore turbans. To participate in a ceremony to which they had been "invited", in their opinion, sufficed to accommodate the state's demand. However, most participants who were female adults or schoolchildren are somewhere between these two extremes. To show their affiliation with the state, village health volunteers and members of housewives' groups wore sweatshirts printed with an emblem of their group or organization. To show their commitment to Islam, they wore headscarves. But these adult women fell short when it comes to the articulation of their Malay descent as well as of their status as the king's subjects. It was the schoolgirls who articulated all the subjectivities requested, as seen in the case of Faara.

As a Malay, Faara wore a traditional Malay dress, and as a Muslim, she wore a headscarf. She has no idea what a Thai citizen looks like, but she did not turn down the T-shirt a female paramilitary ranger had given her to wear on top of her beautiful Malay dress. On the front of the T-shirt is printed the phrase, "the kind-hearted Paramilitary Rangers 41", the unit that had hosted the ceremony, and on the back is printed "Peaceful Yala" both in Thai and in Yawi script. As such, regardless of Faara's intention, the state had found a way to manifest itself on her body — the body of a girl whom the state regarded as its citizen. This manifestation was strengthened by the paper flag she held in her hand. In addition to the flag's three colors, which refer to the three elements of state ideology, one side of the flag was printed with the phrase "Long Live the King", expressing Faara's allegiance to the king as his subject. Taken together, Faara is a girl of Malay descent who embraces Islam, who at the same time is a Thai citizen who is loyal to the king as his subject.

Asked if she felt anything in particular about the T-shirt or the national flag, Faara said, "No". She did not feel that her traditional Malay dress was

SUBJECTIVITIES ON THE RISE 153

FIGURE 3.2
Faara

somehow being overshadowed by the T-shirt. Nor did she feel that it was any problem to tuck the ends of the headscarf into the top of the T-shirt. To her, none of the things she wore, nor the national flag she held and waved, created any tension. Multiple subjectivities share their expression on her.

However, the expression of multiple subjectivities on Faara's body did not go unnoticed by the people there. One woman observed that it was a pity to hide such a beautiful traditional Malay dress behind a plain T-shirt. A female teacher added that the paramilitary rangers should have told them beforehand, so that they could have told the students to wear ordinary dress, or the rangers should have given the T-shirts to students in advance so that they could have worn them from their homes. Apart from such aesthetic and practical concerns, a man commented that the T-shirt obscured the Malay identity of the schoolchildren. He thought that it was the state's attempt to assimilate these children into a Thai identity. To this man and others who think like him, tensions are embedded in these different subjectivities that cannot be easily resolved.

It is noteworthy that the questions of subjectivity that residents of the Deep South have been faced with are far more complex than simply the tension between Malay ethnicity and Islamic religion on the one hand and the Thai Buddhist state on the other. Rather, tensions emerge even among different strands of Islam, and especially between the local beliefs and rituals that make up what we call Malay culture, and some strands of Islam. Southern residents since the 1970s have been compelled to decide which strands of Islamic faith they should follow, and what parts of their local beliefs and rituals they must adjust or discard to be in compliance with the "correct" Islam. The questions have become even more complicated since 2004, when the Thai state and the monarchy became vigorously involved with Malay culture and Islam so as to secure the people's loyalty amid the unrest. These are the "clashes" I will examine in the following chapter.

Notes

1. The notions of merit and sin are commonly known among Malay Muslims of southern Thailand. However, rather than subscribing to an Arabic concept of merit (*ajr*), Muslims of southern Thailand follow the concept as indicated by the Patani Malay word *pahalo* (derived from Sanskrit) in their search for equivalence with the Buddhist notion of merit, or บุญ (*bun*) in Thai (Joll 2012, p. 86). Christopher Joll also argues that, rather than a sign of syncretism, this illustrates how Muslims have attempted to think Islamic thoughts in languages associated with other religious traditions (2012, pp. 17, 88), and that the notion of *pahalo* is Islamic as it is replete with Islamic ideation (2012, pp. 91–100). Regarding the issue of merit

in relation to the month of Ramadan, Joll (2012, pp. 159–67) demonstrates that merit-making elements are rewarded more than usual according to the "Ramadan scale of merit", although there is no consensus on the details of the scale. He also points out that sinful deeds are also punished more severely during the month of Ramadan, as all devils are chained during the month and Muslims therefore can no longer blame the devils for their sinful deeds. Joll writes: "[T]he continuation of shootings and bombings in South Thailand during Ramadan led some to believe that those who committed these acts were either thoroughly bad ... or convinced that their actions were meritorious (for which they would be even better rewarded in Ramadan)" (2012, p. 164). Guba residents are familiar with the notion of merit as well, and, as will be seen, they also find it difficult to answer whether killing in the name of Islam in the month of Ramadan will bring more merit, or more sin, to Muslim perpetrators.
2. How Islam is related to the recent unrest is a subject of debate among scholars. Wattana Sugunnasil (2006) argues that global Islamic radicalism coupled with domestic Islamic resurgence drove some Malay Muslims to violent actions in the name of jihad. Zachary Abuza (2003; see also 2005, 2009) takes this position a step further, arguing that the insurgents established relations with other extremist groups, notably Al-Qaeda. Many observers (Andre 2013, Barter 2011, Gunaratna, Acharya and Chua 2006, Gunaratna and Acharya 2013, Porath 2011, Rappa 2013) pursue this line of argument, locating the insurgency in global jihad and terrorism. However, the International Crisis Group (2005) argues that the unrest is "insurgency not jihad", and Michael Connors (2006) points out how "terrorism analysts got it wrong." Joseph Chinyong Liow (2006) argues that, although coloured by global Islamic radicalism, the unrest remains rooted in the political ideology of nationalism and separatism. Duncan McCargo (2008) maintains that, although Islamic concepts such as jihad surfaced, they did not transform the unrest into a religious conflict. The insurgency is "a war over legitimacy" in which Islam is a rhetorical source the perpetrators selectively invoked and interpreted for their political ends. However, Christopher Joll (2015) maintains that, although the unrest cannot be explained in religious terms, to assert that Islam plays no role in violence is equally erroneous. Although it is not my aim in this book to participate in this debate, I have found attempts to tie the recent unrest to global jihad and terrorism untenable mainly because no Okhrae Dalae in Guba were associated with these movements, and the rhetoric of global jihad has not circulated in Guba.
3. Jemaat Tabligh or Tablighi Jamaat is an Islamic grassroots *dakwah* (missionary) movement that originated in a rural village in India in the mid-nineteenth century as part of an Islamic reform movement emphasizing religiosity, observance and personal devotion with a focus on the replication of the prophetic lifestyle (Liow 2009, p. 140). Its inception is a response to Hindu revivalist movements of the time, which were considered a threat to vulnerable Muslims, and as a result its primary aim is to bring Muslims closer to the practices of the Prophet. It expanded from local to national to a transnational movement with followers in over 150 countries.

In Thailand, Jemaat Tabligh was established in Bangkok in the 1920s through Pakistani immigrants (Raymond Scupin, cited in Joll 2012, p. 48). Then it spread to the south; when Haydar Ali and his brothers reached Yala in their expansion of Jemaat Tabligh from Kelantan to southern Thailand in the late 1970s, they found that members of the Pakistani community in Yala had already established Jemaat Tabligh there. The Pakistani mosque in Yala continued to serve as Jemaah Tabligh's base in southern Thailand until the construction of Markaz Besar (Joll 2012, p. 48) or Markaz Dakwah Jemaat in Yala in 1993 (Liow 2009, p. 141), which is the largest *markaz* (an Arabic term meaning "centre") in Southeast Asia (Farish A. Noor, cited in Joll 2002, p. 48) and the largest Jemaat Tabligh centre in the Asia-Pacific region (Liow 2009, p. 143). It is estimated that Jemaat Tabligh's network in southern Thailand includes 800 mosques (Joseph Chinyong Liow, cited in Joll 2012, p. 49; see also Horstmann 2007a, 2007b for studies of Jemaat Tabligh in southern Thailand).

4. Although Babo studied Islam in Saudi Arabia like many Malay Muslims of southern Thailand of the period, he is not part of "Islamic reform and revival" movement propagated by other Malays who studied in Saudi Arabia. There were two waves of this movement: first, the Jawi Ulama network, starting in the 1930s, and second, the Salafi PhD graduates of the 1980s (Aryud 2014, pp. 83–115, 119–55). In addition, Babo's religious orientation is more "traditional" than "reform" or "revival", although he never identified with any Islamic school of thought or movement.

5, The New Group Yaakob mentioned is the second and latest wave of Islamic reform in southern Thailand. The first wave is represented by the Jawi Ulama network advocated by four Malay Muslims who studied Islam in the Middle East, led by Haji Sulong, who began to carry out religious activities in the region in the 1920s (Aryud 2014, pp. 68–115). The New Group is represented by Ismail Lutfi Chapakia, who has carried out Islamic reform in southern Thailand since 1986, when he first returned from Saudi Arabia. (Aryud 2014, pp. 116–89). However, rather than the Wahhabism that Yaakob mentions as the New Group's foundation, Dr Lutfi rejects this association, given Wahhabism's pejorative connotations, and called his movement "Salafi" instead, referring to the followers of the Salaf, as the early companions of the Prophet were known (McCargo 2008, pp. 22–23). The Salafi reformist movement urges Malay Muslims to return to and strictly follow the sacred sources, including the Koran and the Sunnah, and purify Islamic ideas and practices, which had become sullied by later innovations and accretions of past Indic cultures. The movement aims to reform Islam in three areas, namely Islamic theology, socio-political relations within the Thai state, and interreligious relations in the region. It seeks to promote reform through education, epitomized by the founding of Yala Islamic College in 1998, which attained the status of university in 2002 and was renamed Fatoni University in 2013. Dr Lutfi was the institution's founder and remains its rector (Aryud 2014).

6. The New Group's virtual absence in Guba stands in contrast to its increasing popularity elsewhere in region. Although initially Dr Lutfi was rejected by local

Malay Muslims, his position became more mainstream over time (McCargo 2008, p. 22). This is mainly because he and the Salafi movement have adjusted their Islamic intellectualism to suit local circumstances and realities, and they have utilized an Islamic reformist discourse that allows them to engage with changes brought by modernity (Aryud 2014, pp. 157–69, 197–98), enabling them to draw support from both villagers and townspeople. That the New Group remains absent in Guba despite its flexibility and adjustment to suit local circumstances is tied to how the residents position themselves with respect to Islam and Malay culture, an issue that will be discussed later.

7. Whether the female circumcision rite is Islamic is a subject of debate. However, given Guba residents' understanding and explanation of the ritual, it is taken here as part of Islam tradition rather than a local custom.
8. Thailand held the first Children's Day fair on 3 October 1955 in compliance with a United Nations' resolution to have its member countries hold such a fair to promote children's rights and welfare. Initially, the fairs were held on the first Monday of October, but since 1965 they have been held on the second Saturday of January because October is in the late rainy season, which sometimes makes it difficult for children to attend, and Monday is a working day, which makes it hard for working parents to take children to the fair. In addition to schools, various government agencies (particularly those under the Ministry of Interior) and the military simultaneously hold Children's Days nationwide (Sapha Sangkom Songkro Haeng Prathet Thai 2014).
9. Ya Sin is the 36th of 114 chapters of the Koran and is regarded by Muslims as "the heart of the Koran". The chapter is read in ceremony not only at critical moments of a person's life such as in this case but also for spirits of the dead as a way of making merit. As Christopher Joll (2012, p. 111) pointed out with respect to the Malay Muslims of Cabetigo: "You read Ya Sin when someone is dying, or you can read it to send to the spirit of the dead ancestors — sending the merit to them."
10. The Jalanan Baru project (Khrongkan Yalannan Baru, โครงการญาลันนันบารู, or Khrongkan Thang Sai Mai, โครงการทางสายใหม่, New Path project) was created out of concern over the spread of drugs among youths in the southernmost region during the recent unrest. The Office of the Narcotics Control Board (ONCB) found that, along the insurgency, various kinds of drugs — even heroin, hardly found at all in other parts of the country — had increasingly spread throughout the South. The ONCB believed that the drug problem would only serve to compound existing problems like poverty, lack of educational opportunity, and unemployment, making it easier for the insurgents to attract young people. The ONCB then sought the cooperation of the Internal Security Operations Command (ISOC) Region 4 Forward Section, which oversees the area, to conduct a collaborative drug prevention project with state security as an additional rationale. The Jalanan Baru project was launched in 2007. Initially, it did not aim to treat drug addicts but to provide knowledge to youths who were at risk of getting involved with drugs.

Later, it expanded its mission to cover drug treatment and vocational training. Its website <http://www.yalannanbaru.com/index.php>, which includes the banners of both the ONCB and ISOC Region 4 Forward Section, details thirteen specific activities under the programme and their successes.

11. ISOC is a military agency in charge of national security. It was established in 1973 after the Communist Suppression Operations Command (CSOC) was abolished. Initially, its mission was the suppression of communists, as had been that of its forerunner. After the downfall of the Communist Party of Thailand in the early 1980s, however, ISOC's mission shifted to drug suppression, border security, security-focused development, minority groups and illegal immigrants, and the southern border provinces. ISOC is administratively divided into four regions; Region 4 is the southern region which includes the border provinces. It is under the supervision of the Office of the Prime Minister, and the prime minister serves as director.

12. In addition to the urgency of the insurgency problem in the South, the reason why the Ministry of Defense and other security-related agencies such as ISOC were allocated twice the budget they had received before involves political changes in the country; the military reestablished its paramount role after staging a coup in 2006 (ousting Prime Minister Thaksin Shinawatra), and the Democrat Party, whose priority is to protect the establishment, came to power. These political shifts also explain why the Royal Thai Police was allocated with a smaller budget (just over 1 billion baht) than the military. While in power, Thaksin, himself is a retired police lieutenant colonel, tasked the police with critical roles in tackling the southern unrest while reducing the role of the military in this matter. After overthrowing Thaksin in 2006, the military reestablished its primary role in the Deep South, as reflected by the budget allocations.

13. This special budgetary category has continued to be utilized in subsequent fiscal years, with some changes. For fiscal year 2017, the name of the category changed to "Programme on Integrated Solutions to the Problems of the Southern Border Provinces" (แผนงานบูรณาการขับเคลื่อนการแก้ไขปัญหาจังหวัดชายแดนภาคใต้), with many additional state agencies added (from twenty-eight agencies in 2016 and earlier to fifty agencies in 2017), significantly excluding the National Intelligence Agency. Although the amount of the budget of this category decreased to 12,510,110,300 baht, the overall budget addressing the insurgency continues to increase every year, especially after the military coup of 2014. The overall budget allocated for the insurgency in fiscal year 2017 is 30,886,000,000 baht, compared to 16,507,000,000 baht in fiscal year 2010. (*Phraratchabanyat Raichai Pracham Pi Ngoppraman B.E 2560*)

14. The "sufficiency economy" is King Bhumibol's philosophy of development, which emphasizes subsistence and equilibrium rather than economic growth. He first mentioned the concept in his address to the graduating class at Kasetsart University in Bangkok on 18 July 1974. However, he significantly emphasized the concept in his birthday address of 4 December 1997 as a solution to the Asian financial

crisis, which had started in Thailand (the crisis was dubbed "Tom Yam Kung Crisis" or *wikrit tom yam kung*, วิกฤติต้มยำกุ้ง), and it has become the country's approach to development since then. The sufficiency economy was incorporated in the Ninth National Economic and Social Development Plan (2002–06), which clearly stated the king's encouragement of the approach. The tenth (2007–11) and eleventh (2012–16) plans also incorporated the sufficiency economy, although not as vividly as the ninth plan. In addition, the sufficiency economy was outlined in Article 75 of the constitutions of 2007 and 2017. As a result, the approach has been practised nationwide, primarily through government agencies' initiatives and support but also by non-governmental organizations, community organizations, and private individuals. While being praised, both rhetorically and academically, the sufficiency economy has been criticized for being vague and not in line with economic reality, being a function of state propaganda, and being a rhetorical tool of the 2006 coup leaders (for a critical treatment of the sufficiency economy, see Isager and Ivarsson 2010*b*, pp. 223–39; and Walker 2012, pp. 4, 182–88, 222).

15. Red Cross fairs are put on by the Thai Red Cross Society, which was founded on 26 April 1893 with the support of King Chulalongkorn, with the intention of providing medicines and other necessities for Thai soldiers who were fighting the French at that time. The fair was first held on 31 March – 8 April 1923 at Sanam Luang in Bangkok to encourage membership in the Thai Red Cross Society. It was then held annually and began to stage "choosing games" (เกมส์สอยดาว) in 1929 to provide enjoyment for attendees. During the period 1938–56, it was held at Queen Saovabha Memorial Institute and the National Stadium before moving to Suan Amphon in 1957, where it has been held annually ever since. Additionally, each province in collaboration with its Provincial Red Cross Chapter (เหล่ากาชาดจังหวัด) holds provincial Red Cross fairs every year at different times. Red Cross fairs, both at Suan Amphon and in the provinces, are aimed primarily to provide enjoyment for people, especially lower-income people, and to earn revenue for the Thai Red Cross Society and Provincial Red Cross Chapters. In the southernmost provinces since 2004, the aim to provide enjoyment is particularly important because the recent unrest has deprived the region of cheerfulness. The government has tasked itself with bringing "happiness" back to the region, and annual provincial Red Cross fairs, staged with the assistance of government agencies and private-sector groups, work toward accomplishing this task.

16. Since the revolution of 24 June 1932, which changed the country's polity from absolute monarchy to democracy, Thailand has occasionally been under civilian governments. This significantly started with the Chatichai Choonhavan government (1988–91), followed by the Chuan Leekpai government (1992–95), the Banharn Silpa-archa government (1995–96), the Chavalit Yongchaiyudh government (1996–97), and a second Chuan government (1997–2001), before culminating in the Thaksin Shinawatra government (2001–06) followed by the Abhisit Vejjajiva government (2008–11) and ending with the Yingluck Shinawatra government (2011–14), which ended with the military coup of 22 May 2014. Of these civilian

governments, Thaksin, Abhisit and Yingluck have in turn presided over the country since the recent insurgency began in 2004.

17. The Saiburi Dam construction project was conducted by the Royal Irrigation Department (RID). The project's feasibility study was conducted in 1987, two years after King Bhumibol visited the area and suggested that there be an irrigation dam across the Saiburi River to collect water for agriculture and household consumption. The dam construction project cost about 100 million baht and consisted of eight 12.5 × 6 metre floodgates and a control building. Although the official purpose of the dam was to supply water for agriculture, many residents believed that it was part of a larger scheme to drain water out of the wetlands in the region. They believed that it was aimed to get fresh water from the Saiburi River to cleanse the acidic sulfate soil in dried wetlands under royal initiatives in Narathiwat's Bacho district. Ironically, acidic sulfate soil results from draining water out of wetlands, which was a primary task of wetlands-related royal development projects a few decades earlier. King Bhumibol's involvement in the dam construction project was always cited by the RID to justify the project and to threaten residents who opposed it (Chalita 2013, pp. 73–74).

18. The Village Scouts (Luk Seua Chao Ban, ลูกเสือชาวบ้าน) are a state-supported volunteer group. It was founded in 1969 by the Border Patrol Police and has been sponsored by the monarchy since 1972. Initially, the Scouts aimed to train rural villagers to safeguard their villages, defend themselves, and surveil the border: to be the "eyes and ears" of the state against the communist insurgency, which was the primary security concern at the time. The Scouts were also tasked with standing up for the monarchy, which gave Scouts scarves and flags in return of their reverence and loyalty. As such, when the nation and especially the monarchy were perceived to be in jeopardy, Scouts were deployed along with other right-wing organizations and political vigilantes to defend these two institutions. This sometimes led to violence, as at Thammasat University on 6 October 1976 when students who were deemed a threat to the state and the monarchy were massacred. Although Village Scouts no longer play a crucial role in political conflicts or social movements, they remain an integral part of the royalists, as seen in their audience at the queen's 2004 address. (For studies of the Village Scouts as a right-wing movement, see Bowie 1997, 2005).

19. Tanyong Limo is village 7 of Tanyong Limo subdistrict of Narathiwat's Ra-ngae district. It is widely known for an incident in which two marines were seized and stabbed to death there. The incident started on the evening of 20 September 2005 when men in a passing pick-up truck opened fire on a teashop, which left one person dead. Shortly afterward, two marines who were stationed nearby drove a car to the village, and their car broke down. Residents of the village found the two marines and thought they had been involved with the shooting, so they held them hostage in the village multi-purpose building through the night. The following morning, the villagers prevented security forces from entering the village by blocking the main road with a log. Some women gathered nearby, holding placards

denouncing the government and security forces. Government officials and local politicians attempted to negotiate the release of the two marines, but without success. The villagers had also demanded that journalists from Malaysia come and report on the incident because they did not trust the Thai media. However, before the journalists arrived, the two marines were beaten and stabbed to death. Those who were involved in the killing fled the scene, and later some were caught while others turned themselves in. However, it is still unclear whether the shooters at the teashop were the soldiers, as the villagers claimed, or whether they were insurgents who wanted to discredit state authorities, as the officials claimed.

20. While Tanyong Limo is a Malay Muslim village, it is located only 3 kilometres from Pa Phai village, which is the only Thai Buddhist village in the subdistrict. It is possible that the women the queen talked about in her address are Thai Buddhists from Pa Phai village.

21. Khru Razak had no ties to either PULO or Bersatu, which were both active in the Deep South at the time. However, given the respect he had earned and his position of leadership among Malay Muslims, he was suspected by state authorities of being involved with the separatist movements. Such sweeping and groundless suspicions of innocent people and the subsequent harsh measures taken against them have had the opposite effect of turning many ordinary citizens into antistate fighters.

22. "Thai nation development participants" (*phu ruam phatthana chat thai*, ผู้ร่วมพัฒนาชาติไทย) are former Communist Party members and sympathizers who were granted amnesty and assistance according to the prime minister's Order no. 66/2523. The order was aimed to end the war between the Communist Party of Thailand (CPT) and the Thai government by eliminating injustice in society and treating communists as "misguided" fellow citizens. In addition to amnesty, these former communists were granted farmland, money to get started in earning a living, and other kinds of assistance. The order also provided an opportunity for students who had fled to the forest after the massacre at Thammasat University on 6 October 1976 to turn themselves in and resume normal lives. This measure led to the decline of the communist insurgency in Thailand (Thomas 1986, pp. 17–26). Although Jasim had never joined the CPT, he was nevertheless considered to have been "misguided" by communism and was therefore eligible for amnesty and assistance after turning himself in.

23. Although subdistrict headmen and SAO chief executives are similar in that they are elected and are part of local government, they differ from each other in that the former are under the direct command of district chiefs, who are government officials, whereas the latter are not under such direct command. See note 2 in Chapter 1 regarding subdistrict headmen and note 12 in Chapter 2 regarding SAO chief executives.

4

The Clashes

In 1993, a leading scholar of international relations, Samuel Huntington, published an article, "The Clash of Civilizations?" in *Foreign Affairs*. He argues that, rather than ideological differences or economic competition, the fundamental source of conflict in the future would be differences among civilizations. The state as a source of identity is weakening, whereas religious and other cultural identities that make up civilizations will replace the state in primacy; cultural identity tends to be less mutable, less able to be compromised, than political or economic identities. Differences among civilizations strike at the core of human singularity and are increasingly evident, given that the world is becoming a smaller place. The clash of civilizations will dominate global politics in the twenty-first century, and the fault lines between civilizations will become the world's new battle lines. Huntington specifically points to conflicts between Islamic civilization and Western civilization to illustrate how the clash of civilizations will come to dominate global politics.

Huntington's thesis garnered broad attention. The general public and mass media were terrified by such speculation. Many scholars from various disciplines embraced the prophecy, pointing to the possibility of wars between different "civilizations". However, some scholars, especially those working on Islam and Muslim politics, questioned Huntington's thesis. John Esposito (1999) maintains that the thesis overlooks the plural nature of Islam, the diverse political realities of the Muslim world, and its diverse relations with the West. He argues that disputes and civil wars have more to do with political and socio-economic grievances than with religion and that there are similarities and constructive connections between Islamic civilization and the Western world. Bassam Tibi (2001) contends that Islam as a civilization is composed of a variety of local cultures and, as such, to take Islam as monolithic vis-à-vis the West is misleading. He adds that Islam is both a religious faith and a cultural system but not a political ideology. It is not Islam or Islamic civilization but the politicization of Islam that is not only hostile to other civilizations but is also a threat even to Islam itself. The heterogeneity and "clash" within Islam are emphasized by Robert Hefner (2001; 2002), who points to struggles within Muslim societies, especially Indonesia, where the proponents of civil society and democracy have clashed with the supporters of an anti-pluralistic Islamic state in imagining the Muslim public.

Such "clashes" also took place in Guba. As discussed earlier, rumour had it that the insurgents had spread leaflets prohibiting Muslims from tapping rubber on Friday morning, citing the Koran as their authority. However, Daessa refused to follow the alleged order, saying that she could not find such a prohibition mentioned in the Koran. Likewise, the imam of the Pahong Gayu mosque thought that it was inappropriate to have non-Islamic elements, like royal grave soil, used in an Islamic burial ceremony. But he kept silent, knowing that he might otherwise be targeted by the military. It is these "clashes" between different sources of subjectivity or in other words different forms of sovereignty that Guba residents have had to deal with in everyday life amid the recent unrest.

4.1. Different Strands of Islam

On the surface, Islam in Guba is observed by everyone. The compulsory nature of the Five Pillars of Islam is never questioned, the need for complementary religious practices such as Koran classes and evening preaching is agreed upon, and the staging of major religious events such as Hari Raya is a collective commitment. However, tensions lie beneath the apparent consensus, some of which can be resolved but many of which resist any easy solution.

Yaakob, a New Group practitioner, said that the New Group disagrees with certain beliefs and practices of traditional Islam, including prayer methods, Mawlid,[1] and the notion of merit. For the New Group, Mawlid should not be held, because the ceremony celebrates the Prophet as if he were himself a supreme being like Allah. The New Group also holds that there is no concept of merit in Islam. Such a concept actually is a remnant of Brahmanism, Hinduism and Buddhism, which have long been so intertwined with Islam that they have become part of it. Informed Muslims should discard any practice such as rituals aimed to make merit for the dead where the notion of merit is reinforced.

Such differences notwithstanding, Yaakob has never brought the issues to the fore, nor has he ever forbidden any residents from practising what the New Group deems not in line with Islam. He said: "We just do what we think is right according to Islam. They [other residents] will stop doing wrong when they know Islam better." Given that New Group practitioners keep a low profile, there is no severe "clash" between the New Group and the Old Group in Guba, as there is in some places in the Deep South.[2] In addition, Yaakob said that even in areas where conflicts between the two groups were once acute, now people have adjusted their religious beliefs and practices to each other. New Group practitioners began to accept and participate in rituals they once categorically refused.[3] Old Group practitioners as well as Muslims in general discarded or modified certain beliefs and practices they had long held so as to meet the "correct" Islam advocated by the New Group. According to Yaakob, the Deep South has survived conflict between the two groups, and Islam in general is now flourishing in the region.

Although Yaakob has never forced anyone to practise Islam as prescribed by the New Group, he frequently comments on how people have been led astray from "true" Islam. He criticizes residents who hang out at the teashops and rebukes the Red-Whiskered Bulbul contest. To him, many people still live their lives like animals, or like those with no religion. Sometimes, he acts as if he were an "Islamic rule-enforcement officer". However, when Yaakob comments on or criticizes others for not practising Islam correctly, he does not cite the New Group as an example to follow. Rather, he identifies himself with the Dakwah movement, and tension between Dakwah and traditional Islam occasionally surfaces in Guba.

Ishak says that Dakwah is commendable because, in general, it neither proposes new, unfamiliar practices nor opposes existing ones. However, he decided to return home while in the middle of his first Dakwah mission after learning that Dakwah practitioners "put their ideas in their preaching. I don't want to listen to it." In addition, many residents often comment negatively on some practices of Dakwah. Jamal said that he is fine with Dakwah's teaching, because it is not in conflict with Islam. But he, like most people in Guba, has never completed a Dakwah mission. Instead of feeling guilty for falling short in this regard, Jamal criticizes Dakwah practitioners on missions, especially the long, forty-day sojourns, saying: "They don't have to take responsibility for anything. It's not good because they go off and leave life's burdens to those behind. I can't do that because I still have a daughter to take care of." In addition, he does not like that Dakwah practitioners wear long beards, because such facial hair looks scary to him, regardless of their claim that they are seeking to emulate the Prophet. Nor can he accept the way Dakwah practitioners eat their food, piled together in a single tray, with their fingers, although, again, they claim that this is how the Prophet ate his meals. Jamal is supported by his close friend Dahari's argument that the Prophet did not usually eat food in a tray with his followers; rather, he ate food in individual plates like most people. The only times when the Prophet ate food in a tray with his followers was during wartime, because, said Dahari, "there were many people and they had to eat fast." Importantly, Dahari said that Dakwah is wrong to focus exclusively on practices, without thoroughly studying the religion behind them first. "Even the Prophet", he said, "didn't perform prayer right away, but he studied it thoroughly first."

Tensions between Dakwah and traditional Islam came to a head during the first Dakwah gathering in Guba. There are always Dakwah missions in Guba, mostly at the northern Guba mosque but sometimes at the southern one. However, these Dakwah meetings are small scale, comprising perhaps fifteen Dakwah members each and not involving Guba residents in general. But on one occasion, Tok Zaki, Guba's Dakwah leader, invited a Dakwah missionary group to lead a gathering in Guba so that Guba residents could get involved. It was during this first major event that tensions between Dakwah and traditional Islam surfaced.

Three nights before the Dakwah gathering, I sat chatting with the chairman (Azlan) and two key members (Hanif and Fathi) of the village 1 Red-Whiskered Bulbul Club. After discussing a few general topics, I raised the topic of the upcoming Dakwah gathering and asked if they would participate. Hanif and Fathi did not hesitate to express their negative attitude towards Dakwah practitioners. Hanif said that Dakwah practitioners were lazy and irresponsible because they did not work, leaving the mundane burdens of everyday life for their families to cope with, especially their wives. Fathi supported this observation and added that Dakwah practitioners were selfish, taking advantage of other family members and using religion as an excuse not to get involved. "They leave problems behind. They leave their home for forty days without taking any responsibility or knowing anything," he said. Azlan said nothing but later called on Yaakob, who at one point walked by on the road, to join them. I greeted Yaakob and told him that we were talking about Dakwah. Then I asked him what he thought about criticisms that Dakwah focused exclusively on practice without first studying the underlying religion. He said: "Actually, Dakwah is a way of learning. During the mission, there are people who preach, and we attend sessions for studying the Koran. Dakwah is learning while doing." Then I asked him what he thought about comments on Dakwah practitioners' laziness, selfishness, and irresponsibility. Yaakob vehemently responded that critics are good for nothing. Dakwah practitioners followed the Prophet's path and helped strengthen Islam. They were doing good things, whereas their critics were doing the contrary. Azlan, Hanif and Fathi did not respond. They turned their faces away from the conversation, casting their gaze to the road outside and leaving the conversation to Yaakob and me.

The Red-Whiskered Bulbul Club is not Dakwah's main opponent in Guba. Rather, it was the southern Guba mosque committee and members whom Dakwah found to be the major obstacle to their first gathering in Guba. As the host, the mosque facilitated the Dakwah missionary group by renovating the place for their stay, procuring kitchen utensils and firewood for their cooking and eating, coordinating food donations, recruiting residents to participate in their prayers and preaching, and other helpful preparations. The mosque in turn sought to earn revenue from the event. A teashop and other shops were set up in front of the mosque, and a donation box was put inside the mosque where Dakwah practitioners stayed and performed religious services. It was the teashop and other revenue-earning establishments that generated tension between Dakwah practitioners and the mosque.

In the late afternoon of the first day of the Dakwah gathering, the teashop was crowded with arriving Dakwah practitioners as well as Guba residents. When it came time for the evening prayer, the teashop and other shops were temporarily vacated as the mosque committee and members joined the Dakwah practitioners in the mosque, leaving me, the only Thai Buddhist at the event, to look after the shop alone. The committee and members left the mosque and reopened the shops as soon as they had finished the prayers, followed by Dakwah practitioners who later crowded the teashop although the preaching was still underway. These religious services seemed to proceed hand-in-hand with the economic activities just outside the mosque until the second night. While Hakeem, the mosque secretary, was opening the teashop after the evening prayer, a Dakwah group leader spoke through a loudspeaker asking for cooperation not to open the shops while the preaching was still underway so as not to distract the Dakwah practitioners. Initially, Hakeem and other mosque members closed their shops as requested. But later they gradually reopened the shops, following the wishes of some children who wanted to buy *roti*. It did not take long for the teashop to be crowded again with Dakwah practitioners, although the preaching was not finished yet.

"Why did you guys open the shops against the Dakwah's request?" I asked Dahari, a mosque committee member, and he said because many people, including Dakwah practitioners themselves, had requested it. In his opinion, instead of asking for the teashop to close, the Dakwah group should have told its members not to hang out there during the preaching. He added: "Dakwah people just come and go. They don't have to take responsibility for any expenses involved. The mosque has to pay for water and electricity bills and all other expenses. So we have to make money to cover these expenses." Mosque members continued to disobey the Dakwah's demand the following night, which was the last night of the gathering; they opened the teashop as soon as they finished the evening prayer in the mosque. Again, Dahari explained: "We still have seven kilograms of flour left to make *roti*. If we were to close the teashop according to their demand, we would lose all the flour. Who will pay for this, if not us?" Interestingly enough, the Dakwah leaders did not respond to this disobedience. Dakwah practitioners, like the night before, crowed the teashop during the preaching, and they quietly left the mosque in the morning of the following day.

It was not the Dakwah practitioners but Yaakob who vehemently criticized the mosque members' behaviour. Two days after the gathering, while sitting and chatting in front of his roadside grocery with me, he said:

> What a shame on Guba people! How can we now face people from other places who know that we sought advantage from the Dakwah gathering? They were here to observe their religious duties, but we were busy making money off them. The mosque people didn't agree with Dakwah in the first place, because they come from the old *pondoks*. But they agreed to let Dakwah hold the gathering at their mosque, because they thought they could make money from it.

He said that the mosque members put "emotion above reason" in that "they shut the shop's door loudly because they were dissatisfied with Dakwah's demand. This is emotional and irrational. Dakwah had a sound reason for their request, but these people did not listen; they just wanted to do their business and they got emotional." I did not interrupt Yaakob, although I had witnessed Hakeem closing the door and believed that he never intended to slam it; the noise it made is just how an iron door normally sounds when it is opened and closed. Yaakob continued with his comments on a couple of other issues before ending by addressing the Arzeulee SAO chief executive's involvement with the mission. He said:

It's also a shame that we cannot find a sufficient number of villagers to join the next Dakwah mission. The SAO chief executive promised that he would take care of the matter but apparently he can't. This is because he doesn't have faith in Dakwah in the first place. He has never performed a Dakwah mission. But he agreed to support this Dakwah gathering because the SAO election is imminent; he wanted to show that he supports religious activities and to please Dakwah people.

While it is unclear to what extent Shakib, the Arzeulee SAO chief executive, has faith in Dakwah, and how much his support for it is related to the upcoming SAO election, it is evident that many mosque members do not subscribe to Dakwah. They hung around the teashop and joined Dakwah practitioners in the mosque only during the evening prayer. Most of them left the mosque as soon as they finished the prayer, since they considered the preaching as something newly added by Dakwah that they were not obliged to stay for. In addition, they commented sceptically about the preaching. As Dahari put it:

Dakwah's preaching is unintelligible because it is unorganized. The preacher talks without structure. There is no topic and no core. All are details of nothing. This is mainly because they don't study religious texts, which would provide them with topics and a structure for preaching. They only focus on practices but ignore study. If they had studied religious texts, their preaching would be more organized and intelligible. The police inspector [and Dakwah group leader] preached well because he has knowledge about religion, because he studied religious scriptures when he was a deputy at Raman police station.

Given that a close examination of religious texts is a focus of the *pondoks*, where Dahari and many other mosque members studied, whereas Dakwah tends to emphasize practice, tension between these two strands of Islam in Guba continues.

Added to these tensions is the insurgents' invocation of Islam in their operations. Rather than identifying themselves with established organizations such as PULO, the BRN, or BRN-Coordinate (the latter who are thought to be behind the recent unrest), insurgents in the leaflets they distribute often identify themselves more directly with Islam, for instance calling themselves the "Islamic Warriors of the Fatoni Darussalam State". Among the demands they present in the leaflets is the call for the founding of an Islamic state, for instance the "Fatoni Darussalam State". In recruiting members, they emphasize how Islam has historically been oppressed by the Thai state. One young man who was approached by insurgents told me:

> Okhrae Dalae always searches for good boys like those performing prayers five times a day. They will approach these boys and tell them how Islam is badly oppressed and how there is an urgent need to liberate Islam. I was once approached by them. They are all my friends. They talked to me about Islam and the history of Islam in the region. They told me that now it is oppressed and intimidated very strongly. They talked to me like this a couple of times. Then one day they came to me and invited me to join them. Actually, I never realized before that they are Okhrae Dalae. I began to suspect them when they repeatedly told me about how Islam was oppressed. But I refused to join them. I told them that these days I've already done my duties for Allah and Islam. So they left me without any threats and never came back again. It's their policy not to force people in their recruitment.

The insurgents' use of the oppression of Islam in their recruitment of members gets various feedback from villagers. Many do not agree with the method. Dakwah leader Tok Zaki said that Islam has been well supported by the state, and the insurgents' claim that Islam is being bullied is groundless. Mana observed that, although insurgents were increasingly using religion as a tool to draw support, Islam in fact was not discriminated against in the Deep South. Residents like Daessa hold the same opinion. She said that the Thai state treats Islam well. She has the freedom to observe her religious duties. Islam is not harried or treated in any discriminatory fashion. So she does not agree with the insurgents' use of religion to recruit members. Teashop owner Talib insisted that the insurgents' claim is untenable, as Islam is not bullied. Rubber trader Abidin said that now was not an appropriate time to wage jihad, as Islam was not under oppression and he still had the freedom to perform his religious duties. He added that Islam in fact was a relatively late arrival to the region and that other religions were already established here before that. Another rubber trader, Effendi, said that Islam had been treated well, saying that women could wear headscarves to schools and universities as well as to all government agencies and buildings. In addition, he observed:

> Prior to Patani, there were other kingdoms and religions such as Brahmanism, Hinduism and Buddhism in the region. The *tupa* we eat during Hari Raya belongs to the Buddhist tradition. Thai Buddhists in Nakhon Si Thammarat make and eat *tupa* when they hold the tenth lunar

month ritual. This land was not ours from the beginning. Islam arrived here later than others, although it has been here for many hundreds of years.

However, other residents did not categorically deny the insurgents' claim. Yaakob admitted that the Thai state had treated Islam well but observed: "It is all right at the policy level, but there may be problems at the operational level. Some state authorities may maltreat Islam, and those who are hot tempered cannot accept it." Likewise, while Dahari insisted that Islam was not being bullied and was in fact treated well like other religions in Thailand, he thought that the insurgents were expressing an "ideology" in saying that Islam was being oppressed. He said: "I don't study religion much, whereas many Okhrae Dalae have higher education in religion, or different kinds of religious education that I don't know about. They may understand or interpret the situation differently from me. So their claim is not totally groundless."

Importantly, some residents agreed with the insurgents. Mamdoh, a man who had held various state appointments, vehemently said that Islam had been oppressed throughout the course of its history. He added that "Islam states clearly that if the religion is bullied, Muslims must fight with their lives." Village 1 SAO member Mohammed, who had said previously that he disagreed with the insurgents' method of using of Islam's alleged oppression as a recruitment tool, was now uncertain. This was primarily because, he said: "There are so many cases in which Muslims are bullied and defamed so much that they have to fight or flee to the forest. Injustice has taken place through the course of history. So it is difficult to argue against them. There really are [many examples]. It is not just a fault but injustice." He added that, according to Islamic principles, Muslims must fight to the death if they face injustice. He admitted that he knew very little about religion compared to some insurgents. As such, he said: "I have no idea how to argue against them."

Another controversial issue involving the manner in which the insurgents utilized religion is their self-expressed right to kill with impunity in the name of Islam. For example, one leaflet stated, "If we kill, we kill for Allah", which implies that the killing is justified. The issue occasionally surfaced, significantly during the month of Ramadan in 2009, as discussed in Chapter 3 above. Asked about the upsurge of violence during the period in an interview with the media, the Fourth Region Army commander pointed to the belief that killing in the name of Islam was acceptable as a major cause. He said that young Muslim insurgents were indoctrinated that any action they took on behalf of Islam during

Ramadan, especially killing, would bring them double merit. So they killed more during Ramadan.

I raised the issue with many residents and found that their positions are varied. Mana dismissed the notion that killing at any time generated merits by saying that killing was sinful, and Islam can coexist with other religions. Likewise, Abidin insisted that such beliefs were false because Islam, with Allah being compassionate and merciful, is a religion of peace and does not encourage or condone any form of violence. In addition, the month of Ramadan is a holy month during which Muslims are encouraged to refrain from committing any sin. As such, he concluded, instead of getting double merits for killing during the month of Ramadan, Muslim insurgents received double sin instead. However, Yaakob said that "sometimes I think such a principle may really exist. You know, some insurgents received higher education in Islam, which ordinary Muslims like me don't have a chance to get. Maybe such a belief is really stated somewhere in Islam. I don't know." Aiman attempted to clarify the issue by saying that, in general, killing is a sin in Islam. But in certain circumstances it is not only allowed but also encouraged and praised, for instance killing while on "the path of the Islamic warrior". As he put it: "In Islam, if you are the warrior and kill the enemy or those oppressing Islam, you are not committing a sin but are carrying out a praiseworthy mission. If you die in that holy war, you soul will be blessed and go to heaven." Similarly, Saifuldin said: "If the warriors fight for religion while it is being oppressed, they don't commit a sin but they will gain double merit during Ramadan. So the commander's opinion is not groundless."

However, the insurgents' utilization of Islam as a recruitment tool and a justification for killing does not affect the villagers for the most part. Rather, it is their alleged prohibition of work on Friday morning that the residents found affected them the most. As discussed earlier, there were rumours of insurgent leaflets forbidding Muslims to work on Friday morning on the ground that it is not in line with Islamic principles. Most residents followed the instruction, despite having never seen the leaflets. However, some questioned the religious grounds of the prohibition. Daessa said that, to her knowledge, nowhere in Islamic teaching is it stated that Muslims are forbidden from working on Friday morning. But, aware that her knowledge of Islam was minimal, she was uncertain whether such a prohibition might be stated somewhere other than where she had read in the Koran. She asked her close friends what they thought but failed to get a decisive answer; they were just as uncertain as she was. And, given the fear and distrust generated by the unrest, the issue was barely discussed in public and was not addressed by religious leaders in the mosques. People were left to respond to the unseen leaflets and their rumoured prohibition as they saw best.

Apart from these three issues — the use of Islam's oppression as a recruitment tool, the use of Islam as justification to kill with impunity, and the rumoured prohibition of work on Friday mornings — the insurgents have never intervened in residents' religious beliefs and practices. Traditional Islam is left largely untouched by the insurgents, although some parts of it are not in line with the stricter versions of Islam they advocate. Dakwah practitioners are able to carry out their missions across the Deep South without fear of being attacked, and so far only a few Dakwah practitioners have been killed by the insurgents. Only religious leaders and scholars who are explicitly associated with the state are targeted.

It is noteworthy that the most serious Islam-related conflict in Guba is not so much religious as political. As mentioned earlier, there are two mosques in the settlement, one in the north and the other in the south. Initially, there was only the southern mosque. However, according to Mana, problems arose with respect to administration, as the two village headmen — of village 1 and village 2 — had to share the same mosque in performing some of their duties. A northern Guba mosque was then built in 1999 to serve as village 1's official mosque, so that the village 1 headman could use it exclusively.

But the story is much more complex. As mentioned earlier, it is widely believed that Mana built the new mosque because he wanted his brother-in-law to be the imam after he had lost to Babo's son in the election to become the imam of the southern Guba mosque. However, the new mosque raised a sharp conflict among the residents. Once the northern Guba mosque was completed, most northern and central Guba residents switched from the southern Guba mosque to the northern one — some for the sake of proximity but many others due to political allegiance — and conflicts between two mosques' attendees sprang up. In addition to attending their respective mosques, the two distinct groups of worshippers avoided participating in rituals and feasts at the same time. Saifuldin said that when tensions were high, he had to invite the two mosques' attendees to rituals and feasts his family held at different times, otherwise no one would come. Mohammed said that some mosque attendees did not invite attendees of the other mosque to join their religious rites and cultural activities. These conflicts had nothing to do with differences in religious belief or practice, because the two groups practised the same Islam — the traditional version — although the practices of the southern Guba mosque, due to Babo's influence, are more grounded in religious texts.

Although such open conflicts have eased as years have passed, tension still lurks. It is common to hear leading members of the two mosques make unfavourable comments about each other. Dahari, a southern Guba mosque committee member, said that the reason why there is no mosque gate decoration at the northern Guba mosque during Ramadan is that "they don't care about it. Even if they have a permanent gate, they still can put some decoration on it." Likewise, a northern Guba mosque attendee said: "Unlike people at the southern Guba mosque, we are easy and friendly to each other. There are a lot of conflicts among those at the southern Guba mosque, as many of them think they are better than others. But here we don't have that kind of thinking. We are friends." Such sniping is especially prevalent with respect to special religious services at the mosques in the night-time during the month of Ramadan. Northern Guba mosque attendees said that their mosque has a full *tarawih*[4] performance, as this is encouraged in Islamic teaching, whereas southern Guba mosque attendees said that performing a full *tarawih* at the mosque was optional. In addition, northern Guba mosque attendees proudly talked about their procurement of a special imam to perform religious services at night in the mosque for the first time, something that, in their opinion, villagers at the southern Guba mosque would never be able to afford even if they wanted to.

4.2. Islam and Malay Beliefs and Rituals

A feature of some Islamic reform movements in southern Thailand is the purification and prioritization of Islam vis-à-vis Malay beliefs and rituals. In terms of purification, reform seeks to purge Islamic practice of what are considered non-Islamic elements, regardless of how long those elements may have existed in the region prior to the arrival of Islam. In terms of prioritization, Islamic reform seeks to abandon or adjust many Malay beliefs and rituals considered not in line with Islam, even if they have long been embedded in the residents' way of life.

This reform process has taken place in Guba as elsewhere in the Deep South. Aiman said that, in the past, people performed a bathing ritual near the cemetery on various occasions, for instance having successfully avoided conscription, performing circumcision rites, and more. But later the bathing ritual was abolished on the grounds that the bathing water, which according to religious principles is considered impure, will infiltrate the graves at the nearby cemetery, which are to be kept pure and free from pollution. Merit-making ceremonies conducted near the cemetery in the belief that sacred beings are around were abandoned as, according to Islam, there are no wandering spirits in this world; spirits go to either heaven or hell after death. Aiman added that certain rituals acknowledging teachers of the performing arts that involve performing those arts for them, such as mak yong (*mayong*, มะโย่ง), were discontinued on the grounds that Islam does not allow the reverence of any beings other than Allah.

The purification and prioritization of Islam in Guba, however, is far from complete. Beliefs and rituals that reformists consider non-Islamic are still broadly held and practised. Beliefs in spirits are an exemplary case. Many people establish designated locations for spirits to stay in their houses to prevent these spirits from disturbing or harming them. These places are generally inconspicuous and not in any recognizable form; they are simply wooden planks or bamboo cuttings hung from the ceiling or laid on crossbeams, with no offerings given. No rituals are regularly held for these spirits; only once in a while do villagers hold rituals. In one case, a ritual was held in response to the behaviour of a frightened, rampaging horse, as mentioned briefly above.

Aiman raised eight horses, primarily for recreation. Sometimes, he took the horses to participate in parades in town. Occasionally, he entered two of the stronger horses, a male and a female, in horse races. An unprecedented incident occurred before one such race, leading to the performance of a ritual for ancestral and other spirits.

Two days before the horse race, Aiman wanted to transport the female to an open field for training. At first, she obediently followed instructions; she stepped up in the pick-up's bed on her own. After binding three bamboo rods to the truck's side balusters to make a makeshift horse cage, four boys and I joined the horse in the bed while Aiman got into the cab with Najmudin, the driver, and the journey began. However, the horse became restless as soon as we left the house. We soon needed to stop the truck and collect some tree branches along the roadside, to use to calm down the horse. But the horse continued to rampage. We stopped again, and Aiman got out the truck to calm her down himself, but to no avail. The horse continued to jump around and only calmed down after she severely hurt her leg. Considering the severity of the wound, Aiman decided to take the horse back home for treatment, cancelling plans to race her.

The news about the horse going a rampage spread very quickly. Many acquaintances came to the family's house to discuss the issue. Initially, it was "scientifically" assumed that the horse was so concerned about her baby — she had recently given birth to a colt — that she resisted the separation. But this reasonable assumption could not provide a satisfactory explanation for those involved, leaving room for alternatives, especially of a supernatural nature. Daessa, the family's rubber tapper, said that the incident could have resulted from the fact that Aiman's family had not offered anything to the ancestors in particular for quite some time; the family just mentioned the spirits collectively, not specifically by name, when holding rituals for them. The incident was a warning sign from these spirits. Aryani, Aiman's paternal younger aunt, agreed with Daessa and added that she had made several vows to ancestral spirits but had not fulfilled them yet. She said that she would offer chicken if Aiman held a ritual for the spirits. Others also agreed with this theory, and an agreement to hold a ritual for the ancestral spirits the following day was unanimously reached.

The ritual was held at the back of the main house. Jaafa was in charge of the overall proceedings, while Osman took measures to appease any spirits or ghosts, particularly bad ones, that might disrupt the ritual. Participants included family members and acquaintances of all ages. The ritual began with a joint recitation of part of the Koran, followed by Jaafa's solo chant. Then the main (and final) part of the ritual — the giving of the offerings — was conducted, with Aiman acting as Jaafa's assistant, since he knew to whom the offerings were being given. There were eight trays of the offerings for eight recipients, seven of whom were different *tok* and the eighth being the Prophet. The seven *tok* included Tok Nik or Toh Nik, the Raman ruler; Tok Guba, the village founder; the paternal and maternal great-grandparents; the dagger master; and the art master. The offerings for each *tok* included white and yellow cooked sticky rice, traditional local sweets, a betel leaf painted with white lime, a betel nut, a glass of water, three bananas, popped rice, and a roasted chicken. However, the offering for the Prophet did not include the betel leaf or nut because the Prophet, as an Arab, did not indulge in it. Flowers were offered instead. Jaafa performed a *dua* prayer while Aiman was touching the offering trays, one by one, and reciting the names of the recipients in turn. After being symbolically given to the spirits, the offerings were then distributed among the participants to eat. Jaafa ate a little bit and was given a piece of cloth and a bag of rice grain as a gift before he left. I asked Aiman how he felt after holding the ritual, and he said, "Now I feel very much better. We shouldn't have forgotten to do it." Likewise, Jamal, Aiman's maternal younger uncle, said that it was good to hold the ritual because "it satisfied the ancestral spirits and, as such, they will not cause us any trouble."

However, it is the spirits of neither the ancestors nor the village founder nor the Raman ruler but the spirits of art masters that most frequently manifest themselves among the residents — mostly in the form of spirit possession. It is common to see one or two villagers, usually women, possessed by a spirit during cultural performances, especially *silat* and *mak yong*, and it is here that belief in the spirits of the art masters is still strong. I had an opportunity to witness a spirit possession during a teacher acknowledgement ritual that my wife and I hosted for our *silat* teacher, Ishan, in a courtyard in the inner part of central Guba.

As soon as my wife finished performing *silat* with her counterpart in the courtyard, there were shouts that some people at Ishan's house had been possessed by a spirit. So we halted the performance and ran to the house to see what was going on there. We found that both Daessa and Ihsan's daughter were acting wildly. However, Ihsan's daughter was not as wild as Daessa; she just wept and lay down wriggling on ground. It was Daessa who was acting so madly that an exorcism was deemed necessary. Aiman assumed a role of the exorcist and asked Daessa why she was acting so wildly. Daessa replied in a male-sounding voice that she was dissatisfied that the ceremonial hardened-clay jug was not filled with water, which she needs to cure people's sicknesses. Aiman responded that no one was sick, and thus there was no sickness to cure, and then commanded the spirit to leave Daessa's body. Daessa did not listen; she still acted wildly. So Aiman whipped Daessa with a piece of cloth he had earlier used in the teacher acknowledgement ritual and chanted along until Daessa calmed down.

I asked Daessa, when she became herself again, if she knew or remembered what had happened to her, and she said, "No". She said, as the youngest daughter of the family, she had inherited the spirit possession tendency from her mother, who had inherited it from her mother. In addition to Malay cultural performances, there are other situations where she tends to be possessed by spirits. For example, she recalled, on one occasion she went to use the bathroom at a Buddhist temple and saw some sentences written on the wall, and she went rampant; it took awhile for the people with her to calm her down. She did not remember what had happened, and no one knew what that spirit was. Usually, the spirits stay with her for awhile before leaving on their own, without any need for exorcism, and while she may feel a little bit tired afterward she recovers quickly with no need for any cleansing ritual, although there is no way to "cure" her of her tendency towards spirit possession. However, there are some circumstances, such as a rampage that is too violent or that lasts too long, when the possession requires an exorcist, who is usually Jaafa and sometimes Aiman. She added that, besides her, there are many other villagers, all women, who are prone to spirit possession. And, besides Jaafa and Aiman, there are other local men who are capable of performing exorcisms, the best known being Qasim of southern Guba.

I first met Qasim when accompanying Jamal to a dinner party to celebrate a tug-of-war competition that I had partially sponsored (Jamal's and my team finished third). While watching three team members cook in front of a nearby house, Saifuldin, who came later, called me from the upstairs and asked me to join him there. I went into the house and found that Saifuldin was sitting and chatting with an elderly man who had asked Saifuldin to call me up there as well. The man and I had a friendly talk during which he put a prayer cap he had been wearing on my head as a sign of an invitation to join Islam; we talked for about ten minutes before I left and rejoined the party downstairs. It was not until Jamal, many weeks later, wanted a *bomoh*[5] to exorcise a spirit from his older male cousin Jek that I learned that the elderly man was Qasim, who is widely known for performing exorcisms. Actually, Jek had been diagnosed with a disease in his brain, and the doctor said that he required brain surgery. But his wife, children and relatives opposed the doctor's advice on the grounds that it would do more harm than good, and they decided to bring him back home from the hospital and treat him with a combination of modern medicines and traditional medicine. Interestingly enough, his condition was improving, except for only one problem — a spirit possession. Jek raved at night that he was a Thai Buddhist who had come from a Buddhist temple. But he did not remember these ravings when he awoke the next morning. He also had the notion that his two legs were not of the same length. His wife said that he sometimes identified himself as someone else and spoke in languages that were incomprehensible to her. Together, his relatives, and Jek himself, concluded that he was possessed by a spirit and in need of an exorcism. Although he lived in a village about 10 kilometres from Guba, Qasim, given his reputation as an exorcist, was proposed to take care of the matter.

Feeling welcomed by Qasim in our first meeting, I told Jamal that I would accompany him, along with Jek and his wife, to Qasim's house to watch the exorcism. As expected, not only did Qasim greet me with gladness but he also encouraged me to shoot a video of his exorcism when I asked for his permission. The exorcism began with Qasim "inquiring about and diagnosing the symptoms and illness of the patient", to borrow a medical phrase, for a few minutes. Then he turned to us and confirmed that Jek was possessed by a spirit. He explained that three *kuman thong* (a Thai word for a child spirit) had been unleashed at the school compound to look after the football field. But one of them is roguish and sneaks out at night to possess the weak. Qasim said that he would perform an exorcism to expel that *kuman thong* from Jek's body.

He led Jek to one corner of the house and had him sit down. Then he chanted a spell while walking around and sweeping Jek with a velvet cloth he uses for prayer. Jek did not respond; he just sat silent with empty eyes. It took about fifteen minutes for the exorcism to be finished. Qasim said that the exorcism had been effective in that the child spirit had been swept from Jek's body, and Jek was now protected from possession in the night. However, he added that we needed to wait to confirm the result, although Jek said that he now felt that his legs were equal in length and that his pain had abated. Then he gave a bag of consecrated rice grains and a bag of holy water to Jamal, to give them to Jek for taking a bath with as a supplementary measure to prevent the spirit possession from recurring. Jamal thanked Qasim and gave him 100 baht as a gift. At first, Qasim said that the amount was too much, but he accepted it at Jamal's insistence. Qasim then said goodbye to me before greeting another client, who had been waiting for her turn since the middle of Jek's exorcism. Jamal told me while we were on our way home that the second client was a southern Guba woman who had come with two bags of mangoes as a gift to have Qasim cure a pain in her body.

Another famous *bomoh* in Guba is Nah, a grade 12 female student at a private Islamic school in Pattani's Saiburi district. Differing from other *bomoh* in the area, Nah was born with a gift that enables her to see anything, anywhere she wants. She first realized this gift when she was in kindergarten and first used it to find a missing item that a villager had lost. After she found the missing item using her gift, villagers quickly came to know about her special capability, and has been sought after for various kinds of help ever since. She said that her gift had developed over time; in the past, she had to run and then sit still for awhile for her premonition to emerge, but now she just sits still for one or two minutes and it comes naturally. In addition to locating missing items, which is her specialty, her services include healing certain kinds of sickness, making charms, curing people suffering from black magic, and more. However, she does not perform exorcisms or tell fortunes because, she said, she is unable to know anything in advance as everything is determined by Allah, and he alone knows what will be, and how. What she can do is to alleviate what has already happened. Most of her clients are women of Guba and nearby villages who come to her with marriage or love affair problems. However, sometimes Thai Buddhist male clients from faraway places come to seek her help with business matters. Most people she helps are major or minor wives; other cases involve getting jobs and locating missing items. She said that, actually, she does not want to charge her clients for her services; she wants to make merit and help suffering people. She cannot touch the money, either. But clients always urge her to accept it. When she grows up, she wants to be a psychiatrist so that she can help suffering people.

I had a chance to observe Nah perform a service once. It was a ritual held for a female Tadika teacher in her late twenties who wanted to commit herself to love. Two men, one a lay Muslim and the other a religious teacher, had been in love with her for a couple of years without her reciprocation, and now she wanted to start a special relationship with one of them — the religious teacher. However, the problem was that despite her decision, she felt uncertain about herself and could not let herself love the man she had chosen. This worried her deeply, because she did not want to lose him, as he was a good and knowledgeable man. So she, according to her friend's suggestion, came to Nah for help — she wanted Nah to help her love the religious teacher, as a first step towards marriage. The ritual started with Nah bathing the teacher with water from a jar. Then Nah put consecrated rice grains into the jar and bathed the teacher with water from it while chanting "Bismillah"[6] and verses from the Koran. The bathing ritual took about fifteen minutes. Then Nah gave her a bag of consecrated rice grains to mix with water when taking a bath at home so as to cleanse "karma", impurity, and evil from her body. Nah told the teacher to come for another bathing ritual the following week. The teacher thanked Nah and gave her 120 baht as a gift, and left.

Other than Qasim and Nah, there are other *bomohs* in Guba who are thought to have fewer skills. These *bomohs* usually heal common illnesses and perform basic rituals such as preventing rain when people want to hold ceremonies outdoors. However, some of them provide specific services that Qasim and Nah do not offer, one interesting example being the healing of male impotence. Yusri, village 1 SAO member, is widely known as "a dead-penis *bomoh*" for his specialization in treating this ailment. He inherited his knowledge from his paternal grandfather, curing the condition by chanting sentences in Malay, which are actually verses from the Koran, over a betel leaf or juice from a young coconut, and then having the patient eat (or drink) it. His clients include both Guba men, many of whom he said have impotence problems, and men from nearby and faraway villages alike, including Thai Buddhists. He has provided this service for fifteen years and treated about eighty cases, many of which he said he had treated successfully.

The service charge varies; it may be 20 or 50 baht but sometimes can be 100 baht, depending on a patient's willingness and capacity to pay. He said that, in addition to him, two other *bomohs* in Guba can cure impotence: one is Babo of southern Guba and the other is the imam of the Pahong Gayu mosque. Babo cures the condition by having the patient chant phrases from the Koran, whereas the imam himself chants phrases over coconut juice, then having the patient drink the juice. Yusri said that he cannot eat papaya salad, as that would cause his magic to disappear. So he has to eat mango salad instead.

Of all the *bomohs* in Guba, Aiman is the exception. Unlike other *bomohs*, who have little or no formal education (except for Nah, who is on her way to earning higher education), Aiman obtained a bachelor's degree in performing arts from Prince of Songkla University, Pattani Campus. In addition, while other *bomohs* can provide only services involving basic applications of magic and medicine, Aiman extends his services to include the provision of special items that he makes himself. As secretary of the Burong Kueteetae subdistrict *kris*-making group, he is always carving pieces of wood into *kris* handles or hilts (*hulus*), which are later assembled into *kris* daggers that are sold on behalf of the group. With respect to his role as a *bomoh*, his friends and acquaintances frequently ask him to produce items with applications in supernatural beliefs and magic. His production of wooden penises is a case in point.

One day, I saw Aiman carving a piece of wood and noticed that it was a wooden penis. Curious, I asked him if that was really what he was making, and he said, "Yes". He added that an old college friend living in Hat Yai asked him to make twelve wooden penises for 50 baht each; this was the third time he had made them for this friend. However, he said he just carves the pieces of wood into a penis shape and then sends them to his friend, who will have others finish the pieces by adding inscriptions; his production of the basic forms involves no supernatural belief or magic. He said that he could not refuse his friend's request for fear of being rebuked and that this friend also occasionally asked him to produce specifically religious images such as renderings of the Hindu deity Ganesha and others. He added that, for pious Muslims, such images are not allowed. But he has ways of dealing with this contradiction, which I will return to later.

The *bomohs* listed in Table 4.1 provide their services as normal activities in Guba. However, they have sometimes come under criticism, especially by New Group members. Yaakob, for example, said that the belief that Nah was born with a gift is not in line with Islam. Abidin said that her gift is not real, because she is not Allah, who knows everything. Tensions along

TABLE 4.1
Bomohs in Guba and Their Services and Specializations

Bomoh	Services	Specializations
Jaafa	Exorcism, praying *dua* for the Prophet in fulfilling a vow, removing fish bones from a person's throat, praying in *kenduri* for a boy before he undergoes circumcision, blessing those frightened by accidents and similar occurrences, tearing white cloth used in wrapping corpses, make yellow threads for children to wear around their neck.	Opening rituals and praying in *kenduri*
Qasim	Exorcism, making amulets such as *ta krud* (tiny rolled pieces of metal inscribed with magic words) and *pha yun* (cloth inscribed with magic words), identifying auspicious times for holding ceremonies and trading, performing shop-opening ceremonies, making charms (for reconciliations), returning stolen animals (by making the thieves feel guilty and returning the animals voluntarily, or having them face bad fortune if they do not return the animals).	Exorcisms, changing bad fortunes
Aiman	Preventing rain (for those who wish to hold ceremonies outdoors), curing sickness generated by the dissatisfied spirits of art masters by having patients chew a concoction of betel leaf and nut, performing *kenduri*.	Performing a variety of rituals
Babo	Locating missing animals, curing drug addicts (using consecrated honey), preventing rain, praying *dua*, making charms for reconciliations (using consecrated salt), exorcisms, identifying auspicious times, lead prayer rituals over people who have died, curing male sexual impotence.	Praying *dua* in rituals
Nah	Locating missing animals and other properties, making charms.	Locating missing animals and other property
Nahdi	Curing sinus and tooth pain and other common ailments.	Curing common sicknesses
Yusri	Curing male sexual impotence.	Curing male sexual impotence
Jalal	Curing asthma in children using medicinal herbs.	Curing asthma in children

these lines remain, although *bomohs* have modified their practices in the wake of Islamic reform, an issue I discuss in Chapter 5.

4.3. MALAY-MUSLIM IDENTITY AND THAI CITIZENSHIP

Despite attempts to separate traditional Malay beliefs and rituals from Islam in the name of Islamic reform, the two worlds are still inextricably intermingled and deeply embedded in people's way of life. Residents of the Deep South call themselves "Okhrae Nayu" (Orang Melayu in standard Malay, which means "Malay people"), while calling the conversion to Islam "Masok Nayu" (Masuk Melayu in standard Malay, which means "to enter Malay"). Likewise, while calling the language they speak "Yawi", which is the Malay language written in modified Arabic script, people call the male circumcision rite "Masok Yawi" (Masuk Yawi in standard Malay, which means "to enter the Malay language"). It is through the Yawi script that people learn Islam.

Malay and Islam provide people in the South with an ethno-religious identity, which is expressed primarily via language, clothing, food, and religious practices. Residents speak Malay, which represents their Malay ethnic identity and connects them with their brethren in Malaysia. They embrace Islam, which articulates their religious identity and at the same time links them with their fellow Muslims around the world and in the Ummah (Islamic community). Malay-Muslim identity transcends and sometimes comes into conflict with national identity, which is largely built on Thai ethnicity and Buddhist religion. Although the Thai state no longer imposes a forced assimilation policy, which once created resentment and resistance across the region, tension between the two assemblages of identity remains.[7] Guba is no exception.

Late one morning while feeding pigeons in front of the house, Saifuldin raised the issue of race. He asked me why Chinese were allowed to mention their race in their Thai ID cards whereas Malays were not. He added that, although ID cards are no longer an issue because they no longer specify the race of the cardholders, he is still not allowed to identify himself as Malay when filling out official documents. He said that he once filled in the word "Malay" in the blank space after the word "race" in one official document, but the official present said that was not right and told him to replace it with the word "Thai". He had to conform to this "suggestion" by the official, despite the fact that, he said, "our ancestors are Malays, not Thais". His cousin Mihran, who was there at the time and joined our conversation, supported

Saifuldin's position and vehemently asked, "What is their reason for denying our race?" He added that, actually, the recognition of the Malay race had once been demanded by Haji Sulong[8] but without success, and as a result the issue is no longer addressed by anyone. Filled with resentment and desperation, Mihran said: "Thailand sucks the blood out of its people and will be punished by God." The issue of race continued to haunt Saifuldin for the rest of the day. When we were watching television later, he searched in a drawer and produced his gun licence, which he showed to me. He pointed to the space after the words "race and nationality", which said "Thai-Thai"; he said: "If you were Chinese, you could put 'Chinese-Thai' in the blank. But if you are Malay like us, you cannot do that. You have to say that your race is Thai. It's totally unfair."

Added to Malay ethnicity is the issue of the Malay language. Despite the government's attempts to demonstrate its support for the Malay language, many people comment on how their language is ruined by the state, for instance in translating and transliterating Malay into Thai. Aiman always felt outraged when we drove past signs showing village names. Many village names in Malay-speaking regions are in fact actual words that have meanings beyond simply being the names of the respective villages — a village might be named for a geographic feature, for instance, or a plant or animal. However, when rendering these village names in the Thai alphabet on road signs, the Thai authorities translated them (giving the Thai word for the meaning of Malay word) rather than transliterated them (giving the closest approximate sound of the Malay word in Thai letters). Aiman said that, actually, the government should have used Thai transliterations of the Malay names, so that the original village names could be read and pronounced properly by outsiders and those just driving by. But the reason why the government did not do so is that, he said, "they didn't ask local Malays. They asked only Thai Buddhists who lived along the road they cut." Aiman added that the official village names, which are often different from the signposted names and which are indeed Thai transliterations of Malay, create problems as well. This is because many of them are inaccurate transliterations that have totally different and at times indecent and nasty meanings when sounded out in Malay. This caused residents of many villages to change their official village names back into names that, when sounded out, are closer to the original Malay pronunciations; Guba is one such case.

The Thai government authorities in charge of such matters originally gave Guba the official name กาเบา, which, when read aloud, sounds like "Gabao". However, this sounds very much like the Malay word *kerbau*, which means "buffalo". Guba football players were mocked with this name by their competitors in football matches. The players then told their parents to inform those in charge to change the village name. The parents accommodated their children's demand; they went to meet with SAO members and asked them to change the village name. The SAO members promised to work on the issue, and after about a year of effort, especially on the part of Saifuldin, their petition to change the official Thai village name from กาเบา (Gabao) to กูบา, which sounds more like "Guba", was officially approved.

Thai renderings of Malay also create problems with regard to people's names. Yaakob has commented that many beautiful and meaningful Arabic and Malay names lose their meaning when written in the Thai alphabet. This is partly because Thai officials do not know Malay or Arabic, and partly because the Thai alphabet is incapable of accurately rendering Malay and Arabic sounds. He suggested that, along with the Thai alphabet, Malay names should be written in Arabic script on national ID cards. It is noteworthy that, given the problems associated with the Thai transliteration of Malay, there is always confusion when Thais attempt to pronounce Malay names as written (in the Thai alphabet) on the ID cards. For example, in one incident that I witnessed, Thai provincial livestock officials had a hard time calling out the names of Malay residents who had come to get compensation checks for animals they had lost. In addition to calling the recipients' first names at least twice or three times, they also had to repeat the surnames several times, given the difference between pronouncing the transliterated Thai, which the officials were reading, and the actual spoken Malay, which the check recipients were listening for. In some cases, officials had to additionally identify recipients by checking them against their pictures on their ID cards.

Most Malay speakers in the South do not pay much attention to the Thai transliterations of their Malay names. Some might complain about it occasionally and then let it go without doing anything about it. But Saifuldin is an exception. One day he said that he intended to change his official name, which is pronounced "Samfuldin" when reading the Thai transliteration (ซัมฟุลดิน), partly because the pronunciation is incorrect and has no meaning either in Arabic or Malay and partly because, now that Guba's official village name has been changed, so his personal name should be changed also. Two weeks later he went to the Raman district office to have his name changed, which, as it turns out, was easy. A Malay Muslim official asked him why he wanted to change his name, and he explained to her exactly what he had explained to me. He said that he knew religion (his name has a religious meaning) better than she or other Malay Muslim officials did, so he was not afraid of any questions he might be asked.

He proudly showed me his new ID card with his new name, Saifuldin (ไซฟุลดิน), displayed.

Saifuldin also raised other topics concerning the Malay language. For example, one day, while we were taking a look at an Arzeulee SAO-sponsored banner of Hari Raya, he told me that if he had seen it earlier he would not have approved it. This is because, he said, "for pious Muslims, it is unacceptable to put the Thai language above Malay like this." Likewise, he once rebuked Yaakob for speaking Thai with his daughter on the grounds that, he said, "we are Malays, so we have to speak Malay, not Thai", although Yaakob responded that "speaking many languages is beneficial to one's life".

The issue of Malays speaking Malay, however, usually arises with regard to officials rather than ordinary residents. Alif, a central Guba woman, said that the Malay nurses at Saiburi Hospital were not good, not only because they do not take good care of patients but also because they always talk to patients in Thai, even though they (and their patients) are Malays. This has caused patients, especially those who are elderly, to be afraid to talk to them. Likewise, during a meeting held by NGO workers, Nadia, a native of Pattani, told the participants that, given that this was a subdistrict-level meeting which some Thai residents might be attending (in fact there were none), she would speak in Thai rather than Malay. She added that her selection of the Thai language was in line with the principle of multiculturalism that her organization was promoting. However, after the meeting had gone on for awhile, some elderly participants asked Nadia if she could speak Malay in addition to Thai, because it was difficult for them to follow her in Thai. Nadia said that, actually, she was more comfortable with Malay herself, and then she switched to Malay. However, she spoke in Malay only for a few minutes before switching back to Thai and continuing in that language until the end of the meeting, forgetting that she had promised to speak Malay. Daessa said after the meeting that the participants, mostly female elders, were dissatisfied with Nadia. They said, according to Daessa, that Nadia "acted as if she were not Malay. Didn't she know that we are not fluent in Thai?"

However, Malays in the South do not categorically deny Thai or other languages. Rather, many of them attempt to improve their skill in Thai as well as a foreign language like English whenever there is a chance. As the only person in Guba who spoke Thai as a first language, I was a resource for people who wanted to practise the language. Mohammed, a village 1 SAO member, said that one reason he liked to talk to me was that he wanted to improve his Thai. He said:

My Thai is not good, because I learned it in school a long time ago and don't use it in everyday life. But I want to practise it because when I attend big meetings with government officials they always ask that if anyone has an opinion or suggestion please raise your hand. I want to raise my hand and speak out, but I don't dare because my Thai is not good enough. It's good to have you here because I can practise my Thai with you.

Likewise, Tahir, village 2 SAO member, was always asking me how to say some Malay words in Thai. He also asked me if I could help him improve his Thai; in my opinion he is already fluent in Thai, but he said: "I want to speak without an accent when dealing with government officials." In addition, given my training in English abroad, during the first stage of my research I taught an evening English class, in response to the requests of some residents who wanted to study English. Seen in this light, people in Guba are aware of the importance and necessity of languages other than Malay in their lives and can separate the usefulness and benefit of these "second languages" from their threat to the continued use of Malay.

Like Malay language and identity, Islam is sometimes in tension with state ideology, but from a different angle. While Malay cannot be designated as a "race" in official documents, Islam is accepted as a religion that Thai citizens are free to embrace, and it receives various forms of support from the state. However, it is also because Islam is officially under the state's patronage that tensions arise.

Guba residents do not regard the Chularajamontri, the royally appointed Muslim supreme leader, as having any real authority over them. Rather, many of them view him as a function of the state, and they occasionally make disparaging comments. Ishak said that there had frequently been conflicts over the starting dates of the month of Ramadan between those announced by the Office of the Chularajamontri and those followed locally. In such cases, the residents disregarded the official dates and followed the local ones, which they believed were more in line with Islam.[9] Likewise, they observe Mawlid during a period that differs from that designated by the Office of the Chularajamontri. In the afternoon of 1 November 2008, for example, I by chance tuned in a television channel which was broadcasting live the opening ceremony of Mawlid in Bangkok. The ceremony was being staged by the Office of the Chularajamontri, who was present, and presided over by the crown prince. After watching participants praying for the Prophet, followed by a *dua* prayer for the king and the queen, I turned off the television and went outside to see if any local people were observing their religious duties regarding this event. Village life was proceeding as usual; nothing was being done in particular to mark the beginning of Mawlid. I learned that evening from Dahair that the reason why no one had done anything on that day was because they observe Mawlid at a different time. He added: "Our Mawlid period is more in line with religious principles than that of the Office of the Chularajamontri. I have no idea how they came up with this period. But they do theirs and we do ours."

The unrest since 2004 has added greater tension, as seen in the case of a royal grave-soil laying ceremony. After participating in the ceremony, held for two village security team members at Pahong Gayu cemetery, many residents commented critically. Saifuldin fervently said that he totally disagreed with the ceremony on the grounds that it was not in line with Islam. Mohammed added that people disagreed with the ceremony because, according to Islam, it is forbidden to pitch tents on a graveyard and to allow Thai Buddhists, especially females, to walk around there. He added that there had never been a ceremony like this before the recent unrest and that this was the first to take place at Guba. He said that he had no idea whether or not the dead would accrue greater merit by being honoured by such a ceremony. But he had to let it go because he had spoken with the Tok Imam, who had told him "not to 'bark'. It's like a dog barking at an airplane, and no one hears him." Likewise, Rushdi, the *bilal* of the northern Guba mosque, vehemently protested that the ceremony was not in line with Islam, but he chose to remain silent when he was around state authorities and, he said, "there's nothing we can do and I don't want to get suspected."

Schools are another crucial site where Islam is at times in tension with state ideology, especially in the form of Buddhism. One day, during morning activities in front of the school flagpole before classes started, for example, a female teacher clarified to schoolchildren whether or not the *wai* — the traditional Thai way of greeting by holding the palms together — is allowed in Islam. She said that the *wai* was not in conflict with Islam as long as it is not done above the head — which is an act of reverence only for sacred objects and supernatural beings. She showed how to perform a *wai* correctly and in a way that was inoffensive to Islam, telling the schoolchildren that they should do this when greeting school guests — mostly Thai Buddhist government officials — as well as the school's only Thai Buddhist teacher (who later was shot dead and burned near the school). The schoolchildren demonstrated no objection, not so much because they agreed with the lesson as because they were more interested in other things at the time. I raised the issue with Saifuldin that evening, and he said that, although he did not oppose the teacher's attempt to clarify the issue, he does not and will not *wai* anyone, because he considered this form of greeting and paying respect to be associated with Buddhism. How Guba residents deal with these tensions and others is the topic of the following chapter.

Notes

1. Mawlid is the celebration of the birthday of the Prophet Muhammad, which is in the third month in the Islamic calendar. Although most denominations of Islam approve of this celebration, some denominations such as Wahhabism and Salafism disapprove of it, regarding it as an unnecessary religious innovation. As a practitioner of Salafism locally called the New Group, Yaakob, then, disapproved of Mawlid.
2. Although the conflict between the Old Group and the New Group was severe in many Muslim communities across Thailand, it has not received proportionate attention from academia. One of a few academic writings addressing the conflict is by Sorayut Aim-Aur-Yut (2007), who examines how the advent of the New Group raised tension in a fishery community in Pattani's Panare district when it converged with traditional Islam and Malay customs, and how the convergence led to a new configuration of Islam and Malayness in the community.
3. It is in line with the thinking of the New Group, and of the Salafi movement in general, to adjust its Islamic intellectualism to suit local circumstances and realities (Aryud 2014, pp. 157–69).
4. *Tarawih* are extra prayers spoken at night during the month of Ramadan. They are performed after *isha* (the night prayer). Although *tarawih* are considered optional and can be performed at home, most Guba residents consider them obligatory and perform them at the mosques.
5. A *bomoh* is a Malay shaman, who can be a traditional healer, a sorcerer, or a ritual specialist addressing issues with the weather, farm animals, or the harvest. In the past, they claimed to derive their power primarily from magic spells and spirits. However, as will be seen later, after the advent of Islamic reform, *bomohs* in the Deep South and especially in Guba claim that they derive their power from Allah.
6. "Bismillah" is a phrase in Arabic that means "In the name of God". It is the first phrase in the Koran and is always recited by *bomohs* in Guba to associate their practice with Allah.
7. For studies of Malay Muslim identity vis-à-vis the Thai Buddhist state, see Braam (2013) and Jory (2007).
8. In addition to being part of the first wave of Islamic reform in southern Thailand (Aryud 2014, pp. 101–6), Haji Sulong sought to have Malay recognized as an official ethnic status in the Thai state. On 3 April 1947, he presented a seven-point demand to the Commission of Inquiry aimed at the reconstruction of the Deep South as an autonomous region in terms of administration, language (Malay), courts (Islamic), and tax and revenue. But the government's reaction to his demand was cold, for fear that such an arrangement would loosen its power over the region and

that it would lead to similar demands by other ethnic minorities in the country. On 16 January 1948, Haji Sulong and other prominent Malays were arrested and jailed. Religious leaders' demand for an explanation for the arrest, their insistence on release on bail, and their telegrams to the UN secretary general and the British prime minister yielded no effect. Haji Sulong and the others were charged with treason and slandering the government; their trial ended on 24 February 1949. The court dismissed the charges of treason but imposed a four-year-and-eight-month prison sentence on Haji Sulong for slandering the government in pamphlets he had distributed to local residents in the South. After his release in 1954, he, along with his son and an associate, were mysteriously killed, allegedly by the police, in the same year (Che Man 1990, p. 68; Nantawan 1976, pp. 208–9; Nik Mahmud 1994, pp. 54–56; Uthai 1988, pp. 262–63; Yegar 2002, pp. 104–6). His story was widely told among people in the South, including Guba, which made him more famous as a "local hero" who had fought the oppressive Thai state for the sake of Malay identity rather than as an Islamic reformer.

9. In the past, Malay Muslims of southern Thailand were always reluctant to observe Hari Raya on the day announced by the Office of the Chularajamontri unless it conformed with the opinion of religious teachers in their community. In 1981, for example, about half of the residents observed Hari Raya Aidil Adha a day earlier than that officially announced, following local ulama whom they respected. This is partly because the Chularajamontris have always been Muslims from Bangkok, and partly because they worked through the Thai state, which some local ulama regarded as contradicting Sharia principles. The Chularajamontri's decisions about Islamic law were generally disregarded by Muslims in the South, who turned to local authorities in religious law or to the ulama for the advice of a fatwa (Che Man 1990, p. 165; Surin 1988, p. 197; Yegar 2002, pp. 96–97, 102, 137). Although the situation has improved, especially under the current Chularajamontri, who is a native of Songkhla, residents still tend to listen first to the advice of their own ulama and religious teachers.

5

Living Lives with Multiple Subjectivities

My roommate Najmudin is a fascinating individual. He is a native of Baunae Jeudong village, about 15 kilometres away from Guba. But given that his maternal grandmother and relatives live in Guba, he has travelled to the village since he was young. He spent his youth and early adulthood in Yala city with "unconventional" friends, many of them Thai Buddhists. Then, he worked as a driver for Shakib, the Arzeulee SAO chief executive who at the time was an antique dealer. However, for various reasons, he quit that job and began to work for other people, mostly as a driver. After two years of being a freelance driver, Najmudin settled into the house of the family I stayed with, mostly driving and doing other chores for the family. The day I began my field research in Guba, Saifuldin and other family members assigned me to stay on the second floor of the house. The floor has one room, which belongs to Aiman (the homeowner), and outside the room is an old bed with a shabby mattress and pillow covered by a torn mosquito net, where Najmudin spends the night. The empty space between Aiman's room and Najmudin's area was allocated for me to make a sleeping place with some old mats. It is largely from our before-sleeping talks that I gradually learned how fascinating Najmudin's life is.

In addition to helping the family out with various matters, Najmudin does some work for one *kratom* cocktail producer/seller, getting paid in product. If there is no work in the family, he hangs out with his friends, most of them living on the fringes of the law, during the day and returns home late at night. His life is like a mystery, and many residents regard it as extraordinary. However, he is still committed to being a good Muslim. He regularly performs Friday noon prayers at the mosque, and he attempts to fast during Ramadan despite the pain this causes because of his *kratom* addiction. Meanwhile, he also considers himself a Malay. In addition to participating in various Malay cultural activities with Aiman, he wears a waistband with *ta krud* (tiny, rolled pieces of metal inscribed with magic spells), a local belief he considers not in conflict with Islam, because, he said, "I don't revere it". One day when arriving home from an anti-alcohol camp sponsored by the Thai Health Promotion Foundation in cooperation with the military, he wore a giveaway T-shirt printed with the message "Muslims do not drink alcohol" on the back. When I asked if he felt any contradiction wearing it, he said "No" and explained: "Because now I hardly ever drink beer or whiskey as in the past, and the *kratom* cocktails I drink are not alcoholic; nowhere in the Koran are they prohibited."

Najmudin's life epitomizes how Guba residents live their lives of multiple subjectivities, be it Muslim, Malay, or Thai citizen. To selectively draw on and interpret Islam to fit their routine activities is part of their daily life,[1] and to navigate the possibility of accommodating local Malay belief and rituals within Islam is a constant undertaking. Likewise, Guba residents are forever trying to outsmart the state, observing the rules established by the insurgents and other influential figures as their first priority. How to live these lives of multiple subjectivities has become more pressing in the wake of the recent unrest.

5.1. Negotiating with Allah and Interpreting Islam

Guba residents are Muslims of various kinds. Some are very devout but others are lax, with the majority lying somewhere between the two extremes. Religious leaders have sometimes attempted to reinforce some rules but without success, partly because they are not equipped with the tools to do so and partly because most people tend to regard religious observances as personal responsibility. It is neither religious leaders nor Islamic movements that people feel obliged to answer to. Rather, it is Allah whom they believe they are directly accountable to.

Talib runs a roadside teashop, but his business goes well beyond selling tea, local snacks and sweets, and evening meals. In front of his teashop is a rack holding bottles of gasoline. The gasoline is untaxed. He buys it from a Malay Muslim mobile gasoline trader, who himself buys it from a gas station through a special channel before mixing it with an additive to make it "more powerful". Residents like to buy bottled gasoline because it is convenient, although it costs a little bit more than gas at normal gas stations. In addition, Talib sells smuggled cigarettes. He buys them from a Chinese agent in Raman, who buys them from a Chinese agent in Yala. These cigarettes are smuggled across the Thai-Malaysian border at Wang Prachan checkpoint in Satun Province and Su-ngai Kolok checkpoint in Narathiwat Province. Residents like smoking these smuggled cigarettes, mainly because they are considerably cheaper than Thai cigarettes — they cost around 25 baht a pack, whereas Thai cigarettes cost about 80 baht a pack. Unlike the tax-free gasoline, which is put on display, the smuggled cigarettes are secretly kept in a drawer and sold only to those who specifically ask for them. Although admitting that both of these products are illegal, Talib does not see anything morally wrong with selling them. He regards them as just the way he earns his living. He becomes ethically concerned only with respect to another illegal business — the underground lottery.

Talib says that he has played the lottery, mostly the underground one, since he was young. At first he played it just for fun. But after winning a big prize he became addicted to it, even, he admitted, passionate about it. In the past, he travelled across the Deep South to meet with the lottery number makers and to search for numbers on sacred trees and other miraculous items and venues. He also held rituals in cemeteries at night to derive winning lottery numbers. He said it was not only him but also many other people who packed themselves in pick-up trucks to go searching for lottery numbers in different places. These activities mostly stopped after 2004, when the insurgency restarted and local travel became unsafe. Now, he primarily selects lottery numbers by calling a Chinese agent in Raman, who is a representative of a Chinese lottery syndicate operating throughout Yala, involved in both the Thai and Malaysian lotteries.

Asked if his involvement with the underground lottery was sinful, Talib said, "Yes. But I cannot help it." Asked if any religious leaders had rebuked him, he said, "No. It's my personal right." He added that, as a Muslim, it is only he who must accept the fruits of his deeds, and it is only Allah, he said, "to whom I am accountable". In addition, he said:

> Muslims can cleanse all their sins by making a promise with Allah that they will never do it again. Allah will forgive you if you keep the promise. But the sin will be double if you fail to do so. I will make a deal with Allah when I am old that I will quit playing the lottery, because at the time I will not have the appetite to do so, and my past sins will be cleansed.

Making a deal with Allah is a common practice among Guba residents when it comes to the question of sin. Jamal, a big fan of various kinds of entertainment, said that to indulge oneself in worldly entertainment is sinful in Islam. But he cannot help it. What he can do is this, he said: "I will make a deal with Allah when I am old that I will not get involved with fun things anymore. My past sin then will be cleansed, and I will not be punished for it after I die." Likewise, Ishak said that he no longer played any local performances after making a deal with Allah. He has been able to keep the promise because, he said, "I am already old and I don't want to play it anymore."

The other way to deal with sin is to categorize it along the degree of severity. Some activities are regarded as grave sins, while others are only minor. Most of the "sinful" activities that villagers engage in are considered, especially by the practitioners themselves, as minor sins. Azlan smilingly admitted that it is sinful to hold bird-singing contests on Friday mornings. But there were no other time slots left during which the contests could be held, and so the sin was considered minor. He said that it was acceptable as long as the contest was finished before noon, so that everyone could attend Friday noon prayers at the mosque. The contest was therefore left uncriticized, and it drew about 100–120 contestants every Friday. Likewise, Talib said that buying underground lottery tickets is sinful in Islam, but it is not a grave sin. Some people, including him, then still indulge in the practice with no pressure from others to quit.

In the case of grave sins such as alcohol consumption and drug use, those who are involved try to reinterpret the matter. Wasim, a seventeen-year-old boy, said that he has been addicted to *kratom* cocktails for more than two years. He feels moody and restless whenever he needs it. This is particularly the case when he goes to a bigger town such as Yala city, where *kratom* cocktails are hard to find. However, the desperate need for *kratom* can be relieved by drinking beer. Wasim admitted that beer consumption is a grave sin in Islam as well, but he has found a way to reinterpret the act of drinking alcohol to erase the sin. He said: "People say that drinking a drop of beer invalidates forty prayers. But I think it's OK to drink a glass of beer or whiskey because the drops are too many and too fast to be counted when you pour beer into a glass." Given this way of looking at it, Wasim keeps drinking beer whenever he has to or wants to.

The reinterpretation of Islam is not limited to those engaged in "sinful" activities, nor is it exclusively reserved for religious leaders and ulama. Rather, it is a common practice among Muslims of the Deep South in general. A religion with no mediators between God and his followers, Islam places Muslims practically in the presence of Allah, where not only negotiations with Allah but also interpretations of his commands are an integral part of religious life. I commonly saw Guba residents discussing religious issues and drawing from various sources of reference to support their positions.

One night I visited Daessa's home with Aiman. We intended to discuss her involvement in various state-appointed groups. However, at one point our conversation turned to the topic of contraception. She said that about 80 per cent of married Guba women use birth control — some by getting shots but most preferring to take contraceptive pills. (Her estimate is reliable, given her position as a village health volunteer.) These women try to use contraception secretly, as it is in conflict with religious principles. However, Daessa said that the practice is widely known but has never been brought up for public discussion, by religious leaders or others. In addition, she said that her own use of contraception — getting a birth control shot and having sexual intercourse only within seven days before and after her menstrual period — is allowed, because, she reasoned, "I had two birth surgeries in a row, which makes it dangerous for me to have another child. I have learned from the Koran that, in cases like mine, birth control is allowed." Aiman added that another method of birth control that adheres to religious principles is coitus interruptus, because, he said, "the Prophet did it."

Daessa, on another occasion, also cited the Koran when discussing the issue of not working on Friday morning. She said that, to her knowledge, there is no verse in the Koran that prohibits working during this time. So she continues to tap rubber Friday mornings with no fear of being rebuked, even by devout residents and religious leaders. She lamented, "I am poor. So I have to earn money as much as I can to support my family, to raise my kids. It always rains here. There are not many days when I can tap rubber. So I cannot afford to lose a Friday if it doesn't rain." Her position was supported by Dahari, a southern Guba mosque committee member. He said that the Koran merely states that Muslims, especially men, should make themselves free on Friday morning so they can prepare for noon prayers at the mosque. But the Koran does not prohibit working; Muslims can work on Friday morning as long as they do not fail to perform the noon prayers at the mosque. So Dahari and his wife, a Koran reading teacher, also continue to tap rubber on Friday mornings, as indeed do many other residents.

5.2. Modifying the Malay World

Islamic reform in Thailand's southernmost region since the 1970s has shaped the way in which people carry on with their everyday lives. Many practices deemed not in line with Islam have been abandoned. Ishak said that, in the past, many residents raised dogs for hunting, herding and guarding. He himself raised three dogs to hunt wildfowl and to safeguard the house. He said that everybody was aware that it is sinful to raise dogs, but they still did so as there was no pressure on them to end the practice at the time. Things began to change when people who had received higher education in religion, especially abroad, returned home and started to raise the issue. Many people in Guba, including Ishak, then stopped keeping dogs, and the dogs were left to fend for themselves. Likewise, many beliefs and rituals believed to be in conflict with Islam were discontinued. The bathing ritual held near the cemetery was abolished on the grounds that it polluted the cemetery, and spirit worship was discarded as it is only Allah whom Muslims are allowed to revere. However, as mentioned earlier, these local beliefs and practices are far from extinct. Many Malays in southern Thailand, strongly feeling their Malay roots, have employed various techniques to modify their cultural practices to be in accordance with Islam.[2] Aiman's activities are one example.

Aiman is a person of many talents, but his dominant roles are as a ritual specialist and a local artist. He is frequently sought out by people to perform rituals such as preventing rain and healing sicknesses by using supernatural beliefs and magic. These practices are actually not in line with Islam, but Aiman has employed some techniques to render them acceptable. The first technique is "crediting Allah". Aiman said that his ability to prevent rain does not come from any spell or special gift but from knowing how to request a blessing from Allah, who himself then prevents the rain. Other ritual specialists and *bomohs* have also begun crediting Allah for results once attributed to supernatural powers. Nah said that she does not use magic or spells. She just thinks of or mentions Allah and recites the Koran when she performs rituals or chants incantations over rice grains. Likewise, a traditional masseur at Pahong Gayu said that he chants a certain line in Arabic when massaging those suffering from sprains: "It is not me who performs the massage, but it is God who does it."

The second technique Aiman uses when he performs rituals such that they are in line with Islam is "despiritualization". He said that one specific ritual that may not be in line with Islam is *wai khru*, intended to pay respect to performing arts teachers, because it involves belief in a teacher's spirit. To bring the ritual in line with Islam, he interprets it as paying respect to living teachers, not their spirits. He also explains to his fellow performers who believe that, in their own performance, they are possessed by their teacher's spirit, that the "possession" is in fact about their own minds and thoughts; it has nothing to do with the spirits. As he put it: "I told those who thought they were possessed by their teachers' spirits that it's just about their mind. It is because their mind wants to believe. It is like teens who want to dance when they hear the sound of drums and music. It is the same when they want to move their body when hearing the sound of the flute in *silat*."

Aiman's third technique is "secularization". He employs this technique in cases where beliefs and practices are potentially associated with other religions. For example, Aiman said that pious Muslims would not get involved with a wooden penis, believing it to be associated with Brahmanism and Hinduism, or even Buddhism. But he justifies carving wooden penises for his friend by saying that the activity has nothing to do with any religion or belief. He insists: "I'm not making a Buddha image or a statue of any god. What I make is just a work of art. What my customers do with them afterward is none of my business." Likewise, he said that he has stripped *bungor sireh* of the Hindu notion of Mount Meru, so that the practice involves Malay culture and not religion.

Another technique Aiman uses is "aligning with the Prophet". He said that, although musical performance is considered sinful in Islam, to play a musical instrument like drum is not because drums were played to welcome the Prophet home when he returned from battles. Given that local performing arts consist of playing drums, they are therefore not sinful, he said.

Other *bomohs* sometimes employ different techniques to render their services acceptable. For instance, "Islamization" is similar to Aiman's "crediting Allah" technique in that it attributes the results of certain Malay rituals to Islam or Allah. Qasim strikes those who are possessed by spirits with a piece of prayer cloth while chanting verses of the Koran in order to expel spirits. He said that, in the past, some exorcists chanted spells that had no known origin, but now no one chants these spells because they are not in line with Islam. To him, as a Muslim, Allah is the Almighty, and all that exists in this world, including the spirits, is inferior to Allah. It is the power of Allah that forces spirits to leave possessed bodies, he said.

Given these various techniques employed, Malay beliefs and rituals are still vibrant in Guba, with many people still practising or calling upon them.

5.3. Outsmarting the State

Living in a region where questions of state sovereignty and citizens' allegiance are at stake, Muslims in southern Thailand are in a position to engage with the state to a greater degree and via more channels than their fellow citizens in other parts of the country. In addition to general obligations such as primary education and conscription, they must perform their citizenship via cooperation with government agencies — especially those involving state security — which, after the new eruption of the insurgency in 2004, have come to their door.

Unlike most days, Daessa, on the morning of 3 July 2009, did not tap rubber as usual, but she stopped by the family's house wearing a special outfit — sweat pants and a sweat shirt with the emblem of the village health volunteers printed on it. She said that she was on her way to attend an oath of allegiance ceremony (at which participants swear they will not support the insurgents) to be held at the Pa Ou mosque compound around noon. She further said that the ceremony would be conducted by paramilitary rangers to ensure the allegiance of those in the risk group and that there would be around 500 attendees, mostly from village 5. Asked if she was considered to be in the risk group, she said, "No". The reason why she had to attend the ceremony is that the subdistrict headman, the ceremony's civilian coordinator, had asked state-appointed groups such as the housewives' group and village health volunteers group of each village to send their representatives to attend the ceremony.

Daessa, like Faara, the schoolgirl introduced in Chapter 3, participated in the ceremony as requested. She entered the tent, sat down, and was given a paper national flag by a female paramilitary ranger while waiting for the person who would preside over the ceremony. When this person, Lieutenant General Kasikorn Kirisri, arrived and walked past the tent, she along with other attendees, mostly schoolchildren, waved their flags to welcome him and other senior government officials such as the Raman district chief and a paramilitary ranger commander. She also gave the oath of allegiance, following the subdistrict headman's lead. She hoped, like Faara, that the number printed on her flag would be announced when a paramilitary ranger draw lots for prizes, but she was disappointed in that wish. She got her lunch at a makeshift kitchen and brought the food to eat in the tent with her friends. She chatted with her friends for a bit after lunch before returning home on her motorcycle, accomplishing her mission as a village health volunteer.

I saw Daessa again that evening when she stopped by to meet Maeh at the house. I asked how she felt about the ceremony, and she said that she felt nothing; she just went there in accordance with the subdistrict headman's request. I further asked her about the oath of allegiance she had made, and she said that she felt nothing about that, either; she just repeated the words without paying attention to their meaning and did not remember what they were exactly about. So I asked her if she was not afraid of being targeted by the insurgents for cooperating with the military like this, and she said, "No, because they know that we were forced to attend the ceremony and we didn't mean the oath literally." Her reasoning was shared by Saifuldin, who said that he likewise just repeated the words with no intention and did not mean them literally. He even turned down Mohammed's invitation to meet a paramilitary ranger who was a friend of his for fear of being targeted. Mohammed used a different strategy; he joined those in the kitchen during the ceremony so that he did not have to swear the oath. The military's effort to gain the allegiance of these residents via the oath-swearing ceremony thus failed miserably.

However, Muslims in the South engage with the state in other ways than simply resistance or surrender. Sometimes, they seek to outsmart the state through its mediators. An encounter between Effendi and the district military registrar is a case in point. Effendi is a man with several connections, especially among state authorities. He has used his connections to help out other villagers with a variety of problems. Many elders, he claimed, were receiving their pensions because of his intervention, and many residents got their health care cards after he talked to the officials in charge. He said that he helped people without asking for anything in return. His claims notwithstanding, it is not these "charitable missions" that render Effendi's role critical when it comes to dealing with the state. Rather, it is the services he charges for having to do with the conscription that are indispensable to many residents.

One week before the conscription day in 2009, Effendi told me that he had three customers — one fewer than the previous year — who asked him to get their sons out of the conscription. He said the service charge per case was 50,000 baht, of which 40,000 baht goes to the district military registrar (who would distribute the money among state authorities) and 10,000 baht is his fee. Apparently, two customers had already paid whereas the third promised to pay in two days' time. He said he had been in this business for a couple of years, after a government official he used to work with introduced him to the district military registrar, who later invited him to join the business. He said that the reason why he decided to accept the invitation was not so much about the money, which in fact is substantial, but because he "pitied the villagers". He asked me if I was planning to go watch the conscription at the Raman district office building, and I said, "Yes". He said he would go as well and hoped to see me there.

Effendi arrived at the conscription station in the afternoon. When he saw me, he greeted me and then walked me through the crowd to find a place to sit in front of the district building. Before we reached the building, he met a government official he was familiar with. He introduced me and then talked to the official for awhile before leading me to the district building. We sat and chatted in front of the building for about twenty minutes and then walked to the conscription station, as the red and black card-drawing procedure was imminent. As soon as he saw the district military registrar, he greeted him with a *wai*, and the registrar, who is a Thai Buddhist, *wai*'d him back although he was very busy, implying that they were acquaintances. When the card-drawing procedure was about to begin, Effendi invited me to go inside the station, which was now fenced off by ropes and surrounded by hundreds of relatives and friends of the conscription participants. I declined his invitation, saying that I would prefer to observe the conscription from outside. So he went inside the station alone and sat among soldiers as well as two other Malay Muslim civilians who also had connections with these state authorities. When the card drawing was finished, he said goodbye to some state officials and met me outside the station. We walked back together along with other Guba residents to the pick-up truck that would take us home.

Effendi came to the roadside pavilion in front of the house where I stayed late the following morning. He said that about 1 million baht had been distributed across the conscription station the previous day, as many residents paid soldiers for "special services". It was easy to conduct such business this year, as there were no other state authorities, for instance, medical doctors from Raman hospital who had previously been in charge of medical exams, getting involved with the conscription process. The military was in charge of everything. During our conversation, Effendi's cell phone rang, and he picked it up. The caller was the father of a man who the previous day had drawn a red card and had to perform military service for one year; given that he had obtained a bachelor's degree, that reduced the usual two-year duration of service by half. The father asked Effendi what he should do and if Effendi could help him out with this. Effendi told the father to take it easy and calm down; the problem could be solved, no worries, he would take care of the matter. After hanging up the phone, he smiled and told me that he had previously told the father to pay for his service before the conscription day, but the father decided to take a chance that his son would draw a black card. Effendi said the problem could be solved by having the conscript sign some documents at a military camp in Pattani, and then he could return home. However, the father would have to pay 60,000 baht, which is 10,000 baht higher than regular service charge before the conscription. Effendi added that his business had been growing since the eruption of renewed violence after 2004, because parents did not want their sons to risk getting killed. He said that some even mortgaged their rubber plantations to get together the money for the payment.

State encounters, however, do not necessarily always put people at a disadvantage. Sometimes, the reverse is the case. One way that the state takes care of local people, as described in Chapter 3, is in providing compensation for farm animals who have been killed in flooding or other natural disasters.

One day Jamal told me that Aryani, a wealthy southern Guba resident, was looking for me to see whether I had any pictures of dead cows. I had no idea why Aryani would ask such a thing and simply responded that I had no such pictures. Later, one night when I was sitting and chatting with Azlan and some other people in the courtyard of Azlan's house, I learned why. Aryani, whose home is across the street, came to join us wearing an elegant Malay dress. Azlan greeted and teased her as she found a place to sit next to him. Apparently she had had dinner with the subdistrict headman and his wife earlier that evening, and Azlan asked where they had gone, what she had eaten, and how the food was. Aryani smiled and said that they had gone to a restaurant in Yala and that the food was really good. Everybody laughed, and Azlan said that Aryani should have bought him and the rest of us some food from the restaurant, given that she had recently received a great deal of compensation money for dead cows. Aryani laughed, and then the conversation moved to other topics. She sat with us for about fifteen minutes before returning home.

Aryani's dinner became a topic of conversation after she left. Azlan said that Aryani had gone out for dinner in Yala with the subdistrict headman and his wife to celebrate the compensation money for dead cows she had received a few days earlier. However, she has no cows. She conspired by having her nephew Aiman take pictures of other people's dead cows and then having the subdistrict headman sign the necessary documents for her. So, after receiving the compensation money for the cows, she invited the subdistrict headman and his wife to have dinner at a luxurious restaurant to show her gratitude for his help. Azlan said that Aryani is clever, but he will not follow her example in this regard. Everybody laughed, and the conversation moved to other topics.

Other residents besides Aryani also know how to make use of the mediated state in this way. Meng, village 1 assistant headman at the time, told me when we met at the Yala Provincial Livestock Office that he had come to pick up the compensation checks for Mana's dead cow and his own dead goats. He said that Mana was getting compensation of 8,000 baht for one dead cow (compared to Wae, who got about 8,000 baht for two dead cows, and Roheng, 10,500 baht for two dead cows) and that he himself would collect 14,000 baht for his three dead goats. He added that the compensation money for the dead goats was higher than the regular rate, a result facilitated by a bribe paid to the district livestock official in the amount of 2,000 baht. I asked Meng how many people knew how to make use of this channel, and he said, "Only few in the circle know this." I asked if Mana, his father-in-law, knew that he had paid the bribe, and he said, "No. I didn't tell him about this." I then asked Meng why he did not tell other residents about this channel so they could also make use of it, and he said he could not because, he reasoned, "it is illegal".

To "outsmart" the state sometimes is to break the law. But this does not concern people that much, as many of them do not believe in the law, which is in effect an extension of the Thai state, in the first place.

5.4. Observing the Insurgents' and Strongmen's Rules

As mentioned in Chapter 2, according to Talib, the teashop owner and village 2 assistant headman, local Malays who are involved with the unrest can be divided into three groups – ideological leaders, the operatives and the propagandists. Although the first two groups are no longer active because they are closely monitored by the military and many have fled to other places, the third group is still active, using public spaces, especially teashops, to spread their version of the news and arouse local people. As such, everyone, including himself, must exercise great caution when discussing the insurgency. People must constantly determine how best to observe the rules established by those involved in the insurgency in their everyday lives.

Residents in charge of security find this question most compelling. As in other villages of the Deep South, the village 1 security team was appointed by the Ministry of Interior in response to the unrest. However, this project was doomed to fail from the very beginning. Of thirty positions, only twenty were filled and those only with Mana's strong persuasion, because most residents do not want to get in trouble. In addition, security team members then gradually quit, one by one, partly because they were not getting their monthly salary from Mana, who allegedly pocketed the money himself, and partly because they were afraid they might be killed, as the insurgents' leaflets warned. During 2009–13, there were only a few security team members in village 1, and many suspected that Mana was still receiving monthly salaries for the team totaling 40,000 baht a month.

The situation improved a bit after Meng was elected the new village headman in 2014.

Almost all security affairs are overseen by the assistant village headman for security affairs (*phu chuay phuyai ban fai raksa khwamsangop*, ผู้ช่วยผู้ใหญ่บ้านฝ่ายรักษาความสงบ, ผรส). Their primary task with regard to the insurgency is to guard the childcare centre at the northern Guba mosque compound at night; the centre is regarded as the most valuable state property in the village. Mahrus, the village 1 assistant headman for security affairs, said, while we were chatting at the post in front of the northern Guba mosque compound, that every night three assistant village headmen for security affairs are stationed there to guard the childcare centre. He himself is at the post every night, whereas the other two are on duty every other night. Some nights, Pahong Gayu soldiers come join them until morning. Mahrus said that, so far, there had been no incidents at the post, although there are still some insurgents in the area. He admitted that he is scared but believes that the insurgents will spare him because, he said, "I behave properly. I know that they keep an eye on me all the time. So I need to behave well. Don't make them feel that you are having problems with them or want to be their enemy."

Ordinary villagers also have to "behave properly" according to the insurgents' rules. This code of conduct primarily entails avoiding special or close relationships with the military, pleading ignorance about the insurgents when asked by the authorities, doing nothing to obstruct insurgent operations, and conforming to the insurgents' special demands. For example, Saifuldin refrained from introducing himself to a middle-ranking soldier at the oath-swearing ceremony even though the soldier is his friend's friend, fearful that even such an innocent act might prompt the insurgents to target him. He said, "I would surely be in trouble if he [the soldier] came to visit me at my house afterward. They may think I work with the military, and that means I may as well dig a grave for myself." Jamal said that he is not afraid of the insurgents because he knows how to deal with them: "They are on their business and we are on ours. If we don't block their way, they will not harm us." Likewise, Bakhtiar said that he was not worried about being targeted by the insurgents after talking with some soldiers, because "they know that I was just talking to some Malay Muslims like us. It's just a casual talk; nothing much."

Although most residents find that they are able to observe this code of conduct, some find it difficult, especially when it comes to special demands made by the insurgents. Some people were specifically approached by the insurgents and told to cooperate, whether they were willing or not.

For example, the "Uncle" of Pa Ou village had to make his isolated home available to the insurgents to carry out their operations, although he was unwilling to do so in the beginning. A southern Guba resident said that he had to let the insurgents keep their weapons at his home; otherwise, he and his family would be in trouble. Such acts of compliance are necessary if villagers wish to continue with their normal lives.

In addition to the insurgents or Okhrae Dalae, people must observe the rules established by other influential figures. As mentioned earlier, on one occasion I accidentally stumbled upon a *kratom* cocktail business transaction taking place near the riverbank; the seller, thinking I was spying on him, phoned Saifuldin to call me off. Saifuldin later warned me not to go there again; otherwise, he himself might be accused of sheltering "an undercover policeman". Likewise, Jamal said not to interfere with people in *kratom* cocktail rings. As long as their business did not create severe problems, it was best not to obstruct them, he said. Avoidance was the best policy.

However, the strongman whom people deem the most daunting is not in village 1 or in Arzeulee subdistrict, but is Jasim, the Burong Kueteetae subdistrict headman. As mentioned in Chapter 3, Jasim occasionally exerted his influence over Guba and nearby villages. His alleged vested interests in development projects and the Saiburi Dam construction project had the effect of silencing people. The village 2 headman was appointed with no election; no one dared run against the eventual appointee, given Jasim's support for him. Almost all the village headmen in Arzeulee subdistrict are under Jasim's control and consider Jasim to be their "supervisor". Jasim's influence manifests itself even in cultural spheres, the wedding of Yaakob's niece being a case in point.

5.5. "Puloh Yaakob": Encountering de facto Sovereignty

The wedding of Yaakob's niece, an event that people referred to as Puloh Yaakob, was the biggest event in recent memory in Arzeulee subdistrict. A large, deserted area along the main road, across the road from Yaakob's house, was cleared up about ten days before the event. Eight tents were set up for the guests to sit and eat in, three elevated stages were built for food preparation and dishwashing, three large holes were dug for cooking rice using a special method, five stoves were installed, hundreds of coconuts were brought in, several cows were brought in and tied to poles, and other preparations made. The night before the wedding, dinner was provided for the villagers, and the following morning many either tapped rubber earlier than normal or took the day off in order to help out with the ceremony. The road was lined with dozens of stands and vendors selling snacks, sweets, food, clothes, toys, CDs, and other items, while a mobile merry-go-round was being installed. Guests arrived gradually and soon outnumbered the tables and chairs, paralysing traffic by the afternoon. It was not until darkness fell that the guests stopped arriving, almost 3,000 of them. The focus shifted to a shadow puppet theatre that had been temporarily built along the main road. The shadow puppet show started at about midnight and ended more than three hours later, marking the end of an event that villagers said was the biggest they had ever seen.

What Puloh Yaakob means to Guba residents, however, is not simply the largest wedding they remember ever being held in the area, a fact that many of them take great pride in. More so, it is a crucial event through which Guba residents, especially Yaakob, the host, encountered the power of Jasim, whom they regard as the most influential figure in Raman and nearby districts.

Yaakob told me about two months before the wedding that he wanted the ceremony to be as big as possible, even though it was for his niece, not any of his own children. He said that he planned to invite some 3,000 guests not only from the Deep South but also from nearby provinces such as Songkhla and Satun, where he also has customers for his hajj business. He wanted the wedding to be a perfectly exemplary traditional Malay wedding, and he also wanted to have a *dangdut* band (*dangdut* being a popular Malay musical style) perform on the wedding night to entertain his fellow residents, who, he reasoned, had had little chance to indulge in entertainment given the insurgency. In addition, he wanted to make sure that it would not rain on the wedding day and that the food would be eaten properly, not greedily. Then he told me who in the village had been tasked with what assignments for the wedding.

Aiman, an expert in Malay culture, was tasked with the procurement of the Malay wedding throne and arch. He actually had long planned to buy a set of Malay wedding items from Malaysia to rent out — a business resembling that of a wedding studio. He had done research by studying Malaysia's leading fashion magazines and consulting with experts in Malay weddings. After Yaakob contacted him about the wedding throne and arch, Aiman decided that the time had come for him to start up his dream business. He had Najmudin drive him to Malaysia to buy a Malay wedding set. Then he installed the throne and arch as well as other items in front of Yaakob's house two nights before the wedding, with the assistance of several friends. It took until almost four o'clock in the morning of the wedding day for the installation to be completed.

Despite his expertise in conducting rituals, Aiman was not tasked with performing the rain-prevention ritual. Yaakob said that he wanted Aiman to focus his attention on the wedding itself, and he would have Zarif, another ritual specialist, do it instead. The ritual was performed on the morning of the wedding day. Zarif positioned a set of betel leaves and nuts under a tree next to Yaakob's house and chanted spells over them. Meanwhile, Yaakob's aunt, who had just returned from Saudi Arabia, suggested that a ritual to prevent excessive, wasteful, and greedy consumption be performed and that she would find the practitioner. Yaakob agreed, and the ritual was performed on the day before the wedding; the practitioner chanted incantations over a pile of rice grains and then put those grains on top of the sacks of rice that would be cooked for the guests.

Mamduh, who held many state-appointed positions, was in charge of the water supply system. The day before the wedding, he along with several other men set up a water supply system across from the ceremonial area, near the dish-washing station, rice-cooking stoves, and kitchen. When night fell, two men climbed down to the bottom of the well to set up a water pump, because the village tap water would be insufficient for the wedding activities. On the morning of the wedding, he also called the village 2 headman, who had a good relationship with the local military, asking him to contact the military to provide additional water when it turned out that the well water was running out. The headman came to the wedding to coordinate with the soldiers, who arrived with a military water truck.

These people all performed their assigned tasks efficiently, and everything went as planned. The wedding throne and arch were set up in time and were lauded for their beauty and elegance — many guests took pictures of themselves sitting on the throne, or posing there with the bride and bridegroom. There was plenty of water, even during the peak time when the dishwashers were working hard at their chore. Likewise, it did not rain in Guba, although the rain poured down in surrounding villages. Importantly, Yaakob said to me with a smile on his face two days after the wedding that the guests ate very properly — there was no greedy or wasteful consumption of food — and only nine sacks of rice were cooked and four cows killed for the nearly 3,000 attending guests. Instead of losing money as he had anticipated, he actually profited from the wedding, given the customary cash contributions made by attendees.

While pleased with these successes, however, Yaakob was deeply disappointed with one detail that did not work out: the *dangdut* band.

Despite all his determination, his attempts to procure the band failed miserably. Jasim accounts for the failure.

Three weeks before the wedding day, Yaakob asked me if I could do him a favour. He wanted me to convince Saifuldin to support the idea of a *dangdut* show on the wedding night. He said that Saifuldin disagreed with this idea, on the grounds that it was improper for a *zae*, or hajj pilgrim team leader, to stage a *dangdut* show at a wedding he was hosting (*dangdut* shows being known for their "suggestive" content). I smiled and said, "No worries, I will take care of the matter." At first I thought that Saifuldin was not too serious about the issue, but I was totally wrong. He vehemently expressed his opposition to Yaakob's idea, saying: "I totally disagree with him. He is a *zae* and has been to Mecca several times. He also has a son who is an imam whom many people respect. If he were a layperson, that would be fine and I would not oppose him. What would he say if *ustaz* came and see this? This will make him an object of humiliation." Nevertheless, Saifuldin added that he would be fine with whatever Yaakob decided to do, because Yaakob is his good friend. He was just afraid that Yaakob's reputation would be tarnished.

In addition to Saifuldin, Yaakob's wife and son also strongly opposed the *dangdut* idea. Yaakob's wife is a devout Muslim; she attends Koran reading classes on Tuesday and Sunday afternoons and also performs an extra prayer at the mosque every night during the month of Ramadan. So she disagreed with Yaakob about the *dangdut* performance, saying that it was religiously improper — female *dangdut* singers tend to wear close-fitting outfits and dance sensually. Likewise, his son, who is always sought out to perform the imam's duty during the month of Ramadan, did not support the idea. He said that *dangdut* was improper, as it is too sensual and nasty. Yaakob did not argue with his wife and son, mainly because their reasoning was sound, but he did not give up on his plan, either. Aware of potential risk, he decided not to negotiate for a *dangdut* performance directly. He had Talib and Ghalib, who are well known for their ability to engage with such matters, take care of it.

Talib said that Yaakob, without his wife's knowledge, had given him a sum of 5,000 baht for the hiring of the *dangdut* band, which would cost a total of 15,000 baht. He said that of the 10,000 baht shortfall, 5,000 would be sought from the Arzeulee SAO chief executive and the other 5,000 would be raised from among the villagers. Talib was also tasked with raising this money. So I told him I would donate 500 baht, and he accepted my offer. Talib said further that Ghalib, the SAO chief executive's "right-hand man", would be in charge of contacting the *dangdut* band, given his involvement in that circle.

Yaakob's plan to have Blue Star, a famous *dangdut* band, perform on the wedding night became widely known among the residents. Except for Yaakob's wife and his son, no one else openly opposed his plan or accused him of impropriety. Some elders complained a little bit about *dangdut*'s "modernity", but none of them raised the issue of properness or morality. Ihsan, my *silat* teacher, whose practices often raise a red flag among strict Muslims, laughed out loud when he learned that Yaakob, a respectable *zae* and New Group practitioner, would have a *dangdut* band perform at his niece's wedding. Most people did not see anything wrong with *dangdut* and supported Yaakob's plan, partly because there had not been a musical show in Guba for a long time given the unrest and partly because it was extremely rare to have such a famous *dangdut* troupe perform for free in a rural village like Guba. The *dangdut* show then became the talk of the village, and people awaited it attentively.

The booking of the band went as planned. Talib said that, in addition to me, many other residents donated money to support payment for the band. These included Uday (a major *kratom* cocktail producer/seller), Azlan (village 1 Red-Whiskered Bulbul Club chairman), Effendi (a rubber trader), the village 1 and village 2 SAO members, and the SAO chief executive. Talib also said that Ghalib had returned home and been in contact with the *dangdut* band manager. At this stage, Ghalib was trying to bargain down the price — from the quoted 15,000 baht to 13,000 baht. One day later, Talib shook my hand with satisfaction when I entered his teashop. He said that the deal was done, although the effort to bargain down the price had not succeeded. In a day or two, Ghalib would go meet with the band manager in Yala city to make the down payment. Everyone in the teashop was cheerful. The most famous *dangdut* troupe in southern Thailand was coming to perform in Guba.

This excitement, however, lasted only two days. Two nights before the wedding, my wife and I went to the wedding site to see the preparations, and then we went to Talib's teashop across the street to get updates as usual. Talib was sitting at his usual table in the back of the shop, alone and looking downcast. He raised his head when he noticed us and said only, "We lost", in despair. He said that the verbal deal on the *dangdut* troupe had been cancelled, as the manager that morning had suddenly signed a contract with another customer who had just contacted him two days earlier. The new contract was to perform at the wedding of Lohman Buffalo's daughter, which happened to fall on the same day as that of

Yaakob's niece. Talib said that he and some others had heard about this only yesterday, but the news was confirmed that afternoon when Ghalib met with the manager at the manager's house in Yala after being unable to contact him via cell phone throughout the morning. After learning why the manager had been compelled to renege on his original agreement and sign with a new customer, Ghalib neither tried to negotiate, nor did he blame the manager. The only thing he could do was to leave the manager's house in "defeat", to use Talib's word. Then Talib returned the money I had donated and said that he would reimburse the other donors soon. The *dangdut* affair was over.

The failure to procure the *dangdut* troupe brought disappointment to the villagers. Jamal, a big fan of live entertainment, said that it was a pity, as this was a very rare opportunity to watch a famous *dangdut* band perform in his village for free. Daessa said that she would now have to cancel her plan to sell sweets on the wedding night, as she could only be assured of adequate business if the band was present. However, it was Yaakob who not only felt disappointed but indeed angry when he learned about the cancellation of the deal. On the one hand, he felt angry because he had been through arguments with his wife, his son and his close friends and had risked his reputation as a respectable *zae* to procure the band. On the other hand, he was angry because there was nothing he could do. He could not blame Ghalib, as the circumstances were beyond his ability to control. Nor could he solve the problem through his own influence. He categorically rejected Talib's proposal that some other *dangdut* band be procured, saying that they were not sufficiently noteworthy. If the intended *dangdut* troupe was unavailable, he said, there would be no *dangdut* show on the wedding night. All anyone could do, then, was to leave Yaakob walking furiously back and forth alone across the wedding grounds.

"Lohman Buffalo" is an alias of the Burong Kueteetae SAO chief executive. Although influential in his own right, Lohman Buffalo did not account for Guba's forced capitulation in the matter. Rather, Jasim does. Jasim is Lohman Buffalo's uncle, and, as Burong Kueteetae subdistrict's headman, got him elected the subdistrict's SAO chief executive. The wedding of Lohman Buffalo's daughter, then, had the shadow of Jasim lurking behind it. And, given Jasim's daunting power, it is understandable why Yaakob and others in Guba had no choice but to give up their plan. It is also understandable why the *dangdut* manager had to break his word to Ghalib. Other famous *dangdut* bands in Yala were also summoned to perform at Jasim's event, and about a hundred cars were "invited" to participate in the wedding motorcade so as to show the might of Jasim. No one dared to refuse his "invitation".

As mentioned earlier, Jasim is not a stranger to Yaakob. He spent part of his childhood in Guba at the house of relatives who also had kin relations with Yaakob's mother. Yaakob was advised by his maternal younger aunt that he should deliver a wedding invitation to Jasim at his house (not yet knowing about Jasim's own event on the wedding day). Initially, Yaakob was reluctant to do so because, he said, "I don't want to get involved with the influential figures because they are uneducated, irrational, and difficult to understand and deal with." However, after his aunt's strong insistence and her promise to accompany him, Yaakob eventually decided to go to Jasim's house to deliver the card in person, about two weeks before the wedding day. He said that Jasim's house is big, has a strong perimeter wall, and is guarded by many territorial defence volunteers. It took him awhile to gather the courage to drive his pick-up truck through the gate with his aunt and Talib's older sister. The territorial defence volunteers interrogated him and his passengers for a few minutes before letting them in. Yaakob said that his aunt then led the conversation with Jasim while he just sat listening and answering a few questions when asked. Jasim said that he might not be able to attend the wedding but that he would have one of his wives come instead. (It turned out that his daughter-in-law came on his behalf.) The awkward conversation lasted about ten minutes, and then Yaakob and the others left with relief. This was the first time Yaakob had encountered Jasim in person, and he sensed how powerful Jasim is. The failure to procure the *dangdut* troupe was the second time he experienced that insurmountable power.

Why is Jasim so terrifying in the eyes of Yaakob and other people in Yala? Is it because he is ascribed with authority as a subdistrict headman that enables him to use violence against anyone he wants? Or is it because he is able to suspend the application of law that forces people to comply with his wishes? Judging from people's narratives about Jasim's ability to use violence at the expense of law, the latter seems to be the case.

Giorgio Agamben, as mentioned in the introduction, maintains that, rather than a person within the political order invested with power, the sovereign is the one who decides on the state of exception (1998, p. 11) and who has the power to take life without being considered to have committed homicide or sacrifice (1998, p. 142). Thomas Blom Hansen and Finn Stepputat (2006, pp. 296–97), building on Agamben's notion of sovereign power, propose a notion of de facto sovereignty — "the ability to kill, punish, and discipline with impunity" — as a call to abandon sovereignty as an ontological basis of power and order in favour of sovereignty as a tentative and emergent form of authority grounded in violence. It is these abilities that render Jasim the sovereign among the residents.

As mentioned in Chapter 3, it is widely known among the residents that Jasim is ruthless and "real", ruling over his territory by the use of violence. His ability to suspend the application of law in order to maintain his dominance is the primary reason why people find him daunting. Saifuldin abruptly changed his mind about attending Talib's mother's funeral ceremony after learning that two subordinates of Jasim would be there for fear that, he said, "they will scold me for protesting the dam construction project Jasim has interests in. They carry M16s, and I'm not sure what they might do if they get pissed off." Likewise, Yaakob said in despair that there was nothing he could do about the *dangdut* band if it was wanted by Jasim's relative. He added: "Jasim is the kind of person you should refrain from crossing, or not obstruct, as he can kill you if he wants to. And no one can hold him accountable. You will die at no cost to him." Jasim generates and executes his sovereign power over the residents of Raman and nearby districts by flaunting his ability to take life at will and with impunity.

However, as Hansen and Stepputat (2005, p. 36) point out, de facto sovereignty has multiple forms that are in constant competition with one another. As such, in addition to Jasim, there are other de facto sovereigns who exert their power in Guba. This has particularly been the case during the recent unrest, in which the absence of law enforcement officers has allowed for the prosperity of illegal businesses and crime rings; in such circumstances, order is not maintained by the rule of law as much as by the use of violence. People are terrified by *kratom* dealers because they reinforce their own rules via the use of violence, while the chance for litigation against them is very slim. Likewise, the main reason why the residents observe the insurgents' rules is not so much because they agree with those rules or their justifications as because they are afraid of the insurgents' ability to kill with impunity. Importantly, many people are likewise afraid of state authorities, especially soldiers, not because they direct the enforcement of the law but because they are able to use violence at the expense of the law, rendering them de facto sovereigns in the eyes of the people of the South.

Although the decision to obey these de facto sovereigns is a matter of life and death, how people articulate their obedience is far more complex than simply total surrender. People initiate various strategies that enable them to engage these sovereigns as their subjects and simultaneously obtain agency to accomplish what they wish through these same sovereign powers. I will examine this topic in the following chapter.

Notes

1. Guba residents' selectively drawing on and interpreting Islam to justify their actions can be conceived as part of what John Richard Bowen called "socially embedded forms of public reasoning" (2003, p. 5). According to Bowen, Islam does not consist of "a fixed set of rules" (2003, p. 19). Rather, it is a collection of multiple, diverse and competing norms from which Muslims selectively draw and interpret to justify their acts and arguments. Rather than focusing on the content of major religious texts such as the Koran and the Hadith, he focuses on the "struggles by Indonesians to reconcile, or select among, competing sets of values and norms" (2003, p. 10) to understand how they "justify what they do in specific, generally conflict-ridden, social settings" (2003, p. 7). For example, he maintains, in developing arguments the villagers, jurists and activists present as evidence ideas about what God had said, Umar's *fiqh* reasoning, the diversity of the *adat*, surveys about local norms, how the ancestors think, legal aid cases, village labour patterns, and even "whether Megawati Sukarnoputri could remarry" (2003, p. 261).

2. In examining how tensions over rituals and religious practices between traditionalists/villagers and modernists/townspeople of the Gayo ethnic group in Sumatra were prevented from escalating into open conflicts and violent confrontations, John Richard Bowen (1993) submits that at least three mechanisms were involved. First is the specific logic of the ritual. Rather than confronting a suspected sorcerer or making public accusations, Gayo healers draw on magical resources to covertly counter the sorcerer's activities and exact retribution. This particular selection and recasting of Muslim elements prevent the harsh feelings and accusations directed against purported sorcerers from escalating into large-scale conflicts (Bowen 1993, pp. 151–52, 164). Second is the compartmentalization of the ritual. By splitting rituals into two stages — one involving the secluded specialists' communication and transaction with the spirits, and the other involving public communication with and sacrifice for God — the Gayo were able to ignore one part of the ritual and participate in the other (1993, p. 237) and hold divergent opinions without ever having to confront their differences publicly (1993, p. 181). Third is avoidance. When confrontation is inevitable and irreconcilable, the Gayo resort to social avoidance to prevent confrontation from developing into physical violence. Many villagers avoid the mosques, because worship is conducted in a modern manner (1993, p. 308), whereas controversy over whether regular noon worship should be carried out after the Friday worship led villagers to build new mosques. In some cases, they left their villages if they were unable to settle religious disputes (1993, pp. 309–10). In the case of Guba, tensions are not that high, and it is primarily the *bomohs* who play a crucial role in calming down volatile situations.

6

Engaging with the Sovereigns

The notion of sovereignty has captured attention across academic disciplines, especially in anthropology. Although Thomas Blom Hansen and Finn Stepputat (2006, p. 296) argue that the return of sovereignty as a central concern in anthropology has been informed by the work of Giorgio Agamben, the discussion of sovereignty in anthropology is also informed by Michel Foucault's works. Foucault cautions readers not to view the emergence of governmentality in terms of total replacement. Rather than the elimination of sovereignty by discipline and of discipline by governmentality, what exists, argues Foucault, is a triangularity of sovereignty-discipline-governmentality, which "has as its primary target the population and as its essential mechanism the apparatuses of security" (Foucault 1991, p. 102). Foucault reminds readers of the existence of sovereignty in contemporary power relations, although he has not demonstrated how it operates and converges with the two other modes of power.

Anthropologist Aihwa Ong elaborates on the notion of sovereignty using Foucault as a backdrop. She argues that Agamben conceptualizes the notion of exception too narrowly, regarding it only as a fundamental principle of sovereign rules. The exception, she maintains, can be conceptualized more broadly as "an ordinary departure in policy that can be deployed to include as well as to exclude" (Ong 2006, p. 5). She argues that, in practice, sovereignty is manifested in multiple, contradictory strategies. Rather than a singularity or a simple opposition of normativity and exception, as Agamben suggests, sovereign power is a "shifting and flexible ensemble of heterogeneous calculations, choices, and exceptions that constitute security, life, and ethics" (Ong 2006, p. 10). Drawing on Foucault's notion of governmentality — the right disposition of things, arranged so as to lead to a convenient end

(Foucault 1991, p. 93) — Ong proposes a notion of neoliberal exception, arguing that, rather than simply an economic doctrine, neoliberalism is the most recent development of biopolitics and in particular a governmentality that "relies on market knowledge and calculations for politics of subjection and subject-making" (Ong 2006, p. 13). In addition, Ong maintains that governmentality involves two entangled processes of subjectification: "one is subjected to someone else by control and dependence [subjection], and tied to one's own identity by a conscience of self-knowledge [self-making]" (Ong 2003, p. 15). That is, "while governing technologies are involved in the making of citizens by subjecting them to given rationalities, norms, and practices, individuals also play a part in their own subjectification or self-making" (Ong 2003, p. 16).

While Ong finds Foucault's notion of governmentality helpful in rethinking the notion of sovereignty and subjectification, some writers find it limited in conceiving the ways in which individuals craft subjectivity and obtain and enact agency through the sovereign. Lois McNay (2000, pp. 4–5) argues that the feminist notion of subjectivity and agency, which in part is influenced by Foucault's notion of subjectivation (or two entangled processes of subjectification in Ong's elaboration), is partial, as it remains within a negative paradigm of subjectification. Subject is understood in passive terms as an effect of discursive structures and practices, and agency is regarded as resistance to dominant norms. However, McNay argues, there are circumstances in which subject is crafted and agency is obtained and enacted in active and positive manners. She then proposes a generative paradigm of subjectification examining the ways in which individuals negotiate with meanings and norms that do not necessarily fall into a dichotomy of domination and resistance. Her position has been elaborated by anthropologists working on women's issues in religious spheres.

Sylva Frisk (2009, pp. 12, 14–15), for example, argues that the feminist notion of liberatory subject and subversive agency is inadequate, as it elides women's actions inconceivable by the logic of repression and resistance. Women's religious practices within orthodox Islam do not necessarily challenge the patriarchal structure, nor are women victims of Islamization. Islamic virtues such as shyness and modesty, incompatible with the feminist notion of agency, are the necessary conditions for women's enhanced role in religious and political life. Drawing on McNay's notion of the generative paradigm of subjectification, Frisk examines how urban Malaysian Muslim women's submission to God has transformed them into pious subjects with the agency to enact in religious, political and familial matters.

Guba is a place where sovereigns are engaged in this manner. A full observation of religious duties has turned some ordinary women into pious Muslims ascribed with the authority to exercise in various matters in the name of Allah. Importantly, by crafting themselves as the king's loyal subjects, Guba residents, discontent with state officials, have nevertheless been able to engage them legitimately and authoritatively. This generative subjectification of royal subjects has become pressing in the recent unrest, during which citizens' commitment to state sovereignty is highly demanded.

6.1. Women of Allah

Guba women are anything but stereotypical Muslim women. The middle table in the largest morning teashop is always occupied by three women, whose chatter and laughter dominate the surrounding atmosphere. One of these women, after finishing her breakfast, usually walks across the road to her makeshift office to run her rubber business — buying rubber scrap and rubber milk — until noon. Her overseeing a rubber business is echoed by many other women in Guba who are in charge of various household economic activities ranging from tapping rubber and raising cows and goats to selling agricultural products and managing household incomes and expenses. These women always play a leading role in meetings with state authorities and NGO workers. They constitute the majority of attendees and actively participate in such meetings, while a handful of male participants, who always timidly sit in the rear, only rarely express their opinion or volunteer to join state-appointed groups. In addition, these active women are big fans of and enthusiastic contestants in sports, games and other recreational activities. With only a quick glance, it is easy to be impressed by the ways in which women prevail in Guba.

Guba women also play significant roles in the religious realm. They constitute a large portion of sermon attendees, and there are two Koran-reading classes specifically offered for them whereas there are none for men. Importantly, women tend to urge their husbands to observe religious duties. One husband had to remove a wooden horse from a wooden clock he had purchased before installing it on the wall due to his wife's opposition and suggestion. A male-only meeting about SAO member nominations, which Saifuldin called a *shura*, was stopped when a wife came in and told her husband that it was time for evening prayers. Guba women in turn are only rarely forced by men to perform their religious duties; how to practise Islam is left to their discretion. Some factors contribute to their authority in socio-economic and religious matters; Maeh is a case in point.

Maeh is a woman who has several responsibilities. She gets up early in the morning while her adult children, including Saifuldin and Aiman, are still sleeping, and goes with Wae on a motorcycle to the family's rubber plantations to tap rubber. She returns home with Wae at about eleven o'clock, takes a bath, and puts on clean clothes. Then she goes to the kitchen to prepare lunch for everyone, with her daughters' assistance. Before or while cooking lunch, she often goes out to buy food items such as fish, meat, vegetables, and curry paste as well as sweets and desserts from grocery pick-up trucks. After taking a nap in the afternoon, she does various chores. Sometimes she does housework, such as repairing curtains, airing out mattresses and pillows, sweeping the floors, dusting the walls and ceilings, and so on. Sometimes she does additional chores like peeling and fermenting *sa-tor* (bitter bean) seeds, making durian paste, planting rubber saplings or weeding at the plantation, collecting fruit such as bananas and durians at the family's fruit orchards, and more. She frequently spends time talking with friends and acquaintances in the afternoon and evening before returning to the kitchen to prepare dinner. Her last chore is to wash the dishes after everyone has finished eating dinner.

In addition to her everyday routine, Maeh is in charge of maintaining kin relations. She plays a leading role in taking care of family guests, whether relatives or friends, who visit the home, while Wae joins the conversations quietly. Maeh is the family member who generally pays visits to relatives, either at their homes or at the hospital when they are sick, and she helps with or attends religious rituals such as funerals on behalf of the family. In particular, she is in charge of leading family members in visiting relatives after the end of the month of Ramadan, a custom widely practised across the Deep South.

Maeh is also the family's financial manager. She oversees the family income and savings and makes decisions on what their money should be spent on and how much. She is in charge of taking care of sixteen workers who tap rubber for the family. It is very common to see the family's main house filled with her "employees", which is how these workers refer to themselves.

Maeh's roles extend beyond familial and kinship spheres; they also cover socio-political spaces widely thought to be occupied or dominated by men. For example, she played a crucial role in deciding whether her oldest son, Saifuldin, who was joining a rally in Bangkok at the time, would contest the first SAO member election. Her contribution and support also played a crucial role in the SAO chief executive's victory in the elections.

Why does Maeh figure so large in her family? Why are her roles and engagements accepted among her neighbours? What are the sources of her authority and legitimacy? A primary answer to these questions is her piety.

As mentioned in Chapter 3, Maeh is a devout Muslim. Not only does she regularly perform five prayers a day plus the extra ones, but her prayers are about three times longer than normal. Not only does she fast every day during the month of Ramadan, but she also performs additional fasting during the week after the Hari Raya. She regularly attends Koran reading classes as well as Babo's preaching and special sermons given by religious scholars visiting the mosque. Her piety is widely known among the villagers, especially her "employees", who know not to bother her with any business during the two prayer times in the evening. Her observances of religious duties are to be respected.

One Thursday night, while watching an Indian music programme on TV, Saifuldin switched the channel after realizing that it was almost nine o'clock and then called Maeh, who was in the kitchen, to remind her that her religious programme was coming on. This Malaysian programme, *Forum Perdana Ehwal Islam*, airs from 9:00 to 9:30 every Thursday night, and Maeh is a big fan. It is unanimously agreed in the family that the TV is reserved for Maeh during this time, regardless of what anyone else may be watching. As Saifuldin said after switching from his show to hers, "We need to give her the first priority." Then Maeh came to join the people gathered around the TV, not only family members but also neighbours who tended to hang around the house in the evening. Everyone, especially Maeh, watched the programme with attention and delight, chiming in with opinions here and there. Maeh sat with others for a little while after the programme ended before returning to the back of the house to resume her chores. Then Saifuldin switched to another channel, usually a Hollywood movie or an Indian musical show.

In addition to ceding the TV to Maeh for religious programming, family members are obliged to accommodate her observances of religious duties. Saifuldin bought Maeh a small radio receiver so that she could listen to religious programmes whenever and wherever she wanted to. Saifuldin himself feels under greater obligation to perform prayers while travelling with Maeh. One day while on our way home, Saifuldin had to drive the truck faster than normal in order to arrive at a gas station that provides a prayer room in time for a scheduled prayer. He said later that, actually, he can skip this prayer and combine it with the next one. But on this occasion he could not do so because Maeh was there. Aiman said, while all of us were waiting for Maeh in front of the prayer room, that Maeh always prays longer than normal because she chooses a long section of the Koran for the optional part. No one complained while we waited, although it was already dark and many were hungry.

Importantly, family members and neighbours feel obliged to accommodate Maeh not only in religious duties but also in other matters — economic, social and political — that she is in charge of or involved with. One day, while helping Maeh cook chicken rice for a feast, Safa, one of her three aides-de-camp, said that she actually had to go to her relatives' house to help them cook for a feast. But she decided to come here instead. Likewise, Daessa, another regular helper, said on another day that a certain rubber plantation owner had offered her family a quota of rubber tapping, but she declined it as she preferred working with Maeh. Yumna told me that she had not yet decided which SAO member and chief executive candidates she would vote for, jokingly commenting that she might vote for those who paid her the highest. But, after being encouraged by Maeh, she said that she would vote for the candidates Maeh supported.

Given these neighbours' self-identification as "employees" of Maeh, their obligation to concur with Maeh's wishes seems analogous to the classical patron–client relationship model. It can be argued that, because Maeh not only provided Daessa with job opportunities but also gave her gifts such as a sarong, sugar and dates during Ramadan and took her on holiday to some tourist destinations on a few special occasions, Daessa is then obliged to demonstrate some degree of loyalty to Maeh. Likewise, it can also be argued that because Maeh allocated labour on a new rubber plantation to Yumna only, Yumna then feels compelled to accommodate Maeh's wish when asked to do so. Clients similarly pay gratitude and loyalty to their patrons for the rare or scarce resources they receive.

However, these neighbours' obligations to Maeh are not constituted within the employer–employee relationship alone. Rather, they are significantly created out of their relationship with Maeh as fellow Muslims. I asked these villagers why they felt obliged to accommodate Maeh's needs and wishes, and all of them replied with almost the same answer — because of Maeh's virtues, the virtues that are part of her pursuing a devout Muslim life. Daessa said that, in addition to being a very good employer, Maeh was an example of a good Muslim — praying several times a day, regularly attending Koran reading classes, always attending the sermons of visiting religious scholars — that Daessa herself sought to emulate. Although another rubber plantation owner had offered her a better employment deal, she preferred working with Maeh because, she said, "Maeh is a good person." Likewise, Yumna said that Maeh was a very good Muslim and that Maeh's allocation of a new plantation to Yumna's family was a way of making merit according to Islamic principles, which she really appreciates. In this regard, Daessa's and Yumna's obligation to Maeh is not so much based on their employee–employer relationship with Maeh as on their understanding of the Islamic moral order, in which Maeh occupies a high ground. Theirs is an obligation to Maeh's moral authority, which is grounded in Islamic virtue.

Women's authority derived from piety has increasingly gained attention from many scholars and observers. In her study of how Malaysian Muslim women cultivate themselves as pious Muslims ascribed with agency, Sylva Frisk (2009, pp. 12–15) outlines the research into "creative aspects of submission" within the Muslim and Christian traditions. She maintains that, aware of the serious limitations of the secular and liberal notion of subject and agency championed by feminists, many studies adopted more generative approaches to understanding women's subjectivity and agency in the realm of religion. For example, Saba Mahmood (2001; see also 2005) argues that Islamic virtues such as modesty, shyness and patience that Egyptian women sought to cultivate and that are contradictory to the secular and liberal notion of agency are in fact these women's form of agency. Phyllis Mack (2003) maintains that Quaker women insist that their actions are done not as acts of will but as acts of obedience to God. She writes: "Quaker women defined agency not as the freedom to do what one wants but as the freedom to do what is right. Since 'what is right' was determined by absolute truth or God as well as by individual conscience, agency implied obedience as well as the freedom to make choices and act on them" (Mack 2003, pp. 156–57). Likewise, Marie R. Griffith (2000), in response to the assumption that North American Christian women are participating in their own victimization and internalizing patriarchal ideas about female submission, maintains that these women believe that the doctrine of submission leads them to freedom and transformation. Through submission, they become God's obedient daughters, whose pains and sorrows are eased and whose marriage relations transformed. It is "mediated agency" obtained from their submission to God that has enabled these women to attain freedom and effect change.

Drawing on this body of literature, Frisk (2009) examines pious Malaysian Muslim women's agency as an active submission to the will of God. She argues that, while acknowledging male dominance and authority, Malaysian women, by assuming the identity of a *mukmin* — a true believer — simultaneously emphasize men's and women's equal responsibility towards God and as such are enabled to challenge male interpretations of the Koran.

Through Islamic discourses on and practices of piety, Malaysian women are enabled to negotiate gender relations, shape their lives in correspondence to orthodox Islam, and transform Islam in Malaysia — creating a female space within the male-dominated mosque environment and enhancing spaces for women to enter positions of religious authority.

How do Maeh's life and religious practices fit in these theoretical frameworks and ethnographies?

Like Muslim women discussed elsewhere, Maeh's agency is largely derived from her submission to God as a pious Muslim. Saifuldin gave her the first priority in viewing the religious television programme, because he regards her viewing of the programme as part of her pursuit of a pious life. Aiman and the others did not complain while waiting for her in front of the prayer room precisely because they thought that praying longer than normal is a feature of her piety, which everyone must accommodate. Her employees have no problems waiting until eight o'clock in the evening to meet and talk to her about rubber-related business, as they deem her observance of religious duties so important that their worldly business can wait. Her virtues, which are part of her pious life, shape the decisions and commitments of her family members, relatives, friends and acquaintances not only in the religious realm but also in social, political, and economic spheres. By submitting to God as a pious Muslim, or becoming a *mukmin*, Maeh is enabled to influence the residents on various matters.

However, unlike the Muslim women examined in the scholarly literature, most of whom are educated, urban middle-class professionals, Maeh is and regards herself as an unschooled rural peasant. She did not go to public elementary school, and she did not attend a Tadika either. She said: "My knowledge about Islam is very rudimentary", when I asked her why she attended Koran reading classes on Tuesday and Sunday afternoons. She has never performed the hajj while her husband and sons have, because, she said, "I don't have money", an explanation I do not take literally given that she is the family's financial manager. Importantly, while Muslim women of urban Malaysia quit their professional careers and become full-time housewives in order to spend more time on religious studies, a Malay Muslim woman of rural Thailand like Maeh performs all these tasks and duties altogether. Maeh does not find that the numerous chores and housework she performs conflict with her pursuit of a pious life. She finds that it is not necessary to quit her jobs in order to become a "full-time housewife" and to perform her religious duties.

In addition, Maeh has never participated in the Dakwah mission, which requires the abandonment of work and household responsibilities for a certain period of time. Nor did she join the group of women outside the southern Guba mosque to listen to the sermons of various notable preachers from the loudspeakers during the Dakwah gathering in Guba. She preferred to pray alone in her corner in the house, as she always does, during the Dakwah sermons at the mosque because, she said, "it is all right to pray at home". Importantly, she has never attempted to create a female space in the male-dominated mosque environment. She always attends religious talks and sermons at the southern Guba mosque but never thought of setting up religious classes or Koran reading classes exclusively for women there. Nor does she wish to have a position of religious authority, such as a religious teacher, as most such positions are occupied by men.

In other words, Maeh crafted her religious subjectivity not only in an orthodox Islamic context but also given the existing socio-economic conditions. And the fact that her agency is not enacted either in expanding women's space in formal religious settings or in changing women's roles in the family and society points to the complexity of power relations Maeh engages with. Men's religious positions, such as imam, do not automatically lead to authority, whereas women's roles and responsibilities in the family enable women to engage with various matters with legitimacy. Rather than leaving the secular, occupational, domestic realms, Maeh strengthened her position in these realms with agency she obtained from the religious sphere as a pious Muslim, which at the same time enabled her to pursue her religious path in a way that differs from those dominated and led by men.

However, the agency Maeh derives from being a pious Muslim is recognizable only among those who acknowledge Allah's supremacy. In other words, Allah's sovereignty, through which Maeh obtained and enacted agency, is legible and effective only among those who comply with Allah's power and order. In addition, given that there are several strands of Islam in which Allah's order is interpreted and reinforced differently, the agency obtained and enacted via the observance of a given strand of Islam is subject to debate. Some residents, especially the New Group members, regard Maeh as an ordinary Muslim who is still in need of "correct" knowledge of Islam and as such has not yet acquired authority through Allah's sovereignty. Those residents who reinterpret Allah's order in subversive manners do not recognize Maeh's agency that is mediated through Allah. This is not to mention those outside the realm of Islam, such as Thai Buddhist state authorities and Chinese Thai merchants in Raman, to whom Allah's sovereignty is incomprehensible; as such, they regard Maeh simply as an uneducated rural villager with no authority to conform to.

To put it another way, the agency mediated through the sovereign is in large part tied to the sovereign. To what extent and in what ways the agency is enacted and recognized are due largely to the degree to which the sovereign is submitted to. In this regard, the discussion of agency and subjectivity of this kind has to consider the sovereign and examine how the three are related. How the residents crafted their subjectivity and obtained and enacted agency through the sovereign monarch is an exemplary case.

6.2. "We Love Mr King": Crafting Subjectivity and Enacting Agency through the Exceptional Sovereign

On the morning of 25 June 2009, a main street in Raman was crowded with hundreds of Tadika schoolchildren and teachers, SAO members and executives, and government officials who were parading to a sports field in front of the district building for the opening ceremony of Tadika Samphan, a sporting event. Parade participants — mostly local Malay Muslims — were in glamorous and colourful costumes. Schoolgirls who carried subdistrict nameplates wore exquisite, traditional Malay dresses, and female teachers were in formal Malay dress with headscarves on. Male teachers wore Malay-style short-sleeved shirts and long pants. Students were in school uniforms and sports outfits, while government officials, many of whom were Thai Buddhists, wore formal clothing. Some parade participants carried gold and silver flowers, likening the parade to a royal procession of Malay rulers in the past, whereas others held national flags as well as images of King Bhumibol in their hands to represent their current status as citizens of Thailand and their allegiance to the king. In addition, representatives of the Tadikas of each subdistrict carried delicately decorated ceremonial footed trays, some inscribed with words revering the king.

Once arriving at the sports field, the parade was split into rows, each representing the Tadika of each of the subdistricts participating. The participants now stood facing a flagpole and a makeshift ceremonial stand, where the footed trays were placed among other ritual items including a large image of King Bhumibol and Queen Sirikit and two national flags. There was a tent in which senior government officials — most of whom were Thai Buddhists — sat on comfortable couches. The official opening ceremony of the Tadika Samphan began with the Raman district chief's reading of a report to the deputy governor of Yala Province, the latter presiding over the ceremony. The background of the event was outlined and the aims explained in terms of creating love and unity among people in the province in times of unrest.

After the district chief finished his report, the deputy governor walked to the ceremonial stand to light candles in order to pay respect to the king's and queen's images. This ritual was followed by the raising of the national flag, during which all participants, including the government officials, stood to attention and sang the national anthem. Afterward, everyone sang the royal anthem and the *Sadudi Maharaja* song to pay respect to the king and queen, marking the end of the opening ceremony and the beginning of the sports activities, which lasted until the evening.

As a state ceremony, the parade and especially the opening ceremony were aimed at reinforcing the subjectivity of the participants as citizens of Thailand as well as their loyalty to the nation. This was done by means of having the participants carry national flags and especially standing to attention and singing the national anthem while the flag of Thailand was raised. Following the lyrics of the national anthem, attendees were reminded that they are Thais, obliged to sacrifice their lives for the nation.

The Thai state, however, does not correspond solely to the nation — it also corresponds to the monarch. The Thai state ideology consists of the three elements of nation, religion and monarch, and the monarch is the most important of the three. On the one hand, the monarch is regarded as the "centre of all Thais' hearts", implying that the nation cannot exist without him. Instead of the nation, as suggested by Benedict Anderson (1996, pp. 6–7), it is the monarch whom Thai soldiers usually declare they are willing to die for. On the other hand, the monarch is constitutionally regarded as the "Upholder of Religions", meaning that no religion can prosper in the kingdom without his support and protection. The ideological significance of the monarch in relation to the nation and to religion is reified in the design of the national flag, in which the dark blue stripe that symbolizes the monarch is placed in the middle, with the two white stripes symbolizing religion above and below it. The red stripes, symbolizing the nation, are outermost. This shows that, although the monarch is not explicitly addressed in the lyrics of the national anthem, he is — literally — the most central element, as shown in the Thai flag. See Figure 6.1.

In the context of the ceremony described above, in addition to the flag-raising ritual during which the king is addressed as an element of state ideology along with religion and the nation, he is also addressed by means of items and rituals that are directly associated with him. Some parade participants carried images of the king and ceremonial footed trays inscribed with words revering him. Importantly, all participants stood to attention

FIGURE 6.1
The Thai Flag

and sang the royal anthem, whose lyrics praise the king and strengthen the loyalty of his subjects. Below is a translation of the royal anthem.

> We, servants of His Great Majesty,
> prostrate our hearts and heads
> to pay respect to the ruler, whose merits are boundless,
> outstanding in the great Chakri dynasty,
> the greatest of Siam,
> with great and lasting honour.
> (We are) secure and peaceful because of your royal rule.
> The result of the King's care
> (is) people in happiness and in peace.
> May it be that
> whatever you will,
> be done
> according to the hopes of your great heart
> as we wish (you) victory, hurrah!

The opening ceremony of the Tadika Samphan is therefore a spatio-temporal dimension in which the monarch becomes manifest both as an element of state ideology as well as through items and rituals that are directly related to him. As a result, the subjectivity that the ceremony reinforces is not so much citizens of the Thai state, but rather subjects of the king. This is also the main reason why Guba residents chose to inscribe the sentence "เรารักนายหลวง" (*rao rak nay luang*) on the footed tray they had made for the Tadika Samphan.

When I asked Aiman, who was in charge of the making of the tray, why the sentence *rao rak nay luang* was inscribed on it, he said that it was not because district authorities had required it. The district, he explained, had only asked for a beautiful footed tray for the parade and the opening ceremony, leaving the Tadikas of each subdistrict the freedom to create a tray of their own imagination. He said that the sentence had been proposed by Daessa, who in turn said that she wanted to imitate the ceremonial footed trays she had seen during state ceremonies she had attended on behalf of her state-supported groups — especially those made by Thai Buddhists and government agencies. Other village health volunteers and housewives' group members who were there agreed with her idea on the grounds that such a sentence is commonly seen in state ceremonies. They said that to be Thai is to express loyalty to the king — especially at these kinds of events. The Tadika schoolchildren who had helped make the tray also had no objection, as the sentence was very familiar to them from school textbooks and activities as well as from the various mass media they habitually consumed. Aiman further claimed that Daessa's idea had been a majority decision. He added that, as a "cultural specialist" and "local artist", his duty was only to decorate the footed tray.

The tray held cooked sticky rice dyed in three colors, representing the three fundamental institutions of Malay Muslims — white their religion, red their nation, and yellow their race. However, Aiman explained that, in addition to their race, yellow also refers to the raja — the king — because "race" refers to a group of people who by nature are ruled and led by a raja, as it would be difficult or almost impossible for a race to exist and prosper without the rulership and guidance of such a person. Also in the tray, on top of the sticky rice, was a hard-boiled egg, which symbolizes life. Taken together, the footed tray conveys the meaning that Malay Muslims' life is based on or supported by the three pillars of religion, nation, and "race" or raja. Aiman said that the tradition of making such ceremonial trays has existed for centuries. He added that, originally, the conical shape of the rice heaped in the tray represented Mount Meru, which has a specific meaning in Hindu mythology, but that after their ancestors adopted Islam, this symbolism was abandoned even though the trays were still made and the conical shape retained.

FIGURE 6.2
Ceremonial Footed Tray: เรารัก (*rao rak*) = We Love

FIGURE 6.3
Ceremonial Footed Tray: นายหลวง (*nay luang*) = Mr King

It is noteworthy that the symbolism of the ceremonial footed tray corresponds to that of the national flag. However, while the two red stripes are meant to represent the Thai nation, it remains unclear what nation the red-coloured sticky rice refers to. Aiman himself did not specify what he means by "the nation", leaving me to figure it out for myself. On the one hand, red sticky rice may refer to the Thai nation as in the national flag. On the other hand, it may denote the Malay nation to which separatists in previous decades claimed to belong to and which remains the inspiration of some Malays of southern Thailand. In addition, while the two white stripes are often associated with Buddhism, within this context the white-coloured sticky rice definitely refers to Islam, the religion of the Malays of southern Thailand. It is only in the dark blue stripe (of the flag) and the yellow-coloured sticky rice (on the tray), which represent, respectively, monarch and raja, that these two different claims to symbolism are rendered compatible. In the context of the ceremonial tray, the latter specifically denotes the Thai monarch, as highlighted by the sentence *rao rak nay luang*.

How is the king capable of serving as the common ground to claims that appear so incompatible? Why did Guba residents not feel any contradiction in expressing their love for the king, the way they did when it came to the question of religion and the nation? The answer, I argue, lies in the ideological significance of the king in relation to the state. As I mentioned earlier, the reason why the king is the most important element of state ideology is that without the king, the two other elements — nation and religion — would find it difficult or impossible to survive. The king survives because he has been promoted as transcending all ethno-religious differences. Although he is a Buddhist, the monarch is constitutionally and traditionally regarded as the Upholder of Religions — including Islam. As a result, while Islam finds it difficult to fit into the "religion" category of state ideology because of the state's strong association with Buddhism, it can find support and protection in the "monarch" category. Likewise, although he is an ethnic Thai, the monarch is constitutionally regarded as the head of state, and, more recently, as father of the land, whose benevolence supposedly extends to all the citizens of the country regardless of their ethnicity. While Malay ethnicity is a difficult fit in the "nation" category of state ideology because of the state's association with Thai ethnicity, it can similarly find support and protection in the "monarch" category. This category therefore makes it possible for Malay Muslims to reside within the territory of the Thai Buddhist state, which is notorious for ethno-religious discrimination.

Aiman said that the reason why his fellow villagers find it not difficult to respect the Thai king is that monarchy is a tradition they have long been familiar with — one that they can trace back to the Malay raja era. However, he added that this also has to do with the way the villagers perceived the Thai monarch. He said that, although the villagers in general are "indifferent" to the king, they do not feel oppressed under his reign. They may dislike the state authorities — especially security authorities — but they do not relate state officials or the government in general to the king. Daessa, a member of numerous state-supported groups, similarly claimed that she does not think the king is discriminatory in terms of ethnicity or religion, although she finds that certain state officials are. She added: "It is not only Thais who can love the king. Malays, too, can love the king." Shaari, a grade 6 schoolboy who helped make the footed tray, also claimed that he has no problem with the king because "the king is good to us Malays. He is good to Islam too." In addition, although some villagers — like many people across the country — make unflattering comments and gossip about some members of the royal family, none ever expressed their dislike of the king to me or in public.

The question, then, is why the king is perceived as unrelated to the government and to state agencies despite his involvement in and influence on both. The reason, I argue, can be found in an ad hoc political strategy concocted by the Thai ruling elites precisely for dealing with matters related to ethno-religious differences.

As soon as the borders of Siam were demarcated in the late nineteenth century, the country's ruling elites were preoccupied with finding ways to connect peoples of different ethnicities and religions within their territory. Doing so was particularly important, as the French utilized a racial justification for expanding their control over the Lao and Khmer who they claimed belonged to French Indochina. Faced with such logic of race, King Chulalongkorn and his advisers advanced that the peoples living within Siam belonged to *chat Thai* — the Thai nation — which transcended local linguistic and cultural differences (Keyes 1995, pp. 136–60), and implemented measures to suppress "primordial attachments" among ethnic groups across the territory in favour of a common heritage (Keyes 1997, pp. 551–68). Anyone residing in the Siamese kingdom belonged to the Thai nation as long as they met certain criteria, one of which was to be loyal to the king as his subjects.

Chulalongkorn's "inclusive" nation-building project was, however, not pursued by his successor, Vajiravudh, who associated the Thai nation with ethnic Thais alone and introduced a nationalist ideology through compulsory primary education, state propaganda, the official rewriting of history, militarism, and the affirmation of the identity of monarchy and nation (Anderson 1996, pp. 100–101). Some leaders of the 1932 revolution reinforced such an "exclusive" nation-building project by creating the notion of "Tai", which allowed them to link all the Tai-speaking peoples inside and outside the country's borders under the pan-Thai movement, or Maha Anachak Thai (Great Thai Empire), across the region (Keyes 1995, pp. 136–37; Scupin 1986, p. 126). Thai nationalist ideology was then forcefully promoted under the government of Field Marshal Plaek Phibunsongkhram (Che Man 1990, p. 65; Nantawan 1977, p. 92; Nik Mahmud 1994, p. 290; Uthai 1988, pp. 253, 259–60; Yegar 2002, pp. 90–91) and then discontinued during Field Marshal Sarit Thanarat's government. The latter restored the role of the monarch (Thak 2007, pp. 181–222) and resumed the previous "inclusive" nation-building project. How the Thai nation is defined and built is therefore related to how the king's sovereignty is conceptualized and put into practice.

In early Siamese kingdoms such as Sukhothai, the king's authority and legitimacy derived from the Theravada Buddhist notion of *dhammaraja*, or "righteous king", who modelled his rule after the moral example of the Buddha and whose political function was regarded as being governed by Buddhist moral law (*dhamma*) or the Ten Kingly Virtues (*dasabhidha rajadhamma*) rather than by divine authority. However, the kings of Ayutthaya, the Siamese kingdom that followed Sukhothai, reverted to Brahmanical ideas of the monarch as a *devaraja* — "the king of the deities" — legitimizing their rule by linking themselves with Vishnu, the Hindu god. The notion of *dhammaraja* returned in the early Bangkok period and was cemented by King Mongkut's reform of Buddhism in the encounter with science and Western culture, resulting in de-emphasizing the supernatural Brahmanical cults. However, such cults continued to be associated with kingly power and constitute the discursive context from which the god-king discourse re-emerged in the reign of King Bhumibol (Jackson 2010, pp. 35–37).

Although King Prajadhipok lost royal sovereignty in the 1932 revolution, superseded by Phibun, who fashioned himself as the country's leader, royal power has been restored since Sarit's 1957 coup, which laid the foundation for the return of god-king discourse (Jackson 2010, p. 32). Initially, young King Bhumibol led the country as a *dhammaraja* (Ivarsson and Isager 2010a, p. 7), but he was later resacralized as *devaraja* or god-king by means of royal ceremonies, state propaganda, and mass media (Ivarsson and Isager

2010*a*, pp. 9-10; Jackson 2010, pp. 37-48; see also Thongchai 2008, p. 21). Before his death in 2016, King Bhumibol had power or prerogative that was far greater than what the English-modelled constitutional monarchy would allow.

The question of the king's as well as the monarchy's involvement in politics is often framed in two ways. On the one hand, it is framed in terms of how the monarchy has been used instrumentally by political leaders — and especially by army generals — in order to serve their own interests, without the monarchy's involvement. This strand of thinking is evident in scholarly works focused on how Sarit sought legitimacy by attaching himself to the monarchy after ousting Phibun by coup d'état (Thak 2007, pp. 181-222). On the other hand, it is framed in terms of how the monarchy itself has become a major political actor in Thai politics. This strand of thinking is evident in scholarly works that examine the monarchy's role in politics since General Prem Tinsulanonda's era. Initially, these works were framed within Antonio Gramsci's notion of hegemony, arguing that the king's initiatives were employed to create royal hegemony (Chanida 2007, p. 456). The monarchy's modus operandi was then examined by Duncan McCargo (2005, pp. 499-519) through his notion of "network monarchy", which proposed that the monarchy operates through an informal network of elites composed of military leaders, bureaucrats, and the "palace" centred around General Prem, the president of the Privy Council. McCargo maintained that this network reinvented itself in order to cope with the process of democratization that followed the Black May incident of 1992, in which about fifty people demonstrating against the administration of General Suchinda Kraprayoon were killed in a military crackdown. Eugénie Mérieau (2016, pp. 445-66) argues that McCargo's notion of "network monarchy" is unable to adequately conceptualize the institutionalized basis of Thailand's elite network, evident in the 2006 and 2014 coups. Drawing on the concept of the "deep state", she argues that judicialization — especially through the Constitutional Court — has been an attempt to institutionalize Thailand's deep state in order to protect it from the challenges of democratization and royal succession.

I pursue the latter line of thought but in a different direction, focusing instead on the king's sovereignty. Given the identicalness between the king and the state discussed earlier, the question of the king's sovereignty can be framed as a question of the sovereignty of the state. It is an anthropological discussion of sovereignty with regard to the "state of exception" that I find relevant here.

As mentioned at the beginning of this chapter, Aihwa Ong argues that neoliberalism is the most recent development in biopolitics and is a governmentality that "relies on market knowledge and calculations for politics of subjection and subject-making" (Ong 2006, p. 13). She further argues that this kind of governmentality is exercised in a state of exception because, in encountering global markets, regulatory institutions and transnational NGOs, many Third World states have no choice but to resort to creating special economic zones where they allow the criteria of other sovereign powers to be imposed. In this state of exception, Ong argues, the state becomes a "graduated sovereignty" as it moves from "being administrators of a watertight national entity to regulators of diverse spaces and populations that link with global markets" (Ong 2006, p. 78).

Taking cues from Ong's notion of "neoliberal exception", I advance that the Kingdom of Thailand can be conceived as a state of exception that Thailand, as a democratic state, created in dealing with the question of ethno-religious difference. As mentioned earlier, faced with European colonial expansion and with the question of how to connect peoples of different ethnicities and religions in a newly demarcated territory, Chulalongkorn created an "inclusive" nation, claiming that everyone living in the kingdom belonged to the Thai nation. Although disrupted by subsequent rulers, this project has resumed. There is, however, a difference between the "inclusive" nation created by Chulalongkorn and the nation that existed following the 1932 revolution. During Chulalongkorn's reign, the kingdom coincided with the state, and sovereignty belonged to the absolutist king. After the revolution, the kingdom and the state separated, because, following the democratic model, sovereignty belongs to the people. Despite this, the concept of "kingdom" has remained intact along with that of a democratic state, as manifested in the country's official name — the Kingdom of Thailand — and in the state ideology, which stresses the importance of the monarch.

The reason why the concept of the kingdom has been kept intact has a lot to do with how the Thai state deals with the question of ethno-religious difference. Rather than functioning as a democratic state committed to equality and the rights of its citizens, the Thai state defers to the monarchy on questions of ethnicity and religion. The monarch is constitutionally regarded as the Upholder of Religions and as head of state, whose benevolence covers all his subjects, whereas the Thai state, which is only associated with Buddhism and ethnic Thais, is notorious for ethno-religious discrimination. However, given the identicalness of the state and the monarch, it is misleading to place the two in contraposition to each other. Rather, the monarch should be read as a configuration or the embodiment of the Thai state on questions of ethnicity and religion. Or, to put it in Ong's words, the Thai state has resorted to a "state of exception" by creating a "special political zone" — the Kingdom of Thailand — when it must deal with ethnicities and religions other than Thai and Buddhism and can look to the monarch as its embodiment. This allows the criteria of other ethnicities and religions to be imposed on its peoples and places along with those of the sovereign monarch.[1]

Although allowing the criteria of other forms of sovereignty to be imposed, the sovereignty of the Thai state in such a state of exception is not exercised in a flexible manner. Rather than the kind of "graduated sovereignty" suggested by Ong, the Thai state in its disguise is still "undifferentiated sovereignty" and continues to take the nation as its major concern as manifested in state ideology in which the king is directly associated with the nation. This is particularly the case if we take into account the ways in which the king's sovereignty is conceptualized in the country's polity. Instead of being placed under the constitution according to the principle of constitutional monarchy, the king is placed above the constitution, as clearly stated in section 6 of the Constitution of the Kingdom of Thailand of 2017: "The King shall be enthroned in a position of revered worship and shall not be violated. No person shall expose the King to any sort of accusation or action." What this entails is that the king is legally placed outside the law or he is inside and outside the law at the same time. At this point, I find Agamben's discussion of sovereignty to be of great relevance.

As mentioned in Chapter 5, Agamben maintains that the nature of the sovereign is paradoxical in that the sovereign is simultaneously inside and outside the juridical order; having the legal power to suspend the application of law, the sovereign legally places himself outside the law (Agamben 1998, pp. 11–12). Because the Thai monarch is constitutionally placed outside the law, or inside and outside the law at the same time, he is the sovereign in Agamben's sense.[2]

As an embodiment of the Thai state in a state of exception, the Thai monarch is supposed to exercise his sovereign power in a flexible and fragmented manner. This would at least seem to be the case if we consider the Thai monarch's status of Upholder of Religions and head of state — a status that is flexible or fragmented enough to cover all ethnicities and religions. However, if we take into account the Thai monarch's juridico-political status as articulated in the country's constitution and Code of Criminal Procedure, things appear to be slightly different. With the exclusive or exceptional power to suspend the application of law, indeed, the Thai monarch's sovereign power cannot be differentiated or shared. Paradoxical notwithstanding, the Thai monarch is a sovereign through whom people in the Deep South craft their subjectivity and enact agency while engaging with state authorities.

One day while we sat chatting at a roadside pavilion, I asked Daessa what she meant by the word *rao* (เรา), or "we", in the sentence *rao rak nay luang* (เรารักนายหลวง), and she said that she was referring to "Malay people". I then asked her if she felt uneasy, given that the sentence is seemingly designed primarily for Thai people, and she said: "No. It's OK for Malays to love the king. We Malays can love the king, too." I asked Moh, who had helped make the ceremonial footed tray, if she agreed with Daessa, and she replied that she did. She added: "We reside in Thailand, so we are Thai too." This position was shared by others at the pavilion. No one said that Malays did not like the king.

While the meaning of the word *rao* is straightforward, that of the phrase *nay luang* (นายหลวง) is not. Alone with Aiman, I asked what he meant by *nay luang*, and he said that he was referring to "the king." When I asked him further what he meant by the word *nay* alone, he explained that the term can have two different meanings, depending on the language that is used. In the Thai language, he explained, *nay* means "Mister", and the phrase *nay luang* therefore means "Mister Luang", which may or may not denote the king. In Malay, however, *nay* is part of the word *tok nay*, which refers to Thai Buddhist government officials from Bangkok or from other Thai Buddhist-dominated provinces. When combined with *luang*, the Malay word *nay* implies the chief of government officials — that is, the king. However, Aiman added that, given that the phrase *tok nay* is used by Malays of previous generations whereas many of the footed tray makers were young, it is more likely that what they meant by *nay* is "Mister". And given that the word *luang* is usually related to the king, Aiman said that it is likely that many of the footed tray makers meant *nay luang*, or "Mister King".

With Aiman's explanation in mind, I asked other tray makers the same question and received similar answers. Daessa said that what she meant by *nay* was "Mister", because the king is "a man". She also added that local Malays pronounce *tok nay* as *tok nae*, and that *nay* does not therefore refer to *tok nay*. Likewise, Shaari claimed he had hardly ever heard the Malay terms *tok nay* or *tok nae* and that, to him, *nay* is a Thai word that means "Mister". In addition, both Daessa and Shaari agreed that *luang* denotes either the king or something related to the king. As such, for these Malay footed tray makers, *nay luang* is a Thai phrase that, when translated word for word, means "Mister King".

The fact that the phrase *nay luang* denotes the king but literally means "Mister King" is important. It illustrates how the sovereign monarch is put into an exceptional state that allows Malay Muslims to engage with him without compromising their religious principles. That is to say, although constitutionally regarded as Upholder of Religions, the king was resacralized as a god-king especially through royal ceremonies associated with Brahmanism and Hinduism. This mythical and theological feature of the king poses a challenge to Malay Muslims, because, as Muslims, they are not allowed to revere any supreme beings other than Allah. The sentence *rao rak nay luang*, "We love Mr King", therefore makes it possible for them to engage with the king without compromising their religious principles. First, the word "love" denotes an intimate relationship and not an act of solemn worship or reverence. Second, the word "Mister" denotes a human being and not a god or a supernatural being. Taken together, "We love Mr King" is thus the expression of an intimate human relationship and not a solemn reverence of the followers of a supreme being. The expression therefore puts the sovereign monarch into a state of exception by stripping him of his god-like features, in order to render such an intimate human relationship possible.

It should, however, be noted that the footed tray makers did not intend to "strip" the king of his god-like sovereign features in the first place, as they believed that "นายหลวง" (*nay luang*) was the correct spelling. Not only were they surprised when I told them of their spelling mistake; they were also startled when I made sense of, or interpreted, the word. Some said that, although they were simply unaware of the correct spelling and its connotation, they agreed that the word "นายหลวง" (*nay luang*) had no connotations of any god-like sovereign, making it possible for them to engage with the king in a more human fashion. Others said that they did not take it that far. To them, the king is a human being, regardless of what words Thais may use to describe him or refer to him. As one put it: "The king is a human like us. It does not matter what people call him in Thai. He's still a human. So we love him as a human and we don't revere him as if he were God or as a 'Father' as the Thais do."

Whatever the footed tray makers have in mind, the sentence "We love Mr King" has practical effects. The Raman district deputy who oversaw and coordinated the event greeted them with a smile when noticing what was inscribed on the footed tray. He, who seemed not to notice the awkward spelling, said that the king, especially given the unrest in the region, was concerned about their safety and livelihood and that it was therefore appropriate that they had made a ceremonial tray with words revering the king. He added that the king was concerned about all his subjects regardless of their ethnicity and religion. As a consequence, Daessa later commented that the group had made the right decision in inscribing the sentence "We love Mr King" on the tray, as this made her feel confident in participating in the opening ceremony with many high-level government officials. She added that it also helped clear her and other residents from being suspected of sympathizing with the insurgents, or Okhrae Dalae. As she put it: "They [the state authorities] like us to do that [to express love and loyalty to the king] because they don't want us to side with Okhrae Dalae." The sentence "We love Mr King" then allowed these Malay Muslims to engage with state authorities as royal subjects with authority, without having to pay allegiance to these same state authorities about whom many have expressed discontent. This subjectivity and agency are comparable to those discussed in contemporary anthropological studies of women in religious realms.

I maintain that the way in which the footed tray makers crafted their subjectivity and enacted agency via the sovereign monarch through the sentence "We love Mr King" is analogous to how women crafted their subjectivity and enacted agency through their omnipotent God. The king, as the Upholder of Religions and head of state, is not a repressive figure whom an ethno-religious minority like the Malay Muslims of southern Thailand feel compelled to resist. As the embodiment of state sovereignty in a state of exception, the king can also be a means through which agency can be obtained and enacted. This must be read in tandem with the king's loss of his god-like features, which renders him a human being with whom an intimate relationship is possible. As such, rather than resisting, the Guba residents chose to "submit" to the king as his subjects via the sentence "We love Mr King", in effect enabling themselves to engage with state authorities with whom they are discontent.

I discussed the king's sovereign power with the Guba villagers, asking them what they thought about it. Daessa said that the king is the most powerful person in the country because, she reasoned, "the prime minister, the government, soldiers, and police — all those in power — respect and obey the king". Likewise, Nah said that the king is very powerful because, she observed, "he can do what we ordinary people cannot". Their position is in line with that of other residents. Saifuldin said that the king is not part of the government or of state agencies, but that he has power over both. Similarly, Mohammed said that the king is superior to the government and added that "to be the king's men helps protect us when dealing with the authorities". These residents are fully aware of the king's sovereign power in relation to the state and at the same time seek to utilize it when dealing with state authorities, as demonstrated by their inscription of the sentence "We love Mr King" on the ceremonial footed tray.

However, while enabling the residents to authoritatively engage with state officials, to craft subjectivity, and to enact agency through the monarch in a state of exception, this method is self-contradictory, as the subjectivity was crafted by stripping the king of his god-like features, while agency was enacted by treating the king as the sovereign. Moreover, the central feature of the king's sovereign power, namely his ability to suspend the application of law and his standing as a person outside the law, implies privilege and inequality, whereas what the Muslims in southern Thailand have been demanding is equality and justice. As such, rather than the king as the embodiment of the Thai state in a state of exception, it is the Thai state with its fragmented and flexible sovereignty that should be the means through which the Malay Muslims of southern Thailand can address their ethno-religious concerns and realize their political aspirations.

Notes

1. It is noteworthy that "states of exception" were also created in response to other issues in Thailand as well. For example, in dealing with the southern unrest, special legal terrains such as martial law, the Emergency Decree, and the Security Act were invoked. While restricting the rights and freedom of citizens and creating a state of exception across the southern region, these laws exempt state authorities from any charges if they are on duty; in other words, these laws place state authorities outside the law. Likewise, in dealing with political conflicts, section 44 of the Interim Constitution of the Kingdom of Thailand of 2014 provides the leader of the National Council for Peace and Order (NCPO), or the leader of the military junta that staged the 2014 coup, with supreme power that surpasses all existing laws, rules, and regulations, and with exemption from any charges. In this sense, Thailand is now in a state of exception and has the NCPO leader as the sovereign in Agamben's sense: "he who decides on the state of exception" (Agamben 1998, p. 11).
2. The Thai monarch's ability to suspend the application of law, which makes him the sovereign in Agamben's sense, can be seen in his prerogative to revoke the death penalty as stated in Article 262 of the Code of Criminal Procedure.

Conclusion: Sovereignty in Crisis

This book is about how the Malay Muslims of Guba, a village in Thailand's Deep South, live their lives in the wake of the ongoing insurgency that was reinvigorated in 2004. It argues that the unrest is the effect of the way in which different forms of sovereignty converge around the residents of this region. It also argues that the residents at the same time have cultivated themselves and obtained and enacted agency through the sovereigns. As such, rather than asking why the violence is increasing and who is behind it, like most scholarly works on the topic, I examine how different forms of sovereignty impose their subjectivities on the residents, how they have converged in so doing and what tensions have followed, and how people have dealt with these tensions and cultivated themselves and obtained and enacted agency through the sovereigns.

The question of sovereignty in southern Thailand dates back for many centuries. Between the fourteenth and eighteenth centuries, the question revolved around the ambiguity of sovereignty over the region. On the one hand, the region was composed of Malay sultanates, whose sovereignty had to be realized. On the other hand, the region was regarded by successive Siamese kingdoms as vassal states whose sovereignty needed to be recognized as well. A suzerain-vassal relationship was attempted, in order to address the ambiguity, but to no avail, resulting in wars between the Malay sultanates and Siam that recurred over the course of centuries. The question of ambiguous sovereignty was put to an end when the sultanates were incorporated into Siam in a process that began in the late eighteenth century and was only completed at the turn of the twentieth century. Now, Siamese sovereignty was the only form of sovereignty to be realized over the clearly demarcated territory.

However, singular sovereignty over the territory did not put the question to an end. Rather, it generated a new question and a new form of conflict — a question of sovereignty over subjectivity, which led to the emergence of separatist movements. That is to say, although Siam's nation-building project was first launched inclusively, it was later carried out exclusively, associating the nation with Thai ethnicity and Buddhism at the expense of other ethnicities and religions. Alienated by the state's ethno-religious ideology and subsequent assimilation policy, people in the Deep South were later inspired by the rise of independence movements across Southeast Asia after World War II, especially the pan-Malay nationalist movement. This provided Malay Muslims in the region with a strong sense of separatism and led to the emergence of clandestine movements in the 1950s through the 1980s that fought the Thai state, citing Malay identity and later also Islam as causes.

The recent unrest, which primarily began in 2004, shares the same question but frames it differently. On the one hand, although differing from the separatism of earlier decades in terms of anonymity, casualties, and the intensity of Islam as a motivating factor, the recent unrest is largely rooted in the question of sovereignty over the subjectivity of the people who live in the region. On the the other hand, how this question is posed is more pressing than before, and it involved more forms of sovereignty that people need to answer. Guba is one place where various forms of sovereignty imposed subjectivities on the residents in such a manner.

The return of Babo from his religious study in Saudi Arabia in the 1960s, the younger generation's acquisition of religious education from outside and abroad, and the advent of the New Group and Dakwah exposed Guba residents to various kinds of "correct" Islam, which they consequently felt obliged to practise. Largely refraining from the "sinful" activities they had previously indulged in, the residents began to live the lives of "good" Muslims. The Thai state, on the other hand, forged citizens out of Guba residents through various means, primarily education in the case of children, conscription in the case of young men, and "help and care programmes" in the case of the population at large. At the same time, royal initiatives and royal recognitions were implemented in the region to win the "hearts and minds" of the people as royal subjects.

These subjectification processes had long taken place in Guba to some degree, but they were intensified after 2004 in light of the recent unrest. Schools have become part of security force operations through special activities such as Children's Day fairs and through the building of temporary military camps in school compounds. The military along with government agencies also expanded their scope of mission to cover "help and care programmes" and development projects to discourage people from supporting the insurgents. Likewise, the monarchy provided special assistance to the residents, especially those suffering from the unrest, to ensure their loyalty. Meanwhile, the insurgency led to the breakdown of law enforcement in the region, enabling local influential figures such as powerful administrators and leaders of crime rings to exert power of life and death over common citizens. In addition, the insurgents' invocation of Islam has rendered the question of what is "correct" in Islam and what is a "good" Muslim more pressing for the residents.

The intensification of these processes increased existing tensions. The insurgents' claim that they could kill with impunity, and their alleged prohibition of work on Friday mornings, led to conflicting responses among the residents. Some were inclined to agree with the insurgents' claims, believing them to be better educated in Islam than they were themselves. But others disagreed, especially when their ability to work at certain times (and thus their livelihoods) came into question, and they cited the Koran in making their counterarguments. Although tensions among different strands of Islam — the New Group and the Old Group, Dakwah and the mosque group — did not increase, as the insurgents did not subscribe to any school of Islam in particular, the insurgents' invocation of Islam in general concerned the practitioners of these different schools, who did not want their practice to be at variance with that of the insurgents. Likewise, although the recent unrest did not directly increase the tension between Islam and Malay culture, Malay beliefs and rituals that were in conflict with Islam lost support among the insurgents.

Most evident are the tensions that arose between Islam and Malay on the one hand and the Thai state on the other. The transliteration of Malay words and names into the Thai alphabet — part of the Thai state's effort to support "Malayness" — was met with criticism; some said that the transliterations were often inaccurate and led to misunderstandings, whereas others claimed that the practice would ultimately lead to the extinction of the Malay language in Thailand. As for Islam, the royal grave-soil laying ceremony generated discontent among religious leaders as well as local administrators, who deemed that the ceremony was not in line with Islam. But they felt powerless to raise the issue lest they fall under suspicion of being against the state or on the side of the insurgents. How to live the lives of multiple, and often conflicting, subjectivities is therefore the pressing question faced by residents of the Deep South in the wake of the recent unrest.

As Muslims, people in Thailand's Deep South seek to negotiate with Allah, and to select from and interpret Islam, as a means of coping with questions and necessities in everyday life. By "making a promise" with Allah, some felt that they could continue to engage in sinful activities, confident that they could quit those activities at some future time. Women negotiated with and reinterpreted Islamic precepts to make them fit their everyday necessities, especially when it comes to controlling their own bodies in matters such as contraception and in managing their family's earnings, such as by tapping rubber on Friday mornings. Those who were engaged in dubious businesses and activities countered strict versions of Islam by subversive interpretations. As Malays, people in Guba, especially *bomohs*, modified their Malay beliefs and rituals to align with Islam so that they could continue to offer their services. As Thai citizens, Guba residents on the one hand observed state rules and regulations and on the other hand outsmarted the state in subversive ways. And when dealing with the insurgents and other influential figures, people mostly cooperated and conformed so that they could lead their lives as normally as possible in the "territory" of these de facto sovereigns.

However, the residents' engagement with their sovereigns is far more complex than simply balancing resistance with surrender. Sovereigns can be a means through whom people can craft subjectivity and obtain and enact agency. Through the strict observance of religious duties, one woman in Guba earned herself a reputation as a pious Muslim ascribed with agency to act in the name of Allah in religious and other matters. By inscribing the sentence "We love Mr King" on a ceremonial footed tray, a group of Guba residents crafted themselves as royal subjects ascribed with agency to engage state officials under whose authority they are otherwise discontent.

While enabling people to act with some measure of authority, the agency mediated through the sovereigns is limited. Allah-mediated agency can be enacted only among Muslims who recognize Allah's sovereignty, not among state authorities, most of whom are Thai Buddhists. This is particularly the case for the sovereign monarch, because to craft subjectivity and enact agency through the monarch in a state of exception is self-contradictory — the subjectivity is crafted by stripping the king of his god-like features, whereas agency is enacted by treating the king as the sovereign. Moreover, the central feature of the king's sovereign power, his ability to suspend the application of law and to exist outside the law, implies privilege and inequality, whereas what Malay Muslims of southern Thailand have been demanding is equality and justice. As such, rather than the sovereign monarch, who is the embodiment of the Thai state in a state of exception, it is the Thai state with its fragmented sovereignty that should serve as the means through which the Malay Muslims of southern Thailand can address their ethno-religious concerns and realize their political aspirations.

But how possible is this? In 2012, local academics proposed "southern border administration models" as an attempt to solve the southern unrest, but these proposals were rejected by the government and especially by the military for fear that they would lead to autonomy and even talk of independence, despite their emphasis on decentralization as a primary goal. The 2014 coup d'état that ousted Prime Minister Yingluck Shinawatra closed a window of opportunity for reconciliation in the South, as it replaced the "politics leads the military" policy in the region with a renewed emphasis on national security — an overall strategic direction that has prevailed across the country, which has been under military rule since then. In this political climate, it is unity, not fragmentation or flexibility, of state sovereignty that is emphasized, which consequently makes it extremely difficult if not impossible for the southern insurgency to be resolved. This is quite a different situation from, for instance, that of the Moros in the southern Philippines, for whom the central government created the Autonomous Region in Muslim Mindanao, thus resolving at least part of that conflict.

Importantly, the political conflict that began to gather steam in 2005, one year after the eruption of the recent unrest, only exacerbated the situation. In dealing with the political unrest and other issues that arose after the 2014 coup, Thailand's military leaders invoked Section 44 of the Interim Constitution of the Kingdom of Thailand of 2014 to create a "state of exception" — enabling the leader of the newly established National Council for Peace and Order to suspend the application of laws, rules, and regulations and free himself of responsibility for any actions undertaken in the name of state security. Another sovereign was created. Section 44 of the 2014 constitution was retained as Section 265 of the transitory provisions of the 2017 constitution. However, the creation of "sovereigns" in this sense is not in line with the fundamentals of democracy (in which sovereignty belongs to the people) or the rule of law (in which everyone is equal before the law) — basic rights that many Thai citizens have demanded. This is a crisis of sovereignty, which has led to heightened unrest not only in the Deep South but throughout Thailand as a whole, and it cannot be resolved unless sovereignty is exercised following democratic principles.

Bibliography

Abdulaziz Jehmama. "Phawa Phunam lae Botbat Khong Imam nai Kanchatkan Sun Kansueksa Islam Pracham Masjid (TADIKA) nai Changwat Narathiwat" [Leadership and Roles of the Imam in Managing Provisions of Mosque-Based Educational Centers (Tadika) in Narathiwat Province]. Master's thesis, Prince of Songkla University, Hat Yai Campus, 2013.

Abuza, Zachary. *Militant Islam in Southeast Asia: Crucible of Terror*. Boulder, CO: Lynne Rienner, 2003.

———. "A Conspiracy of Silence: Who Is Behind the Escalating Insurgency in Southern Thailand?". *Jamestown Foundation Terrorism Monitor* 3, no. 9. (2005).

———. *Conspiracy of Silence: The Insurgency in Southern Thailand and Its Implications for Southeast Asian Security*. Washington, D.C.: U.S. Institute of Peace Press, 2009.

Agamben, Giorgio. *Homo Sacer: Sovereign Power and Bare Life*. Translated by Daniel Heller-Roazen. Stanford, CA: Stanford University Press, 1998.

———. *Means without Ends: Notes on Politics*. Translated by Vincenzo Binetti and Cesare Casarino. Minneapolis, MN: University of Minnesota Press, 2000.

———. *State of Exception*. Translated by Kevin Attell. Chicago, IL: University of Chicago Press, 2005.

Anderson, Benedict. *Imagined Communities: Reflections on the Origin and Spread of Nationalism*. New York, NY: Verso, 1996.

André, Virginie. "From Colonialist to Infidel: Framing the Enemy in Southern Thailand's 'Cosmic War'". In *Culture, Religion and Conflict in Muslim Southeast Asia: Negotiating Tense Pluralisms*, edited by Joseph Camilleri and Sven Schottmann. London: Routledge, 2013.

Anusorn Unno. "'We Love Mr. King': Exceptional Sovereignty, Submissive Subjectivity, and Mediated Agency in Islamic Southern Thailand". PhD dissertation, Department of Anthropology, University of Washington, 2011.

———. "'Nabee Tak Makae Pinae' (Nabi Mai Kin Mak): Phithikam Kwamchuea Malayu nai Krasae Kan Plian Plaeng" ["Nabi Tak Makae Pinae" (Nabi Does Not Eat Betel Nuts): Malay Rituals and Beliefs amid Changes]. Research report, submitted to the Department of Cultural Promotion, Ministry of Culture, 2013.

———. "'Khuen Ni Mai Mi 'Dangdut': Amnat Nuea Chiwit kab Kan Sang Tuaton lae Kan Sadaeng Ok Sueng Sakkayapap Hang Ton Khong Chao Malayu nai Changwat Chaidaen Pak Tai" ["There Is No *Dangdut* Tonight": The Southern Border Province Malays' Subjectivity and Agency in Relation to Sovereignty]. Research report, submitted to the Thailand Research Fund, 2015.

———. "'Nabee Tak Makae Pinae' (Nabi Mai Kin Mak): Phithikam Kwamchuea Malayu nai Krasae Kan Plian Plaeng" ["Nabi Tak Makae Pinae" (Nabi Does Not Eat Betel Nuts): Malay Rituals and Beliefs amid Changes]. Nonthaburi: Patani Forum, 2016.

Arghiros, Daniel. *Democracy, Development and Decentralization in Provincial Thailand*. New York, NY: Routledge, 2016.

Aryud Yahprung. "Islamic Reform and Revivalism in Southern Thailand: A Critical Study of the Salafi Reform Movement of Shaykh Dr. Ismail Lutfi Chapakia Al-Fatani (from 1986–2010)". PhD dissertation, International Islamic University Malaysia, Kuala Lumpur, 2014.

Askew, Marc. *Conspiracy, Politics, and a Disorderly Border: The Struggle to Comprehend Insurgency in Thailand's Deep South*. Washington, D.C.: East-West Center; Singapore: Institute of Southeast Asian Studies, 2007.

———. "Landscape of Fear, Horizons of Trust: Villagers Dealing with Danger in Thailand's Insurgent South". *Journal of Southeast Asian Studies* 40, no. 1 (2009): 59–86.

——— and Sascha Helbardt. "Becoming Patani Warriors: Individuals and the Insurgent Collective in Southern Thailand". *Studies in Conflict and Terrorism* 35, no. 11 (2012): 779–809.

Barter, Shane Joshua. "Strong State, Smothered Society: Explaining Terrorist Violence in Thailand's Deep South". *Terrorism and Political Violence* 23, no. 2 (2011): 213–32.

Bowen, John Richard. *Muslims through Discourse: Religion and Ritual in Gayo Society*. Princeton, NJ: Princeton University Press, 1993.

———. *Islam, Law, and Equality in Indonesia: An Anthropology of Public Reasoning*. Cambridge: Cambridge University Press, 2003.

Bowie, Katherine Ann. *Rituals of National Loyalty: An Anthropology of the State and the Village Scout Movement in Thailand*. New York, NY: Columbia University Press, 1997.

———. "The State and the Right Wing: The Village Scout Movement in Thailand". In *Social Movements: An Anthropological Reader*, edited by June Nash. Malden, MA: Blackwell, 2005.

Braam, Ernesto H. "Malay Muslims and the Thai-Buddhist State: Confrontation, Accommodation and Disengagement". In *Encountering Islam: The Politics of Religious Identities in Southeast Asia*, edited by Hui Yew-Foong. Singapore: Institute of Southeast Asian Studies, 2013.

Chalita Bundhuwong. "Economic Life of Malay Muslims in Southernmost Thailand amidst Ecological Changes and Unrest". PhD dissertation, Department of Anthropology, University of Hawai'i at Mānoa, 2013.

Chanida Chitbundit. *Khrongkan Phraratchadamri: Kan Sathapana Phraratcha Amnat Nam (B.E. 2494–2546)* [The Royally Initiated Projects: The Making of Royal Hegemony (1951–2003)]. Bangkok: Foundation for the Promotion of Social Sciences and Humanities Textbooks Project, 2007.

Che Man, Wan Kadir. *Muslim Separatism: The Moros of Southern Philippines and the Malays of Southern Thailand*. Singapore: Oxford University Press, 1990.

———. "National Integration and Resistance Movement: The Case of Muslims in Southern Thailand". In *Regions and National Integration in Thailand, 1892–1992*, edited by Volker Grabowsky. Wiesbaden: Harrassowitz Verlag, 1995.

Collins, James T. *Malay, World Language: A Short History*. Kuala Lumpur: Dewan Bahasa dan Pustaka, 1998.

Connors, Michael. "War on Error and the Southern Fire: How Terrorism Analysts Get It Wrong". *Critical Asian Studies* 38, no. 1 (2006): 151–75.

Croissant, Aurel. "Unrest in South Thailand: Contours, Causes and Consequences since 2001". *Contemporary Southeast Asia* 21, no. 1 (2005): 21–43.

Deep South Incident Database. *Statistics on the Incidents in the Southern Border in 2016*, April 2017 <http://www.deepsouthwatch.org/node/10008> (accessed 25 April 2017).

———. *Violent Conflict Situations in the Southern Border (Quarter 1/2017)*, May 2017 <http://www.deepsouthwatch.org/node/10858> (accessed 27 May 2017).

Esposito, John L. *The Islamic Threat: Myth or Reality?* New York, NY: Oxford University Press, 1999.

Farouk, Omar. "The Historical and Transnational Dimensions of Malay-Muslim Separatism in Southern Thailand". In *Armed Separatism in Southeast Asia*, edited by Lim Joo-Jock and Vani S. Singapore: Institute of Southeast Asian Studies, 1984.

———. "The Origins and Evolution of Malay-Muslim Ethnic Nationalism in Southern Thailand". In *Islam and Society in Southeast Asia*, edited by Taufik Abdullah and Sharon Siddique. Singapore: Institute of Southeast Asian Studies, 1988.

Forbes, Andrew D.W. "Thailand's Muslim Minorities: Assimilation, Secession, or Coexistence?". *Asian Survey* 22, no. 11 (1982).

Foucault, Michel. "Governmentality". In *The Foucault Effect: Studies in Governmentality*, edited by Graham Burchell, Colin Gordon, and Peter Miller. Chicago, IL: University of Chicago Press, 1991.

———. *Ethics: Subjectivity and Truth*. Translated by Robert Hurley, et al. New York, NY: New Press, 1997.

Frisk, Sylva. *Submitting to God: Women and Islam in Urban Malaysia*. Copenhagen: Nordic Institute of Asian Studies Press, 2009.

Griffith, Marie R. *God's Daughters: Evangelical Women and the Power of Submission*. Berkeley, CA: University of California Press, 2000.

Gunaratna, Rohan and Arabinda Acharya. *The Terrorist Threat from Thailand: Jihad or Quest for Justice?* Washington, D.C.: Potomac Books, 2013.

Gunaratna, Rohan, Arabinda Acharya and Sabrina Chua, eds. *Conflict and Terrorism in Southern Thailand*. Singapore: Marshall Cavendish Academic, 2006.

Halim, Fachrizal A. *Legal Authority in Premodern Islam: Yahya B. Sharaf al-Nawawi in the Shafi'i School of Law*. New York, NY: Routledge, 2014.

Handley, Paul M. *The King Never Smiles: A Biography of Thailand's Bhumibol Adulyadej*. New Haven, CT: Yale University Press, 2006.

Hansen, Thomas Blom and Finn Stepputat, eds. *Sovereign Bodies: Citizens, Migrants, and States in the Postcolonial World*. Princeton, NJ: Princeton University Press, 2005.

———. "Sovereignty Revisited". *Annual Review of Anthropology* 35 (2006): 295–315.
Hefner, Robert W. "Public Islam and the Problem of Democratization". *Sociology of Religion* 62, no. 4 (2001): 491–514.
———. "Global Violence and Indonesian Muslim Politics". *American Anthropologist* 104, no. 3 (2002): 754–65.
Helbardt, Sascha. *Deciphering Southern Thailand's Violence: Organization and Insurgent Practices of BRN-Coordinate*. Singapore: Institute of Southeast Asian Studies, 2015.
Horstmann, Alexander. "The Tablighi Jama'at, Transnational Islam, and the Transformation of the Self between Southern Thailand and South Asia". *Comparative Studies of South Asia, Africa and the Middle East* 27, no. 1 (2007a): 26–40.
———. "The Inculturation of a Transnational Islamic Missionary Movement: Tablighi Jamaat al-Dawa and Muslim Society in Southern Thailand". *Sojourn* 22, no. 1 (2007b): 107–30.
Huntington, Samuel P. "The Clash of Civilizations?". *Foreign Affairs* 72, no. 3 (1993): 22–49.
Idris, Ahmad. "Tradition and Cultural Background of the Patani Region". In *Regions and National Integration in Thailand, 1892–1992*, edited by Volker Grabowsky. Wiesbaden: Harrassowitz Verlag, 1995.
International Crisis Group. "Southern Thailand: Insurgency Not Jihad". *Asia Report*, no. 98 (2005).
Ivarsson, Søren and Lotte Isager. "Introduction: Challenging the Standard Total View of the Thai Monarchy". In *Saying the Unsayable: Monarchy and Democracy in Thailand*, edited by Søren Ivarsson and Lotte Isager. Honolulu, HI: University of Hawai'i Press, 2010a.
———. "Strengthening the Moral Fiber of the Nation: The King's Sufficiency Economy as Ethno-Politics". In *Saying the Unsayable: Monarchy and Democracy in Thailand*, edited by Søren Ivarsson and Lotte Isager. Honolulu, HI: University of Hawai'i Press, 2010b.
Jackson, Peter A. "Virtual Divinity: A 21st-Century Discourse of Thai Royal Influence". In *Saying the Unsayable: Monarchy and Democracy in Thailand*, edited by Søren Ivarsson and Lotte Isager. Honolulu, HI: University of Hawai'i Press, 2010.
Joll, Christopher M. *Muslim Merit-Making in Thailand's Far-South*. Dordrecht: Springer, 2012.
———. "Revisiting Ethnic and Religious Factors in Thailand's Southern Discomfort". In *The Politics of Scholarship and Trans-Border Engagement in Mainland Southeast Asia: A Festschrift in Honor of Ajarn Chayan Vaddhanaphuti*, edited by Oscar Salemink. Chiang Mai: Silkworm Books, 2015.
Jory, Patrick. "From 'Melayu Patani' to 'Thai Muslim': The Spectre of Ethnic Identity in Southern Thailand". *South East Asia Research* 15, no. 2 (2007): 255–79.
Keyes, Charles F. "Buddhism and National Integration in Thailand". *Journal of Asian Studies* 30, no. 3 (1971): 551–67.
———. "Who Are the Tai? Reflections on the Invention of Local, Ethnic, and National

Identities". In *Ethnic Identity: Creation, Conflict, and Accommodation*, edited by Lola Romanucci-Ross and George A. De Vos. Walnut Creek, CA: AltaMira Press, 1995.

———. "Cultural Diversity and National Identity in Thailand". In *Government Policies and Ethnic Relations in Asia and the Pacific*, edited by Michael Brown and Sunait Ganguly. Cambridge, MA: MIT Press, 1997.

King, Philip. "From Periphery to Centre: Shaping the History of the Central Peninsula". PhD dissertation, School of History and Politics, University of Wollongong, 2006.

———. "A Tin Mine in Need of a History: 19th-Century British Views of the Patani Interior". In *The Phantasm in Southern Thailand: Historical Writings on Patani and the Islamic World*, vol. 1, edited by Patrick Jory and Jirawat Saengthong (conference proceedings, 11–12 December). Bangkok: Chulalongkorn University, 2009.

Kobkua Suwannathat-Pian. *Kings, Country and Constitutions: Thailand's Political Development, 1932–2000*. London: Routledge, 2003.

Liow, Joseph Chinyong. "International Jihad and Muslim Radicalism in Thailand? Toward an Alternative Interpretation". *Asia Policy*, no. 2 (2006): 89–108.

———. *Islam, Education and Reform in Southern Thailand: Tradition and Transformation*. Singapore: Institute of Southeast Asian Studies, 2009.

Mack, Phyllis. "Religion, Feminism, and the Problem of Agency: Reflections on Eighteenth-Century Quakerism". *Signs: Journal of Women in Culture and Society* 29, no. 1 (2003): 149–77.

Mahmood, Saba. "Feminist Theory, Embodiment, and the Docile Agent: Some Reflections on the Egyptian Islamic Revival". *Cultural Anthropology* 16, no. 2 (2001): 202–36.

———. *Politics of Piety: The Islamic Revival and the Feminist Subject*. Princeton, NJ: Princeton University Press, 2005.

McCargo, Duncan. "Network Monarchy and Legitimacy Crises in Thailand". *Pacific Review* 18, no. 4 (2005): 499–519.

———. "Thaksin and the Resurgence of Violence in the Thai South: Network Monarchy Strikes Back?". *Critical Asian Studies* 38, no. 1 (2006): 39–71.

———. *Rethinking Thailand's Southern Violence*. Singapore: National University of Singapore Press, 2007.

———. *Tearing Apart the Land: Islam and Legitimacy in Southern Thailand*. Ithaca, NY: Cornell University Press, 2008.

———. "Patani Militant Leaflets and the Uses of History". In *The Phantasm in Southern Thailand: Historical Writings on Patani and the Islamic World*, vol. 1, edited by Patrick Jory and Jirawat Saengthong (conference proceedings, 11–12 December). Bangkok: Chulalongkorn University, 2009.

———. *Mapping National Anxieties: Thailand's Southern Conflict*. Copenhagen: Nordic Institute of Asian Studies Press, 2012.

McNay, Lois. *Gender and Agency: Reconfiguring the Subject in Feminist and Social Theory*. Cambridge: Polity Press, 2000.

———. "Agency, Anticipation and Indeterminacy in Feminist Theory". *Feminist Theory* 4, no. 2 (2003): 139–48.

McVey, Ruth. "Separatism and the Paradoxes of the Nation-State in Perspective". In *Armed Separatism in Southeast Asia*, edited by Lim Joo-Jock and Vani S. Singapore: Institute of Southeast Asian Studies, 1984.

———, ed. *Money and Power in Provincial Thailand*. Copenhagen: Nordic Institute of Asian Studies Press, 2000.

Mérieau, Eugénie. "Thailand's Deep State: Royal Power and the Constitutional Court (1997–2015)". *Journal of Contemporary Asia* 46, no. 3 (2016): 445–66.

Nantawan Haemindra. "The Problem of the Thai-Muslims in the Four Southern Provinces of Thailand (Part One)". *Journal of Southeast Asian Studies* 7, no. 2 (1976): 197–225.

———. "The Problem of the Thai-Muslims in the Four Southern Provinces of Thailand (Part Two)". *Journal of Southeast Asian Studies* 8, no. 1 (1977): 85–105.

Nattapoll Chaiching. *Kho Funfai nai Fan an Luea Chuea: Khwam Khlueanwai khong Khabuankan Patipak Patiwat Siam (B.E. 2475–2500)* [An Incredible Dream: The Movement of the Siamese Revolutionary Movement, 1932–1957]. Nonthaburi, Thailand: Fah Diew Kan, 2013.

Nik Mahmud, Nik Anuar. *The Malay Unrest in South Thailand: An Issue in Malaysian-Thai Border Relations*. Bangi, Selangor: Institut Alam dan Tamadun Melayu, Universiti Kebangsaan Malaysia, 1994.

Ong, Aihwa. *Buddha Is Hiding: Refugees, Citizenship, the New America*. Berkeley, CL: University of California Press, 2003.

———. *Neoliberalism as Exception: Mutations in Citizenship and Sovereignty*. Durham, NC: Duke University Press, 2006.

Pasuk Phongpaichit and Chris Baker. *Thailand: Economy and Politics*. Kuala Lumpur: Oxford University Press, 1997.

Porath, Nathan. "The Terrorist Insurgency in the South of Thailand". *Bijdragen tot de Taal-, Land- en Volkenkunde* 167, no. 1 (2011): 130–39.

Phraratchabanyat Raichai Pracham Pi Ngoppraman B.E 2553 [Act Budget Fiscal Year 2010].

Phraratchabanyat Raichai Pracham Pi Ngoppraman B.E 2560 [Act Budget Fiscal Year 2017].

Rabasa, Angel M. "Political Islam in Southeast Asia: Moderates, Radicals and Terrorists". *Adelphi Papers* 43, no. 358 (2003).

Rappa, Antonio L. "Urban Terrorism and Political Violence in Southern Thailand: The Case of Pattani, Yala, Narathiwat". *Journal of African and Asian Local Government Studies* 2, no. 2 (2013): 128–42.

Regional Education Office no. 8. *Kho Mun Sarasonthet Thang Kan Sueksa nai Phuenthi Truat Ratchakan thi 8 (Narathiwat, Pattani, Yala, Songkhla, lae Satun) Pi Kansueksa 2559* [Information on Education in Bureaucracy Inspection Area 8 (Narathiwat, Pattani, Yala, Songkhla, and Satun) in Academic Year 2016] Yala: Regional Education Office no. 8, 2016.

Rouse, Carolyn Moxley. *Engaged Surrender: African American Women and Islam*. Berkeley, CL: University of California Press, 2004.
Sapha Sangkom Songkro Haeng Prathet Thai. *Ngan Chalong Wan Dek Haeng Chat Pracham Pi* [Annual Children's Day Fairs]. Bangkok: Sapha Sangkom Songkro Haeng Prathet Thai nai Phra Borom Rachupatham (National Council on Social Welfare of Thailand), 2014.
Scupin, Raymond. "Islam in Thailand before the Bangkok Period". *Journal of the Siam Society* 68, no. 1 (1980): 55–71.
———. "Thailand as a Plural Society: Ethnic Interaction in a Buddhist Kingdom". *Crossroads* 2, no. 3 (1986): 115–40.
Shamsul, A.B. "A History of an Identity, an Identity of a History: The Idea and Practice of 'Malayness' in Malaysia Reconsidered". In *Contesting Malayness: Malay Identity across Boundaries*, edited by Timothy P. Barnard. Singapore: National University of Singapore Press, 2004.
Sorayut Aim-Aur-Yut. "'Man Yak Thi Cha Pen Nayu.': Chatphan Khwammai lae Kan Torong Khwam Pen Malayu nai Chiwit Pracham Wan" [It Is Difficult to be Malay: Ethnicity, Meaning, and Negotiation of Malayness in Everyday Life]. Master's thesis, Faculty of Sociology and Anthropology, Thammasat University, 2007.
Srisak Vallipodom. "Srivijaya nai Rat Patani" [Srivijaya in the Patani State]. In *Rat Patani Nai "Srivijaya" Kao Kae Kwa Rat Sukhothai Nai Prawatsat: Prawatsat "Pokpit" Khong 3 Changwat Chaidaen Phak Tai* [The Patani State in Srivijaya is Older Than the Sukhothai State in History: A "Closed" History of the Three Southern Border Provinces], edited by Suchit Wongdhes. Bangkok: Matichon, 2004.
Srisompob Jitpiromsri and Panyasak Sobhonvasu. "Unpacking Thailand's Southern Conflict: The Poverty of Structural Explanations". *Critical Asian Studies* 38, no. 1 (2006): 95–117.
Srisompob Jitpiromsri and Supaporn Panasnachee. *An Analysis of Data on the Unrest in the Southern Border Provinces in 2015*, August 2016 <http://www.deepsouthwatch.org/node/7942> (accessed 25 August 2016).
Surin Pitsuwan. "The Lotus and the Crescent: Clashes of Religious Symbolisms in Southern Thailand". In *Ethnic Conflict in Buddhist Societies: Sri Lanka, Thailand, and Burma*, edited by K.M. de Silva et al. London: Pinter, 1988.
Tambiah, Stanley J. *World Conqueror and World Renouncer: A Study of Buddhism and Polity in Thailand against a Historical Background*. Cambridge: Cambridge University Press, 1976.
Tan, Andrew. "The 'New' Terrorism: How Southeast Asia Can Counter It". In *September 11 and Political Freedom: Asian Perspectives*, edited by Uwe Johannen, Alan Smith, and James Gomez. Singapore: Select Publishing, 2003.
Teeuw, Andries and David K. Wyatt. *Hikayat Patani: The Story of Patani*. The Hague: Koninklijk Instituut voor Taal-, Land- en Volkenkunde, 1970.
Thak Chaloemtiarana. *Thailand: The Politics of Despotic Paternalism*. Ithaca, NY: Cornell University Press, 2007.

Thomas, M. Ladd. "Communist Insurgency in Thailand: Factors Contributing to Its Decline". *Asian Affairs* 13, no. 1 (1986): 17–26.

Thongchai Winichakul. "Nationalism and the Radical Intelligentsia in Thailand". *Third World Quarterly* 29, no. 3 (2008): 575–91.

———. *Prachathipatai thi Mi Kasat Yu Nuea Kan Mueang* [*Democracy with the King above Politics*]. Nonthaburi: Fah Diew Kan, 2013.

Tibi, Bassam. *Islam between Culture and Politics*. New York, NY: Palgrave Macmillan, 2001.

Uhlig, Harald. "Southern Thailand and Its Border Provinces". In *Regions and National Integration in Thailand, 1892–1992*, edited by Volker Grabowsky. Wiesbaden: Harrassowitz Verlag, 1995.

Uthai Dulyakasem. "Muslim-Malay Separatism in Southern Thailand: Factors Underlying the Political Revolt". In *Armed Separatism in Southeast Asia*, edited by Lim Joo-Jock and Vani S. Singapore: Institute of Southeast Asian Studies, 1984.

———. "The Emergence and Escalation of Ethnic Nationalism: The Case of the Muslim Malays in Southern Siam". In *Islam and Society in Southeast Asia*, edited by Taufik Abdullah and Sharon Siddique. Singapore: Institute of Southeast Asian Studies, 1988.

Walker, Andrew. *Thailand's Political Peasants: Power in the Modern Rural Economy*. Madison, WI: University of Wisconsin Press, 2012.

Wattana Sugunnasil. "Islam, Radicalism, and Violence in Southern Thailand: Berjihad di Patani and the 28 April 2004 Attacks". *Critical Asian Studies* 38, no. 1 (2006): 119–44.

Yegar, Moshe. *Between Integration and Secession: The Muslim Communities of the Southern Philippines, Southern Thailand, and Western Burma/Myanmar*. Lanham, MD: Lexington Books, 2002.

Index

A

Abhisit Vejjajiva, 85, 159n16
absolute monarchy, 24, 107, 159n16
  see also constitutional monarchy;
    monarchy
Abu Zakaria Yahya Ibn Sharaf al-
    Nawawi, 64n8
administrative levels, in Thailand, 31n2
Agamben, Giorgio, 5–6, 209, 212, 231
Al-Azhar university, 51
Al-Qaeda, 155n2
Ananda Mahidol, King, 107
Angkor Empire, 31n1
anti-government movement, 27
Area of the Seven Provinces, 22
Arzeulee Subdistrict Cultural
    Promotion Committee, 103
Arzeulee Subdistrict Government
    Agency Centre, 99
Asian financial crisis, 158n14
Assembly of the Poor, 133
assimilation policy, 4, 28, 33, 182, 237
Association of Malays of Greater
    Patani, *see* GAMPAR
Autonomous Region in Muslim
    Mindanao, 240
Ayutthaya, 11n5

B

Banharn Silpa-archa, 159n16
Beamtenstaaten, 3
Bersatu, 30, 63n3, 161n21
Bhumibol Adulyadej, King, 10n2, 103,
    106–10, 115–16, 118, 158n14,
    160n17, 221, 228–29

biopolitics, 230
bird-singing contest, 81, 193
birth control, and religion, 194, 239
Black May incident, 136, 229
BNPP (Barisan Nasional Pembebasan
    Patani), 29
bomoh, 177–82, 188n5, 195–96, 211n2,
    239
Border Patrol Police, 160n18
Brahmanism, 30, 163, 169, 196, 228,
    233
BRN (Barisan Revolusi Nasional
    Melayu Patani), 29, 63n3, 168
BRN-Coordinate, 51, 63n2–3, 65n14,
    66n15, 168
Buddhism, 2, 4, 8, 24, 30, 163, 169,
    187–88, 196, 226, 228, 231, 236
bungosireh, 103, 105–6

C

Centre for Community Justice, 117
Centre for Sufficiency Economy of
    Arzeulee Subdistrict, 98–99, 106
Chakri dynasty, 223
Chaloemrat Cultural Centre, 103
chanting ceremony, 88
Chatichai Choonhavan, 159n16
chat Thai (Thai nation), 4, 227
Chavalit Yongchaiyudh, 159n16
Children's Day fair, 85–86, 99, 157n8,
    237
children's rights, 157n8
Christian women, 218
Chronicles of Patani, 31n1
Chuan Leekpai, 159n16

Chulalongkorn, King, 4, 159n15, 227, 230
Chularajamontri, 186
circumcision, 76–77, 105, 157n7, 173
"Clash of Civilizations? The", article, 162
"clash" within Islam, 163
code of conduct, and insurgency, 202–3
Code of Criminal Procedure, 231, 235n2
colour symbols, 2
Commission of Inquiry, 188n8
Community Justice Centre, 132
compensation money, 101–2, 118, 200–1
Compulsory Education Law, of 1921, 10n4
conscription, 87–93, 173, 198–99
"conspiracy theory", 63n2
constitutional monarchy, 24, 229, 231
  see also absolute monarchy; monarchy
contraception, see birth control
Council for Democratic Reform, 63n5
Council for National Security, 63n5
coup, 63n5, 65n12, 107, 158n12–13, 159n6, 228–29, 235n1, 240
CPM-43 (Civilian-Police-Military Taskforce 43), 148, 150
CPT (Communist Party of Thailand), 158n11, 161n22
CSOC (Communist Suppression Operations Command), 158n11
"cultural diversity", 93, 104
cultural identity, 162

D

Daily News, 112
dakwah (missionary), 8, 68, 72–75, 78–79, 155n3, 164–69, 172, 219–20, 237–38
"danger pay", 92
"de facto sovereignty", 6–7
"dead penis *bomoh*", 179
death ceremony, for officials, 118–19
Deep South, 3, 5–7, 9, 11n6, 12–13, 16–17, 24, 30, 32n7, 33, 41, 49, 61–62, 63n5, 64n8, 67, 73, 82, 84, 88, 92–94, 96, 102, 104–5, 108–9, 112, 115–16, 118–20, 123, 130, 142, 145, 147, 154, 158n12, 161n21, 164, 169, 172–73, 188n5, 192–93, 201, 204, 215, 232, 236–38, 240
  area of, 10n2
Democrat Party, 158n12
Department of Cultural Promotion, 103
Department of Forestry, 109
Department of Provincial Administration, 31n2, 96
Department of Religion's Order on Mosque Centers for Islam and Ethics Instruction, 10n2
"despiritualization", 195
disaster relief programme, 102
diversity, among Muslims, 77–82
drugs, 11n6, 75, 79, 82, 93, 98, 129, 146, 151, 157n10, 158n11, 181, 193
Dutch East Indies, 3

E

Emergency Decree, 235n1
ethno-nationalistic ideology, 4, 114
exorcism, 176–78, 182

F

farm project, 115–16
Fatoni Darussalam State, 43–44, 168
"Fatoni Muslims", 43
Fatoni University, 73, 77, 156n5
Federation of Malaya, 4, 29
fiscal year budget, for southern provinces, 94–95, 158n13
Five Pillars of Islam, 77, 163
Foreign Affairs, 162

Forum Perdana Ehwal Islam, 216
Foundation for the Promotion of Supplementary Occupations and Related Techniques, 116
flood relief programme, 101, 108
Foucault, Michel, 6, 212
Fourth Region Army, 67, 89, 140, 145, 170
free medical service, 97–98, 101

G

"galactic polity", 11n5
GAMPAR (Gabungan Melayu Pattani Raya), 28
GMP (Gerakan Mujahidin Patani), 29
"good Muslim", 8, 79–81, 190, 217–18, 237–38
"graduated sovereignty", 230–31
grave-soil laying ceremony, royal, 118, 187, 238
Great Thai Empire (Maha Anachak Thai), 4, 228
"grey figures", and illegal businesses, 141–48
"Guardians of the People", 43
Guba
  arson in, 41–42
  bombings in, 40–41
  fear and distrust in, 55–62
  leaflets in, 42–46, 51, 55, 57–58, 63n3–5, 64n8, 113, 163, 168, 170–72, 201
  military camp near, 49–50
  Raman Sultanate, and, 20–25
  security forces operations in, 46–51
  shootings in, 34–40
  villages of, 13–20
  "wild territory", as, 25–30, 34
  unrests in, 34–46

H

Haji Sulong, 183, 188n8
handicraft production project, 119

Hansen, Thomas Blom, 6
Haydar Ali, 156n3
"hearts and minds", winning the, 85–86, 93, 98, 106, 110, 120, 237
"help and care" programmes, 8, 101, 105
Hinduism, 2, 24, 105, 163, 169, 196, 233
holy war, 171
horse race, 174
"house registration", 117
house searches, 47–48
Huntington, Samuel, 162

I

Imam Ibrahim, 54, 58
Imam Nawawi, 44, 64n8
"influential person", 27, 32n8, 148
institutions of Thai society, 83
insurgency, 34–36, 38, 40–42, 48, 51–54, 61, 66n15, 84, 88, 90, 110, 113, 116, 128, 130, 140–41, 145–46, 155n2, 157n10, 158n12, 159n16, 168–72, 192, 197, 201, 204, 237, 240
  code of conduct, and, 202–3
Interim Constitution of the Kingdom of Thailand, 235n1, 240
internal colonialism, 3, 4
Internal Security Operations Command, 116
"interpreters of violence", 66n15
Islam, 3–6, 8–9, 10n2, 13, 31n1, 34, 36, 45, 54–55, 67–68, 104–5, 152, 162, 226–27, 237–38
  "clash" within, 163
  interpreting, 191–94, 211n1
  Malay beliefs and rituals, and, 173–82
  strands of, 15, 69–76, 163–73
  traditional, 72–73, 165, 172
  unrest, and, 155n2
  way of life, 76–82

women in, 214–21
  see also Malay Muslims
Islamic boarding school, 18
Islamic community (ummah), 182
Islamic radicalism, 2, 5, 155n2
"Islamic reform", 84, 194
"Islamic revival", 15
"Islamic Warriors of the Fatoni State", 42–45, 168
"Islamization", 196, 213
Islamo-nationalism, 66n15
Ismail Lutfi, 15, 156n5
ISOC (Internal Security Operations Command), 94, 157n10, 158n11, 158n12

J

Jalanan Baru project, 93, 157n10
Jawi Ulama network, 156n4, 156n5
Jemaat Tabligh, 68, 73, 155n3
jihad, 155n2, 169

K

Kafir Siam, 42–45
Kasetsart University, 158n14
Kasikorn Khirisri, 149, 197
Kaum Muda (New Group), 15, 72–73, 75, 156n5, 156n6, 163, 164, 180, 188n1, 188n2, 188n3, 207, 220, 237–38
Kaum Tua (Old Group), 15, 72, 164, 188n2, 238
Kedah Annals, 31n1
Khru Razak, 25, 27–28, 30, 34, 71, 161n21
  legacy of 120–30
"kingdom", concept of, 230
"King's Man, the", 108
Klong Prem Central Prison, 122
Koran, 2, 69, 76–81, 88, 105, 156n5, 157n9, 163, 166, 171, 175, 179–80, 188n6, 191, 194–96, 206, 211n1, 214, 216–20, 238

Kratom cocktails, 7–8, 11n6, 16–17, 36, 56–57, 59, 68, 75, 79, 129, 141–48, 151, 190–91, 193, 203, 207, 210
  military, and, 145–47
Kratom Act, 11n6
Kriangkrai, Lieutenant, 36, 38
Kromluang Narathiwat Ratchanakarin Military Camp, 5, 30, 33

L

Lang Chia Shu, 30n1
Langkasuka, 13, 24, 30n1
leaflets, 42–46, 51, 55, 57–58, 63n3–5, 64n8, 113, 163, 168, 170–72, 201
Life Quality Development Centre, 132
Local Government Act, 31n2
local politics, 128, 136–38
"Lohman Buffalo", 128, 207–8

M

Maha Anachak Thai (Great Thai Empire), 4, 228
Mahidol University, 112–13
Mahmmud Mayhiddin, 28
Makyong performance, 174, 176
Malay arts, 103
Malay beliefs and rituals, and Islam, 173–82
Malay culture, 105, 106, 154, 157n6, 238
Malay identity, 2, 6, 15, 29–30, 154, 182, 237–38
Malay Muslims, 1–2, 4–9, 10n4, 15, 33, 43–46, 54, 55–56, 62n2, 63n5, 93, 106, 108, 114–15, 118, 145, 147, 152, 155n2, 156n5, 157n6, 157n9, 161n21, 191, 202, 224, 233–36, 239
  Thai citizenship, and identity, 182–88
  see also Islam
Malay ruling elites, 4, 29

INDEX 253

Malay separatism, 108
Malay sultanates, 11n5, 236
Malay world, modifying the, 194–96
Malay writing system, 13, 31n4
Manifesto of the Declaration Day, 42–43
Markaz Dakwah Jemaat, 74, 78, 156n3
martial law, 235n1
Mawlid, 163, 186–87, 188n1
MCP (Malayan Communist Party), 126–27
"mediated agency", 218
methamphetamines, 75, 79, 146
militant Islam, 2
military, and *kratom*, 145–47
military draft, *see* conscription
Ministry of Agriculture and Cooperatives, 96, 101
Ministry of Culture, 96, 103–4
Ministry of Defense, 96, 158n12
Ministry of Education, 10n2, 84, 96, 132, 148
Ministry of Interior, 24, 31n2, 96, 136, 157n8, 201
Ministry of Justice, 96
missionary (dakwah), 8, 68, 72–75, 78–79, 155n3, 164–69, 172, 219–20, 237–38
MNLA (Malayan National Liberation Army), 127
Mon Empire, 31n1
monarchy, 6–8, 11n4, 106–8, 110–11, 150, 154, 160n18, 226–30, 237
    see also absolute monarchy; constitutional monarchy
Mongkut, King, 228
Monthon Pattani (Pattani Circle), 22–24
"moral police", 82
Mosque Center for Islamic Studies, 10n2
mosques, conflicts between, 172–73
multiculturalism, 185

N
Nakhon Si Thammarat, 11n5, 31n1
national anthem, 84–87, 222
National Economic and Social Development Plan, 159n14
National Education Act, 10n2
National Government Organization Act, 31n2
national identity, 182
nationalism, 4, 28, 66n15, 155n2
NCPO (National Council for Peace and Order), 235n1, 240
neoliberalism, 230
"network monarchy", 229
"New Group", *see* Kaum Muda
"New Theory on Agriculture", 109
NIA (National Intelligence Agency), 96, 158n13

O
oath of allegiance, 83, 85, 148, 151, 197
Office of the Chularajamontri, 186–87, 189n9
Office of the Prime Minister, 158n11
Office of the Royal Development Projects Board (RDPB), 108–9
Office of the Rubber Replanting Aid Fund, 50, 96
official leaders, 131–41
OIC (Organization of the Islamic Conference), 115
Okhrae Dalae, 35, 36, 38–39, 41, 46–47, 51–57, 62n1, 155n2, 169–70, 203, 234
Okhrae Hijau, 46, 62n1
Okhrae Hitae, 46, 51, 56, 62n1
"Okhrae Nayu", 182
Old Group, *see* Kaum Tua
ONCB (Office of the Narcotics Control Board), 157n10
Ong, Aihwa, 212–13, 230–31
opium business, 26–27

Outstanding Environment
    Conservation Mother Award, 112
"outstanding mother" award, 111
Outstanding Young Farmer award, 117

P
pahalo, 154n1
Pahong Gayu killings, 38–40
pan-Malay nationalism, 4
Paramilitary Ranger Special Unit 41,
    150, 152
"Patani Malay", 32n6, 154n1
"Patani Mujahideen Warriors", 45,
    66n15
Patani Sultanate, 7, 12–13, 24
paternalism, 22
patron–client relationship, 217
Pattani Circle (Monthon Pattani),
    22–24
peat swamp management, 108–10
People Party, 4
phanphum (tray), offering, 1–3, 7, 9n1,
    11, 224–26
Pikulthong Royal Development Study
    Centre, 109, 115
Plaek Phibunsongkhram, 4, 85, 107,
    228–29
PohYeh, 30
Police Special Branch Division, in
    Bangkok, 121
"politics leads the military", 106, 118,
    240
Pondok schools, 2, 10n4, 65n13, 69–71,
    73, 76, 105, 167–68
"portable" preaching, 68
PPM (Patani People's Movement), 29
Prajadhipok, King, 107, 228
Prem Tinsulanonda, 108, 229
Prince of Songkla University, 96, 103,
    180
Princess of Naradhiwas University, 96
private Islamic schools, 65n13, 76
Privy Council, 229

"Programme for Promoting and
    Developing Religion, Art, and
    Culture", 96
"Programmes for Solving Problems
    in and Developing the Southern
    Border Provinces", 93–94
"Programme on Integrated Solutions
    to the Problems of the Southern
    Border Provinces", 158n13
Provincial Islamic Committee, 132
Provincial Red Cross Chapters, 159n15
public pavilions (*salas*), 19
PULO (Patani United Liberation
    Organization), 29, 63n3, 161n21,
    168

Q
Quaker women, 218

R
"radical Islam", 10n4
"Ramadan scale of merit", 155n1
Raman District Probation Office, 117
Raman hospital, 100, 105
Raman Malay dialect, 13
Raman Sultanate, 7, 12, 34
    Guba, and, 20–25
rao rak nay luang (We Love Mr King),
    1, 7, 9
Ratprachanukroh Foundation, 116
RDPB (Office of the Royal
    Development Projects Board),
    108–9
Red Cross annual fair, 103, 159n16
    see also Thai Red Cross Society
Red-Whiskered Bulbul Club, 81, 133,
    141, 164–66, 207
"red-zone village", 34, 49
revolution, of 1932, 24, 159n15, 228
Revolutionary Council Announcement,
    136
RID (Royal Irrigation Department),
    108, 110, 160n17

"righteous king", 228
ritual offerings, 175
royal anthem, 223
Royal Development Study Centre, 108
royal grave-soil laying ceremony, 118, 187, 238
royal initiatives, 107–10
royal involvement, with the recent unrest, 113–20
Royal Patronage, 116, 119
royal recognition, 111–13
Royal Thai Army, 63n5
Royal Thai Police, 158n12
rubber plantation, 15–16
Runda Kumpulan Kecil (RKK), 53, 65n14

S

Sadudi Maharaja, 83, 87, 151, 222
Saiburi Dam, 110, 160n17, 203
Salafi movement, 15, 156n5, 157n6, 188n1
SAO (Subdistrict Administrative Organization), 50, 61, 65n12, 119, 132–41, 146, 149–50, 161n22, 167–68, 170, 179, 184–86, 190, 206–8, 214–15, 217, 221
Sarit Thanarat, 10n4, 65n13, 107–8, 228–29
Schmitt, Carl, 5
school activities, 83
S.E.A. Write Award, 111
Security Act, 235n1
security forces operations, in Guba, 46–51
separatist movement, 4–5, 7, 28–30, 33, 53, 107, 121, 126–27, 237
shura, 134
Siamese kingdom, 3
silat, 103, 126, 176, 196, 207
Sirikit, Queen, 113–15, 221
Sirindhorn, Princess, 110, 117
Soamsawali, Princess, 111–12

social studies textbook, 83
Songkhla, 22
Sonthi Boonyaratglin, General, 43, 63n5
"southern border administration models", 239
Southern Border Provinces Peace Building Command, 118
sovereignty, issues of, 5–6, 209–12, 229–31, 236–40
"special political zone", 231
"special services", 199
spirit possession, 175–78, 195–96
Srisunthorn forces, 64n9, 64n11
Srivijaya, 31n1
state ideology, 85, 222–23, 226, 230
state intelligence, 53
"state of exception", 5, 229–31, 235n1, 240
state, outsmarting the, 196–201
Stepputat, Finn, 6
strands of Islam, 15, 69–76, 163–73
Subdistrict Council and Subdistrict Administrative Organization Act, 136
Subdistrict Official Administration Act, 136
Suchinda Kraprayoon, 229
"sufficiency economy" project, 98, 115, 158n14
Sukhothai, 11n5
Sulong Abdul Kadir al-Fatani, 29
Sunni Muslims, 15
supernatural beliefs, 175–78, 195, 196
Surayud Chulanont, General, 63n5
suzerain–vassal relationship, 3

T

Tablighi Jamaat, *see* Jemaat Tabligh
Tadika (Taman Didikan Kanak Kanak), 1–2, 10n2, 13, 51, 53–54, 70, 75–76, 97, 105, 132, 179, 219, 221, 223–24

Tambiah, Stanley Jeyaraja, 11n5
Tanyong Limo incident, 160n19
tap water project, 131
tarawih, 80, 173, 188n4
teachers' wages, 10n2
teashops, in Guba, 18–20
"teasing the soil" technique, 109
Ten Kingly Virtues, 228
terrorism, 155n2
Thai citizenship, 82–106
    Malay Muslims, and, 182–88
Thai Health Promotion Foundation, 191
Thai identity, 154
Thai monarchy, revival of, 107
Thai nation (*chat Thai*), 4, 227
Thai national flag, signifies, 2
Thai Ratthaniyom (Thai Customs Decree), 4
Thai Red Cross Society, 159n15
    see also Red Cross annual fair
Thai society, three institutions of, 83
Thailand
    administrative levels, 31n2
    fiscal year budget, for southern provinces, 94–95, 158n13
Thaksin Ratchaniwet Palace, 108, 113
Thaksin Shinawatra, 63n5, 105, 113, 158n12, 159n16
Thamavitya Mulniti School, 51, 65n13
Thammasat University, 160n18, 161n22
Thanom Kittikachorn, 85
Toh Nik, 21–22, 32n5, 175
tok imam, 63n5, 187
Tok Zaki, 74, 78–79, 165, 169
"Tom Yam Kung Crisis", 159n14
traditional Islam, 72–73, 165, 172
tray (*phanphum*), offering, 1–3, 7, 9n1, 11, 224–26
tributary states, 3
troop patrols, 47–49
Tuan Loh The, 32n5

U
ulama, 15, 189n9
ummah (Islamic community), 182
"unauthorized" business, 16, 19
"undifferentiated sovereignty", 231
unrests
    Guba, in, 34–46
    Islam, and, 155n2
    royal involvement, and, 113–20
"Upholder of Religions", 222, 226, 230–31, 233–34

V
Vajiralongkorn, King, 10n2, 111
Vajiravudh, King, 4, 107, 227
vassal states, 236
village headman, 31n2
"village Islam", 72
Village Scouts, 113, 160n18
village security team, 40–42, 50, 58, 61, 64n9, 119, 130, 132, 139, 149, 201
villages in Guba, 13–20
vocational training programme, 82, 93, 129, 146

W
Wahhabism, 72, 156n5, 188n1
waikhru, 195
Wang Phaya–Tha Thong Demonstration Farm Project, 116–17
water management, 108
way of life, and Islam, 76–82
"We love the king", 1, 7, 9
Western Region Community Forestry Network, 112
women in Islam, 214–21
"worldly education", 10n2
World War II, 4, 28, 237

Y

Ya Sin, sura, 88, 157n9
Yala Female School, 104
Yala Islamic College, 73, 77, 156n5
Yala Province, 1, 13, 20, 24
Yala Provincial Livestock Office, 200
Yala Provincial Office of Culture, 103–4
Yala Teacher Training School, 120
Yala Rajabhat University, 120
Yingluck Shinawatra, 159n16, 240

About the Author

Anusorn Unno is currently Dean and Associate Professor in Anthropology at the Faculty of Sociology and Anthropology, Thammasat Univerity, Thailand. His research interests are Malay culture and Muslim communities in southern Thailand and Thai politics and social movements. His publications include "A New Extraterritoriality? Aquaculture Certification, Sovereignty, and Empire", *Political Geography* 31, no. 6 (2012) with which he co-authored with Peter Vandergeest, "'Rao Rak Nay Luang': Crafting Malay Muslims' Subjectivity through the Sovereign Thai Monarch", *Thammasat Review* 19, no. 2 (2016); "'Raya Kita': Malay Muslims of Southern Thailand and the King", *Tokyo Review of Southeast Asia* 22 (2017).

www.ingramcontent.com/pod-product-compliance
Lightning Source LLC
Chambersburg PA
CBHW070024010526
44117CB00011B/1698